D0780115

Red Skin, White Masks

INDIGENOUS AMERICAS

Robert Warrior, Series Editor

Chadwick Allen, *Trans-Indigenous:*
Methodologies for Global Native Literary Studies

Raymond D. Austin, *Navajo Courts and Navajo Common Law:*
A Tradition of Tribal Self-Governance

Lisa Brooks, *The Common Pot: The Recovery of Native Space in the Northeast*

Kevin Bruyneel, *The Third Space of Sovereignty:*
The Postcolonial Politics of U.S.-Indigenous Relations

Glen Sean Coulthard, *Red Skin, White Masks:*
Rejecting the Colonial Politics of Recognition

James H. Cox, *The Red Land to the South:*
American Indian Writers and Indigenous Mexico

Daniel Heath Justice, *Our Fire Survives the Storm:*
A Cherokee Literary History

Brendan Hokowhitu and Vijay Devadas, *The Fourth Eye:*
Māori Media in Aotearoa New Zealand

Thomas King, *The Truth About Stories: A Native Narrative*

Scott Richard Lyons, *X-Marks: Native Signatures of Assent*

Jean M. O'Brien, *Firsting and Lasting:*
Writing Indians out of Existence in New England

Paul Chaat Smith, *Everything You Know about Indians Is Wrong*

Gerald Vizenor, *Bear Island: The War at Sugar Point*

Robert Warrior, *The People and the Word: Reading Native Nonfiction*

Robert A. Williams, Jr., *Like a Loaded Weapon: The Rehnquist Court,*
Indian Rights, and the Legal History of Racism in America

Red Skin, White Masks

Rejecting the Colonial Politics of Recognition

Glen Sean Coulthard

Foreword by Taiaiake Alfred

INDIGENOUS AMERICAS

University of Minnesota Press

MINNEAPOLIS • LONDON

Portions of chapter 1 were previously published as "This Is Not a Peace Pipe: Towards a Critical Indigenous Philosophy," *University of Toronto Quarterly* 77, no. 1 (2008): 164–66, reprinted with permission from University of Toronto Press, www.utpjournals.com; and as "Subjects of Empire: Indigenous Peoples and the 'Politics of Recognition' in Canada," *Contemporary Political Theory* 6, no. 4 (2007): 437–60. Portions of chapter 3 were previously published as "Resisting Culture: Seyla Benhabib's Deliberative Approach to the Politics of Recognition in Colonial Contexts," in *Deliberative Democracy in Practice*, ed. David Kahane (Vancouver, BC: University of British Columbia Press, 2009), 138–54, reprinted with permission of the publisher, copyright University of British Columbia Press 2009, all rights reserved.

Published by the University of Minnesota Press
111 Third Avenue South, Suite 290
Minneapolis, MN 55401-2520
http://www.upress.umn.edu

Library of Congress Cataloging-in-Publication Data
Coulthard, Glen Sean.
Red skin, white masks : rejecting the colonial politics of recognition / Glen Sean Coulthard ; foreword by Taiaiake Alfred.
(Indigenous Americas)
Includes bibliographical references and index.
ISBN 978-0-8166-7964-5 (hc : alk. paper)
ISBN 978-0-8166 7965-2 (pb : alk. paper)
1. Indians of North America—Canada—Government relations.
2. Indians of North America—Canada—Politics and government.
3. Indians of North America—Legal status, laws. etc.—Canada. 4. Indians, Treatment of—Canada. 5. Canada—Ethnic relations—Political aspects. I. Title.
E92.C68 2014
323.1197´071—dc23
2013049674

Printed in the United States of America on acid-free paper

The University of Minnesota is an equal-opportunity educator and employer.

20 19 18 17 16 15 14   10 9 8 7 6 5 4 3 2 1

For
RICHARD PARK COULTHARD
(1942–2012)

CONTENTS

FOREWORD

Taiaiake Alfred

Not so very long ago, in Canada there numbered just less than fourteen million inhabitants: thirteen million human beings, and half a million Natives. The former had the land; the others had the memory of it. Between the two there were hired chiefs, an Indian Affairs bureaucracy, and a small bourgeoisie, all three shams from the very beginning to the end, which served as go-betweens. In this unending colony the truth stood naked, but the settlers preferred it hidden away or at least dressed: the Natives had to love them and all they had done, something in the way a cruel father is still loved by the children who are wounded by his selfish hands. The white élite undertook to manufacture a Native élite. They picked promising youths, they made them drink the fire-water principles of capitalism and of Western culture; they educated the Indian out of them, and their heads were filled and their mouths were stuffed with smart-sounding hypocrisies, grand greedy words that stuck in their throats but which they spit out nonetheless. After a short stay in the university they were sent home to their reserves or unleashed in the cities, whitewashed. These walking lies had nothing to say to their brothers and sisters that did not sound false, ugly, and harmful; they only mimicked their masters. From buildings in Toronto, from Montréal, from Vancouver, businessmen would utter the words, "Development! Progress!" and somewhere on a reserve lips would open ". . . opment! . . . gress!" The Natives were complacent and compliant; it was a rich time for the white élite.

Then things changed. The mouths of Natives started opening by them-selves; brown voices still spoke of the whites' law, democracy, and liberal humanism, but only to reproach them for their unfairness and inhumanity.

White élites listened without displeasure to these polite statements of resentment and reproach, these pleas for reconciliation, with apparent satisfaction. "See? Just like we taught them, they are able to talk in proper English without the help of a priest or of an anthropologist. Just look at what we have made of the backward savages—they sound like lawyers!" Whites did not doubt that the Natives would accept their ideals, since the Natives accused the whites of not being faithful to them. Settlers could still believe in the sanctity of their divine civilizing mission; they had Europeanized the Natives, they had created a new kind of Native, the assimilated Aboriginal. The white élites took this all in and whispered, quiet between themselves over dinner, as good progressive persons of the (post)modern world: "Let them cry and complain; it's just therapy and worth the expense. It's better than giving the land back!"

Now the sham is coming to an end. Native thinkers and leaders are coming on the scene intent on changing things, entirely. With the last stores of our patience, Native writers, musicians, and philosophers are trying to explain to settlers that their values and the true facts of their existence are at great odds, and that the Native can never be completely erased or totally assimilated. This *New Indigenous Intelligentsia* is trying to get settlers to understand that colonialism must and will be confronted and destroyed. It is not 1947; we're not talking about reforming the Indian Act so that we can become little municipalities. It is not 1982; we're not talking about going to court to explore empty constitutional promises.

It is the twenty-first century. Listen: "what is treated in the Canadian discourse of reconciliation as an unhealthy and debilitating incapacity to forgive and move on is actually a sign of a *critical consciousness*, of our sense of justice and injustice, and of our awareness of and unwillingness to *reconcile*." Coulthard is talking about rising up, Seeing Red, about resurgence and the politics of authentic self-affirmation. This is a call to combat contemporary colonialism's objectification and alienation and manipulation of our true selves. He understands that in Canada today "settlement" of conflict means putting the past behind us, a willful forgetting of the crimes that have stained the psyche of this country for so long, a conspiracy of collective ignorance, turning a blind eye to the ongoing crimes of theft, fraud, and abuse against the original people of the land that are still the unacceptable everyday reality in Canada. So how could we settle and accept and not question and challenge the naturalized injustice that frames and shapes and gives character to our lives? There is nothing natural about the dominance of white people on the North American continent and the removal and erasure of our people, our laws, and our cultures from our homelands.

Glen Coulthard is a leading voice of the new Indigenous Intelligentsia, and he has accomplished so much with this book. To have rescued Karl Marx from his nineteenth-century hostage chamber in that room in the British Library and to expose him to the full breadth of history and the light of the human landscape was enough to make this a great work of political theory. He's gone beyond that accomplishment in correcting Jean-Paul Sartre's and Frantz Fanon's narrow vision—something you have to excuse them for given they were doing philosophy while in the midst of a ferocious physical fight— and brought Marx and Sartre and Fanon together with his Dene Elders and me and you, Reader, to show us all how our psycho-affective attachments to colonialism are blocking the achievement of a just society. As such, this book is a profound critique of contemporary colonialism, and clear vision of Indigenous resurgence, and a serious contribution to the literature of freedom.

ACKNOWLEDGMENTS

The research and writing of *Red Skin, White Masks* would not have been possible without the insight and guidance offered by many friends and colleagues. The unwavering support and intellectual guidance provided by professors James Tully and Taiaiake Alfred warrant special mention. If there are any insights to be gleaned from *Red Skin, White Masks*, it's due in large part to the support I received from these two outstanding scholars. I consider both of them to be friends and mentors of the highest order.

I would also like to thank the many people I have met over the years who have influenced my thinking in innumerable ways. In particular, I would like to express my deepest gratitude to my close friends and esteemed colleagues Dory Nason, John Munro, Robert Nichols, Jakeet Singh, and Rita Dhamoon. Your thoughtful comments on various incarnations of this project have been invaluable. You have all been crucial to my intellectual and personal development in ways that I cannot possibly express here.

There are, of course, many others whose words of encouragement and support have indelibly shaped this book. In particular, I would like to start by acknowledging my friends and colleagues in the First Nations Studies Program at the University of British Columbia: Dory Nason, Sheryl Lightfoot, Daniel Justice, Linc Kesler, (the forthcoming) Johnny Mack, Janey Lew, Jie Ie Baik, Hannah Butson, and Tanya Bob. I look forward to many more conversations in the future.

Special thanks are also due to my editor, Jason Weidemann, at the University of Minnesota Press, as well as the series editor for Indigenous Americas, Robert Warrior. Your collective support for this project struck the perfect balance between persistence and compassion.

Credit is also due to the many illuminating conversations I have had over the years with these brilliant interlocutors: Erin Freeland Ballantyne, Leanne Simpson, Audra Simpson, Andy Smith, J. P. Fulford, Duncan Ivison, Melissa Williams, Jeff Corntassel, Michael Asch, Avigail Eisenberg, Jeremy Webber, Chris Andersen, Peter Kulchyski, Paul Patton, Kevin Bruyneel, Richard Day, Harsha Walia, David Dennis, Cliff Atleo, Ivan Drury, Elizabeth Povinelli, Laura Janara, Barbara Arneil, Bruce Baum, Jeffery Webber, Nikolas Kompridis, Brad Brian, Sylvia Federici, Andrej Grubacic, Dylan Rodriguez, Brendan Hokowhitu, Vince Diaz, Stephanie Irlbacher-Fox, Francois Paulette, Stephen Kakfwi, Kyla Kakfwi Scott, Amos Scott, Melaw Nakehk'o, Modeste and Therese Sangris, Toby Rollo, Am Johal, Shyla Seller, Matt Hern, Geoff Mann, Mike Krebs, Denise Ferreira Da Silva, Scott Morgensen, Shiri Pasternak, Chris Finley, Arthur Manuel, Val Napoleon, Mandee McDonald, Siku Allooloo, Nina Larrson, and Jarrett Martineau.

A shout-out is also due to my students at the University of British Columbia and elsewhere. Thanks to Kelsey Wrightson and Matthew Wildcat for the care they put into helping prepare the text, both intellectually and physically, for publication. I have also learned so much from my conversations in and outside of the classroom with Daniel Voth, Jessica Rosinski, Derek Kornelsen, Jessica Hallenbeck, Dawn Hoogeveen, Kelly Aguirre, and Charlotte Kingston.

Finally, I could not have completed this project without the love and support of Amanda Dowling; our children, Hayden and Tulita Dowling-Coulthard; and my mother, Christine Coulthard. This book is for all of you.

I dedicate *Red Skin, White Masks* to the loving memory of my father, Richard Park Coulthard (1942–2012). I miss you more than words can say. *Mahsi cho!*

Subjects of Empire

Real recognition of our presence and humanity would require a genuine
reconsideration of so many people's role in North American society that
it would amount to a genuine leap of imagination.

—George Manuel and Michael Posluns,
    The Fourth World

From "Wards of the State" to
Subjects of Recognition?

Over the last forty years, the self-determination efforts and objectives of
Indigenous peoples in Canada have increasingly been cast in the language
of "recognition."[1] Consider, for example, the formative declaration issued by
my people in 1975:

> We the Dene of the NWT [Northwest Territories] insist on the right to be
> regarded by ourselves and the world as a nation.
>
>   Our struggle is for the *recognition* of the Dene Nation by the Government
> and people of Canada and the peoples and governments of the world. . . .
>
>   And while there are realities we are forced to submit to, such as the existence
> of a country called Canada, we insist on the right to self-determination and the
> *recognition* of the Dene Nation.[2]

Now fast-forward to the 2005 policy position on self-determination issued
by Canada's largest Aboriginal organization, the Assembly of First Nations
(AFN). According to the AFN, "a consensus has emerged . . . around a vision
of the relationship between First Nations and Canada which would lead to
strengthening recognition and implementation of First Nations' governments."[3]
This "vision," the AFN goes on to explain, draws on the core principles outlined in the 1996 *Report of the Royal Commission on Aboriginal Peoples* (RCAP):
that is, recognition of the nation-to-nation relationship between First Nations

1

and the Crown; recognition of the equal right of First Nations to self-determination; recognition of the Crown's fiduciary obligation to protect Aboriginal treaty rights; recognition of First Nations' inherent right to self-government; and recognition of the right of First Nations to economically benefit from the use and development of their lands and resources.[4] Since 2005 the AFN has consistently reasserted and affirmed these guiding principles at its Annual General Assemblies and in the numerous resolutions that these gatherings have produced.

These demands have not been easy to ignore. Because of the persistence and dedication of countless Indigenous activists, leaders, communities, and organizations, we have witnessed within the scope of four decades the emergence of an unprecedented degree of recognition for Aboriginal "cultural" rights within the legal and political framework of the Canadian state.[5] Most significant on this front was Canada's eventual "recognition" of "existing aboriginal and treaty rights" under section 35(1) of the Constitution Act of 1982. This constitutional breakthrough provided the catalyst that led to the federal government's eventual recognition, in 1995, of an "inherent right to self-government,"[6] as well as the groundswell of post-1982 court challenges that have sought to both clarify and widen the scope of what constitutes a constitutionally recognized Aboriginal right to begin with. When considered from the vantage point of these important developments, it would certainly appear that "recognition" has emerged as the dominant expression of self-determination within the Aboriginal rights movement in Canada.

The struggle for recognition has become a central catalyst in the international Indigenous rights movement as well. As the works of Will Kymlicka, Sheryl Lightfoot, Ronald Neizen, and others have noted, the last three decades have witnessed the emergence of recognition-based approaches to Indigenous self-determination in the field of Indigenous–state relations in Asia, northern Europe, throughout the Americas, and across the South Pacific (including Australia, New Zealand, and the Pacific Islands).[7] Although varying in institutional scope and scale, all of these geopolitical regions have seen the establishment of Indigenous rights regimes that claim to recognize and accommodate the political autonomy, land rights, and cultural distinctiveness of Indigenous nations within the settler states that now encase them. Although my primary empirical focus in *Red Skin, White Masks* is Canada, I suspect that readers will find many of my conclusions applicable to settler-colonial experiences elsewhere.

On a more discursive plane, the increase in recognition demands made by Indigenous and other marginalized minorities over the last forty years has also prompted a flurry of intellectual activity that has sought to unpack the complex ethical, political, and legal questions that these types of claims raise. To date, much of this literature has tended to focus on a perceived relationship between the affirmative recognition and institutional accommodation of societal cultural differences on the one hand, and the freedom and autonomy of marginalized individuals and groups living in ethnically diverse states on the other. In Canada it has been argued that this synthesis of theory and practice has forced the state to dramatically reconceptualize the tenets of its relationship with Indigenous peoples; whereas before 1969 federal Indian policy was unapologetically assimilationist, now it is couched in the vernacular of "mutual recognition."[8]

In the following chapters I critically engage a multiplicity of diverse anti-imperialist traditions and practices to challenge the increasingly commonplace idea that the colonial relationship between Indigenous peoples and the Canadian state can be adequately transformed via such a politics of recognition. Following the work of Richard J. F. Day, I take "politics of recognition" to refer to the now expansive range of recognition-based models of liberal pluralism that seek to "reconcile" Indigenous assertions of nationhood with settler-state sovereignty via the accommodation of Indigenous identity claims in some form of renewed legal and political relationship with the Canadian state.[9] Although these models tend to vary in both theory and practice, most call for the delegation of land, capital, and political power from the state to Indigenous communities through a combination of land claim settlements, economic development initiatives, and self-government agreements. These are subsequently the three broad contexts through which I examine the theory and practice of Indigenous recognition politics in the following chapters. Against this variant of the recognition approach, I argue that instead of ushering in an era of peaceful coexistence grounded on the ideal of *reciprocity* or *mutual* recognition, the politics of recognition in its contemporary liberal form promises to reproduce the very configurations of colonialist, racist, patriarchal state power that Indigenous peoples' demands for recognition have historically sought to transcend.

To demonstrate the above claim, *Red Skin, White Masks* will theoretically and empirically map the contours of what I consider to be a decisive shift in the modus operandi of colonial power following the hegemonization of the recognition paradigm following the release of the federal government's infamous *Statement of the Government of Canada on Indian Policy*—also known as the "White Paper"—in 1969.[10] In the two centuries leading to this historic policy proposal—which called for the blanket assimilation of the status Indian population by unilaterally removing all institutionally enshrined aspects of legal and political differentiation that distinguish First Nations from non-Native Canadians under the Indian Act—the reproduction of the colonial relationship between Indigenous peoples and what would eventually become Canada depended heavily on the deployment of state power geared around genocidal practices of forced *exclusion* and *assimilation*.[11] Any cursory examination into the character of colonial Indian policy during this period will attest to this fact. For example, this era witnessed Canada's repeated attempts to overtly uproot and destroy the vitality and autonomy of Indigenous modes of life through institutions such as residential schools;[12] through the imposition of settler-state policies aimed at explicitly undercutting Indigenous political economies and relations to and with land;[13] through the violent dispossession of First Nation women's rights to land and community membership under sexist provisions of the Indian Act;[14] through the theft of Aboriginal children via racist child welfare policies;[15] and through the near wholesale dispossession of Indigenous peoples' territories and modes of traditional governance in exchange for delegated administrative powers to be exercised over relatively minuscule reserve lands. All of these policies sought to marginalize Indigenous people and communities with the ultimate goal being our *elimination*, if not physically, then as cultural, political, and legal *peoples* distinguishable from the rest of Canadian society.[16] These initiatives reflect the more or less unconcealed, unilateral, and coercive nature of colonial rule during most of the nineteenth and twentieth centuries.

Although Indigenous people and communities have always found ways to individually and collectively resist these oppressive policies and practices, it was not until the tumultuous political climate of Red Power activism in the 1960s and 70s that policies geared toward the recognition and so-called "reconciliation" of Native land and political grievances with state sovereignty began to appear. Three watershed events are generally recognized as shaping this era of Native activism in Canada. The first was the materialization of widespread First Nation opposition to the previously mentioned 1969 White

Paper. Instead of serving as a bridge to passive assimilation, the White Paper inaugurated an unprecedented degree of pan-Indian assertiveness and political mobilization. The National Indian Brotherhood (now the Assembly of First Nations) issued the following response to the federal government's proposed initiative: "We view this as a policy designed to divest us of our aboriginal . . . rights. If we accept this policy, and in the process lose our rights and our lands, we become willing partners in cultural genocide. This we cannot do."[17] Although designed as a once-and-for-all solution to Canada's so-called "Indian Problem," the White Paper instead became a central catalyst around which the contemporary Indigenous self-determination movement coalesced, "launching it into a determined [defense] of a unique cultural heritage and identity."[18] The sheer magnitude of First Nations' resistance to the White Paper proposal forced the federal government to formally shelve the document on March 17, 1971.[19]

The second watershed event occurred following the partial recognition of Aboriginal "title" in the Supreme Court of Canada's 1973 *Calder* decision.[20] This landmark case, which involved a claim launched by Nisga'a hereditary chief Frank Calder to the un-extinguished territories of his nation in northwestern British Columbia, overturned a seventy-five-year precedent first established in *St Catherine's Milling and Lumber Company v. The Queen* (1888), which stated that Aboriginal land rights existed only insofar and to the extent that the state recognized them as such.[21] Although technically a defeat for the Nisga'a, the six justices that rendered substantive decisions in *Calder* all agreed that, prior to contact, the Nisga'a indeed held the land rights they claimed in court.[22] The question then quickly shifted to whether these rights were sufficiently extinguished through colonial legislation. In the end, three justices ruled that the Aboriginal rights in question had not been extinguished, three ruled that they had, and one justice ruled against the Nisga'a based on a technical question regarding whether this type of action could be levelled against the province without legislation permitting it, which he ruled could not.[23] Thus, even though the Nisga'a technically lost their case in a 4–3 decision, the Supreme Court's ruling in *Calder* left enough uncertainty around the question of existing Aboriginal rights that it prompted a shift in the federal government's policy vis-à-vis Native land interests. The result was the federal government's 1973 *Statement on Claims of Indian and Inuit People: A Federal Native Claims Policy*, which effectively reversed fifty-two years (since the 1921 signing of Treaty 11 in the Northwest Territories with the Sahtu Dene) of state refusal to recognize Indigenous claims to land where the question of existing title remained open.[24]

The third event (or rather cluster of events) emerged following the turbulent decade of energy politics that followed the oil crisis of the early 1970s, which subsequently fueled an aggressive push by state and industry to develop what it saw as the largely untapped resource potential (natural gas, minerals, and oil) of northern Canada.[25] The federal government's holding of 45 percent equity in Panartic Oils led Indian Affairs minister Jean Chrétien to state that "it is very seldom in public life that a minister of a government presides over that kind of profit."[26] The proposed increase in northern development was envisioned despite concerns raised by the Métis, Dene, and Inuit of the Northwest Territories regarding Canada's proposal to sanction the development of a huge natural gas pipeline to be carved across the heartland of our traditional territories, as well as the resistance mounted by the Cree of northern Quebec against a similarly massive hydroelectric project proposed for their homeland in the James Bay region.[27] The effectiveness of our subsequent political struggles, which gained unprecedented media coverage across the country, once again raised the issue of unresolved Native rights and title issues to the fore of Canadian public consciousness.

In the following chapters I will show that colonial rule underwent a profound shift in the wake of these important events. More specifically, I argue that the expression of Indigenous anticolonial nationalism that emerged during this period forced colonial power to modify itself from a structure that was once primarily reinforced by policies, techniques, and ideologies explicitly oriented around the genocidal exclusion/assimilation double, to one that is now reproduced through a seemingly more conciliatory set of discourses and institutional practices that emphasize our *recognition* and *accommodation*. Regardless of this modification, however, the relationship between Indigenous peoples and the state has remained *colonial* to its foundation.

KARL MARX, SETTLER-COLONIALISM, AND INDIGENOUS DISPOSSESSION IN POST–WHITE PAPER CANADA

What do I mean by a *colonial*—or more precisely, *settler-colonial* relationship? A settler-colonial relationship is one characterized by a particular form of *domination*; that is, it is a relationship where power—in this case, interrelated discursive and nondiscursive facets of economic, gendered, racial, and state power—has been structured into a relatively secure or sedimented set of hierarchical social relations that continue to facilitate the *dispossession* of Indigenous peoples of their lands and self-determining authority. In this respect, Canada is no different from most other settler-colonial powers: in the Canadian context, colonial domination continues to be structurally committed to maintain—through force, fraud, and more recently, so-called "negotiations"—ongoing state access to the land and resources that contradictorily provide the material and spiritual sustenance of Indigenous societies on the one hand, and the foundation of colonial state-formation, settlement, and capitalist development on the other. As Patrick Wolfe states, "Whatever settlers may say—and they generally have a lot to say—the primary motive [of settler-colonialism] is not race (or religion, ethnicity, grade of civilization, etc.) but access to territory. Territoriality is settler colonialism's specific, irreducible element."[28]

In thinking about colonialism as a form of structured dispossession, I have found it useful to return to a cluster of insights developed by Karl Marx in chapters 26 through 32 of his first volume of *Capital*.[29] This section of *Capital* is crucial because it is there that Marx most thoroughly links the totalizing power of *capital* with that of *colonialism* by way of his theory of "primitive accumulation." Challenging the idyllic portrayal of capitalism's origins by economists like Adam Smith, Marx's chapters on primitive accumulation highlight the gruesomely violent nature of the transition from feudal to capitalist social relations in western Europe (with an emphasis placed on England). Marx's historical excavation of the birth of the capitalist mode of production identifies a host of colonial-like state practices that served to violently strip—through "conquest, enslavement, robbery, murder"[30]—noncapitalist producers, communities, and societies from their means of production and subsistence. In *Capital* these formative acts of violent *dispossession* set the stage for the emergence of capitalist accumulation and the reproduction of capitalist relations of production by tearing Indigenous societies, peasants, and other small-scale, self-sufficient agricultural producers from the source of their livelihood—*the land*. It was this horrific process that established the two necessary preconditions underwriting the capital relation itself: it forcefully opened up what were once collectively held territories and resources to privatization (dispossession and enclosure), which, over time, came to produce a "class" of workers compelled to enter the exploitative realm of the labor market for their survival (proletarianization). The historical process of primitive accumulation thus refers to the violent transformation of noncapitalist forms of life into capitalist ones.

The critical purchase of Marx's primitive accumulation thesis for analyzing the relationship between colonial rule and capitalist accumulation in the contemporary period has been the subject of much debate over the last couple of decades. Within and between the fields of Indigenous studies and Marxist political economy, these debates have at times been hostile and polarizing. At its worst, this hostility has led to the premature rejection of Marx and Marxism by some Indigenous studies scholars on the one side, and to the belligerent, often ignorant, and sometimes racist dismissal of Indigenous peoples' contributions to radical thought and politics by Marxists on the other.[31] At their nondogmatic best, however, I believe that the conversations that continue to occur within and between these two diverse fields of critical inquiry (especially when placed in dialog with feminist, anarchist, queer, and postcolonial traditions) have the potential to shed much insight into the cycles of colonial domination and resistance that characterize the relationship between white settler states and Indigenous peoples.

To my mind, then, for Indigenous peoples to reject or ignore the insights of Marx would be a mistake, especially if this amounts to a refusal on our part to critically engage his important critique of capitalist exploitation and his extensive writings on the entangled relationship between capitalism and colonialism. As Tsimshian anthropologist Charles Menzies writes, "Marxism retains an incisive core that helps understand the dynamics of the world we live." It "highlights the ways in which power is structured through ownership" and exposes the state's role "in the accumulation of capital and the redistribution of wealth from the many to the few."[32] All of this is not to suggest, however, that Marx's contributions are without flaw; nor is it meant to suggest that Marxism provides a ready-made tool for Indigenous peoples to uncritically appropriate in their struggles for land and freedom. As suggested above, rendering Marx's theoretical frame relevant to a comprehensive understanding of settler-colonialism and Indigenous resistance requires that it be transformed *in conversation* with the critical thought and practices of Indigenous peoples themselves. In the spirit of fostering this critical dialog, I suggest that three problematic features of Marx's primitive accumulation thesis are in need of such a transformation.

The first feature involves what many critics have characterized as Marx's rigidly *temporal* framing of the phenomenon. As early as 1899, for example, anarchist geographer Peter Kropotkin made note of what seemed to be an "erroneous division" drawn in Marx "between the *primary* [or primitive] accumulation of capital and its *present day formulation*."[33] The critical point here, which many contemporary writers have subsequently picked up on, is that Marx tended to portray primitive accumulation as if it constituted "a process confined to a particular (if indefinite) period—one already largely passed in England, but still underway in the colonies at the time Marx wrote."[34] For Marx, although the era of violent, state dispossession may have *inaugurated* the accumulation process, in the end it is "the silent compulsion of economic relations" that ultimately "sets the seal on the domination of the capitalist over the worker."[35] This formulation, however, clearly does not conform well to our present global reality. As the recent work of scholars as diverse as David Harvey, Silvia Federici, Taiaiake Alfred, Rauna Kuokkanen, and Andrea Smith (to name but a few) have highlighted, the escalating onslaught of violent, state-orchestrated enclosures following neoliberalism's ascent to hegemony has unmistakably demonstrated the *persistent* role that unconcealed, violent dispossession continues to play in the reproduction of colonial and capitalist social relations in both the domestic and global contexts.[36]

The second feature that needs to be addressed concerns the *normative developmentalism* that problematically underscored Marx's *original* formulation of the primitive accumulation thesis. I stress "original" here because Marx began to reformulate this teleological aspect of his thought in the last decade of his life, and this reformulation has important implications with respect to how we ought to conceptualize the struggles of non-Western societies against the violence that has defined our encounter with colonial modernity. For much of his career, however, Marx propagated within his writings a typically nineteenth-century modernist view of history and historical progress. This developmentalist ontology provided the overarching frame from which thinkers as diverse as Immanuel Kant, Georg W. F. Hegel, John Stuart Mill, and Adam Smith sought to unpack and historically rank variation in "human cultural forms and modes of production" according to each form's "approximation to the full development of the human good."[37] As Michael Hardt and Antonio Negri point out, this modernist commitment often led Marx (along with Engels) to depict those non-Western societies deemed to be positioned at the lower end of this scale of historical or cultural development as "people without history," existing "separate from the development of capital and locked in an immutable present without the capacity for historical innovation."[38] As a result, Marx's most influential work tends to not only portray primitive accumulation as a historical phenomenon in the sense that it constituted a prior or transitional stage in the development of the capitalist mode of production, but that it was also a historically *inevitable* process that would ultimately have a *beneficial* effect on those violently drawn into the capitalist circuit. Take, for instance, Marx's often quoted 1853 *New York Tribune* writings on colonial rule in India. There he suggests that, although vile and barbaric in practice, colonial dispossession would nonetheless have the "revolutionary" effect of bringing the "despotic," "undignified," and "stagnant" life of the Indians into the fold of capitalist-modernity and thus onto the one true path of human development—socialism.[39] Just as Hegel had infamously asserted before him that Africa exists at the "threshold of World History" with "no movement or development to exhibit," Marx would similarly come to declare that "Indian society has no history at all, at least no known history."[40] Clearly, any analysis or critique of contemporary settler-colonialism must be stripped of this Eurocentric feature of Marx's original historical metanarrative.[41]

But this still raises the question of *how* to address this residual feature of Marx's analysis. For our purposes here, I suggest that this can most effectively be accomplished by *contextually shifting* our investigation from an emphasis on the *capital relation* to the *colonial relation*. As suggested in his critical appraisal of Edward G. Wakefield's 1849 text, *A View of the Art of Colonization*, Marx was primarily interested in colonialism because it exposed some "truth" about the nature of capitalism.[42] His interest in the specific character of colonial domination was largely incidental. This is clearly evident in his position on primitive accumulation. As noted already, primitive accumulation involved a dual process for Marx: the accumulation of capital through violent state dispossession resulting in proletarianization. The weight given to these constituent elements, however, is by no means equal in Marx. As he explicitly states in chapter 33 of *Capital*, Marx had little interest in the condition of the "colonies" as such; rather, what caught his attention was "the secret discovered in the New World by the political economy of the Old World, and loudly proclaimed by it: that the capitalist mode of production and accumulation, and therefore capitalist private property as well, have for their fundamental condition the . . .

expropriation of the worker" (emphasis added).[43] When examined from this angle, colonial dispossession appears to constitute an appropriate object of critique and analysis only insofar as it unlocks the key to understanding the nature of capitalism: that capital is not a "thing," but rather a "social relation" dependent on the perpetual separation of workers from the means of production.[44] This was obviously Marx's primary concern, and it has subsequently remained the dominant concern of the Marxist tradition as a whole.[45] The contextual shift advocated here, by contrast, takes as its analytical frame the subject position of the colonized vis-à-vis the effects of *colonial dispossession*, rather than from the primary position of "the waged male proletariat [in] the process of commodity production,"[46] to borrow Silvia Federici's useful formulation.

At least four critical insights into our settler-colonial present emerge from the resolution of these first two problems. First, by making the contextual shift in analysis from the capital-relation to the colonial-relation the inherent injustice of colonial rule is posited *on its own terms and in its own right*. By repositioning the colonial frame as our overarching lens of analysis it becomes far more difficult to justify in antiquated developmental terms (from either the right or the left) the assimilation of noncapitalist, non-Western, Indigenous modes of life based on the racist assumption that this assimilation will somehow magically redeem itself by bringing the fruits of capitalist modernity into the supposedly "backward" world of the colonized.[47] In a certain respect, this was also the guiding insight that eventually led Marx to reformulate his theory after 1871. Subsequently, in the last decade of his life, Marx no longer condemns non-Western and noncapitalist social formations to necessarily pass through the destructive phase of capitalist development as the condition of possibility for human freedom and flourishing. During this period, Marx had not only come to view more clearly how certain features of noncapitalist and capitalist modes of production "articulate" (albeit asymmetrically) in a given social formation, but also the ways in which aspects of the former can come to inform the construction of radical alternatives to the latter.[48]

A similar insight informed Kropotkin's early critique of Marx as well. The problem for Kropotkin was that Marx not only drew an "erroneous division" between the history of state dispossession and what has proven to be its persistent role in the accumulation process, but that this also seemed to justify in crude developmentalist terms the violent dispossession of place-based, non-state modes of self-sufficient Indigenous economic, political, and social activity, only this time to be carried out under the auspices of the coercive authority of *socialist* states. This form of dispossession would eventually come to be championed by Soviet imperialists under the banner *socialist primitive accumulation*.[49] I suggest that by shifting our analytical frame to the colonial relation we might occupy a better angle from which to both anticipate and interrogate practices of settler-state dispossession justified under otherwise egalitarian principles and espoused with so-called "progressive" political agendas in mind. Instead, what must be recognized by those inclined to advocate a blanket "return of the commons" as a redistributive counterstrategy to the neoliberal state's new round of enclosures, is that, in liberal settler states such as Canada, the "commons" not only belong to somebody—*the First Peoples of this land*—they also deeply inform and sustain Indigenous modes of thought and behavior that harbor profound insights into the maintenance of relationships within and between human beings and the natural world built on principles of reciprocity, nonexploitation and respectful coexistence. By ignoring or downplaying the injustice of colonial dispossession, critical theory and left political strategy not only risks becoming complicit in the very structures and processes of domination that it ought to oppose, but it also risks overlooking what could prove to be invaluable glimpses into the ethical practices and preconditions required for the construction of a more just and sustainable world order.

The second insight facilitated by this contextual shift has to do with the role played by Indigenous labor in the historical process of colonial-capital accumulation in Canada. It is now generally acknowledged among historians and political economists that following the waves of colonial settlement that marked the transition between mercantile and industrial capitalism (roughly spanning the years 1860–1914, but with significant variation between geographical regions), Native labor became increasingly (although by no means entirely) superfluous to the political and economic development of the Canadian state.[50] Increased European settlement combined with an imported, hyperexploited non-European workforce meant that, in the post–fur trade period, Canadian state-formation and colonial-capitalist development required first and foremost *land*, and only secondarily the surplus value afforded by cheap, Indigenous labor.[51] This is not to suggest, however, that the long-term goal of indoctrinating the Indigenous population to the principles of private property, possessive individualism, and menial wage work did not constitute an important feature of Canadian Indian policy. It did. As the commissioner of Indian Affairs in 1890 wrote: "The work of sub-dividing reserves has begun in earnest. The policy of destroying the tribal or communist system is assailed in every possible way and every effort [has been] made to implant a spirit of individual responsibility instead."[52]

When this historical consideration is situated alongside the contemporary fact that there has been, first, a steady increase in Native migration to urban centers over the last few decades, and, second, that many First Nation communities are situated on or near lands coveted by the resource exploitation industry, it is reasonable to conclude that disciplining Indigenous life to the cold rationality of market principles will remain on state and industry's agenda for some time to follow.[53] In this respect Marx's thesis still stands. What I want to point out, rather, is that when related back to the primitive accumulation thesis it appears that the history and experience of *dispossession*, not proletarianization, has been the dominant background structure shaping the character of the historical relationship between Indigenous peoples and the Canadian state. Just as importantly, I would also argue that dispossession continues to inform the dominant modes of Indigenous resistance and critique that this relationship has provoked. Stated bluntly, the theory and practice of Indigenous anticolonialism, including Indigenous anticapitalism, is best understood as a struggle primarily inspired by and oriented around *the question of land*— a struggle not only *for* land in the material sense, but also deeply *informed* by what the land *as system of reciprocal relations and obligations* can teach us about living our lives in relation to one another and the natural world in nondominating and nonexploitative terms—and less around our emergent status as "rightless proletarians."[54] I call this place-based foundation of Indigenous decolonial thought and practice *grounded normativity*, by which I mean the modalities of Indigenous land-connected practices and longstanding experiential knowledge that inform and structure our ethical engagements with the world and our relationships with human and nonhuman others over time.

The third insight to flow from this contextual shift corresponds to a number of concerns expressed by Indigenous peoples, deep ecologists, defenders of animal rights, and other advocates of environmental sustainability regarding perceived "anti-ecological" tendencies in Marx's work. Although this field of criticism tends to be internally diverse—and some have argued, overstated (I am thinking here of eco-socialists like Joel Kovel and John Bellamy Foster)—

at its core it suggests that Marx's perspectives on nature adhered to an instrumental rationality that placed no intrinsic value on the land or nature itself, and that this subsequently led him to uncritically champion an ideology of productivism and unsustainable economic progress.[55] From the vantage point of the capital relationship—which, I have argued, tends to concern itself most with the adverse structural and ideological effects stemming from expropriated labor—*land is not exploitable, people are.* I believe that reestablishing the colonial relation of dispossession as a co-foundational feature of our understanding of and critical engagement with capitalism opens up the possibility of developing a more ecologically attentive critique of colonial-capitalist accumulation, especially if this engagement takes its cues from the grounded normativity of Indigenous modalities of place-based resistance and criticism.

And finally, the fourth insight that flows from the contextual shift advocated here involves what many have characterized as Marx's (and orthodox Marxism's) economic reductionism. It should be clear in the following pages that there is much more at play in the contemporary reproduction of settler-colonial social relations than capitalist economics; most notably, the host of interrelated yet semi-autonomous facets of discursive and nondiscursive power briefly identified earlier. Although it is beyond question that the predatory nature of capitalism continues to play a vital role in facilitating the ongoing dispossession of Indigenous peoples in Canada, it is necessary to recognize that it only does so *in relation to or in concert with* axes of exploitation and domination configured along racial, gender, and state lines. Given the resilience of these equally devastating modalities of power, I argue that any strategy geared toward authentic decolonization must directly confront more than mere economic relations; it has to account for the multifarious ways in which capitalism, patriarchy, white supremacy, and the totalizing character of state power interact with one another to form the constellation of power relations that sustain colonial patterns of behavior, structures, and relationships. I suggest that shifting our attention to the colonial frame is one way to facilitate this form of radical intersectional analysis.[56] Seen from this light, the colonial relation should not be understood as a primary locus or "base" from which these other forms of oppression flow, but rather as the inherited background field within which market, racist, patriarchal, and state relations *converge* to facilitate a certain power effect—in our case, the reproduction of hierarchical social relations that facilitate the dispossession of our lands and self-determining capacities. Like capital, colonialism, as a structure of domination predicated on dispossession, is not "a thing," but rather the sum effect of the diversity of interlocking oppressive social relations that constitute it. When stated this way, it should be clear that shifting our position to highlight the ongoing effects of colonial dispossession in no way displaces questions of distributive justice or class struggle; rather, it simply situates these questions more firmly alongside and in relation to the other sites and relations of power that inform our settler-colonial present.

With these four insights noted, I can now turn to the third and final feature that needs to be addressed with respect to Marx's primitive accumulation thesis. This one, which constitutes the core theoretical intervention of this book, brings us back to my original claim that, in the Canadian context, colonial relations of power are no longer reproduced primarily through overtly coercive means, but rather through the asymmetrical exchange of mediated forms of state recognition and accommodation. This is obviously quite different from the story Marx tells, where the driving force behind dispossession and accumulation is initially that of *violence:* it is a relationship of brute "force," of "servitude," whose methods, Marx claims, are "anything but idyllic."[57] The strategic deployment of violent sovereign power, then, serves the primary reproductive function in the accumulation process in Marx's writings on colonialism. As Marx himself bluntly put it, these gruesome state practices are what thrust capitalism onto the world stage, "dripping from head to toe, from every pore, in blood and dirt."[58]

The question that needs to be asked in our context, however, and the question to which I provide an answer in the following chapters, is this: what are we to make of contexts where state violence no longer constitutes the regulative norm governing the process of colonial dispossession, as appears to be the case in ostensibly tolerant, multinational, liberal settler polities such as Canada?[59] Stated in Marx's own terms, if neither "blood and fire" nor the "silent compulsion" of capitalist economics can adequately account for the reproduction of colonial hierarchies in liberal democratic contexts, what can?

FRANTZ FANON AND THE POLITICS OF RECOGNITION IN COLONIAL CONTEXTS

To elucidate precisely *how* colonial rule made the transition from a more-or-less unconcealed structure of domination to a mode of colonial *governmentality* that works through the limited freedoms afforded by state recognition and accommodation, I will be drawing significantly (but not exclusively) on the work of anticolonial theorist, psychiatrist, and revolutionary Frantz Fanon.[60] At first blush, turning to Fanon to develop an understanding of the regulating mechanisms undergirding settler-colonial rule in contexts where state violence no longer constitutes the norm governing the process might seem a bit odd to those familiar with his work. After all, Fanon is arguably best known for the articulation of colonialism he develops in *The Wretched of the Earth*, where colonial rule is posited, much like Marx posited it before him, as a structure of dominance maintained through unrelenting and punishing forms of violence. "In colonial regions," writes Fanon, the state "uses a language of *pure violence*. [It] does not alleviate oppression or mask domination." Instead, "the proximity and frequent, direct intervention by the police and military ensure the colonized are kept under close scrutiny, and contained by rifle butts and napalm" (emphasis added).[61] And considering Fanon wrote *The Wretched of the Earth* during one of the twentieth century's most gruesome anticolonial struggles—the Algerian war of independence (1954–62)—it is not surprising that he placed so much emphasis on colonialism's openly coercive and violent features. Given the severe nature of the colonial situation within which *The Wretched of the Earth* was produced one could argue that the diagnosis and prescriptions outlined in the text were tragically appropriate to the context they set out to address.

But this simply is not the case in contemporary Canada, and for this reason I begin my investigation with a sustained engagement with Fanon's earlier work, *Black Skin, White Masks*. As we shall see in the following chapter, it is there that Fanon offers a groundbreaking critical analysis of the affirmative relationship drawn between recognition and freedom in the master/slave dialectic of Hegel's *Phenomenology of Spirit*—a critique I claim is equally applicable to contemporary liberal recognition-based approaches to Indigenous self-determination in Canada.[62] Fanon's analysis suggests that in contexts where colonial rule is not reproduced through force alone, the maintenance of settler-state hegemony requires the production of what he liked to call "colonized subjects": namely, the production of the specific modes of colonial thought, desire, and behavior that implicitly or explicitly commit the colonized to the types of practices and subject positions that are required for their continued domination. However, unlike the liberalized appropriation of Hegel that continues to inform many contemporary proponents of identity politics, in Fanon recognition is not posited as a source of freedom and dignity for the colonized, *but rather as the field of power through which colonial relations are produced and maintained*. This "is the form of recognition," Fanon suggests, "that Hegel never described."[63] Subsequently, this is also the form of recognition that I set out to interrogate in *Red Skin, White Masks*.

OUTLINE OF THE BOOK

With these preliminary remarks made, I will now provide a brief outline of the structure and chapter breakdown of the book. In chapter 1, I use Frantz Fanon's critique of Hegel's master/slave dialectic to challenge the now commonplace assumption that the structure of domination that frames Indigenous–state relations in Canada can be undermined via a liberal politics of recognition. I begin my analysis by identifying two Hegelian assumptions that continue to inform the politics of recognition today. The first, which is now uncontroversial, involves recognition's perceived role in the constitution of human subjectivity: the notion that our identities are formed *intersubjectively* through our complex social interactions with other subjects. As Charles Taylor influentially asserts: the "crucial feature of human life is its fundamentally *dialogical* character. . . . We define our identity always in dialogue with, sometimes in struggle against, the things our significant others acknowledge in us."[64] The second, more contentious assumption suggests that the specific structural or interpersonal character of our relations of recognition can have a positive (when mutual and affirmative) or detrimental (when unequal and disparaging) effect on our status as *free and self-determining agents*. I draw off Fanon's work to partially challenge this second assumption by demonstrating the ways in which the purportedly diversity-affirming forms of state recognition and accommodation defended by some proponents of contemporary liberal recognition politics can subtly reproduce nonmutual and unfree relations rather than free and mutual ones. At its core, Fanon's critique of colonial recognition politics can be summarized like this: when delegated exchanges of recognition occur in real world contexts of domination the terms of accommodation usually end up being determined by and in the interests of the hegemonic partner in the relationship. This is the *structural* problem of colonial recognition identified by Fanon in *Black Skin, White Masks*. Fanon then goes on to demonstrate how subaltern populations often develop what he called "psycho-affective" attachments to these structurally circumscribed modes of recognition. For Fanon, these ideological attachments are essential in maintaining the economic and political structure of colonial relationships over time. This is the *subjective* dimension to the problem of colonial recognition highlighted in *Black Skin, White Masks*. With these two interrelated problematics identified, I go on to conclude the chapter with a brief discussion of an alternative politics of recognition, one that is less oriented around attaining legal and political recognition by the state, and more about Indigenous peoples empowering themselves through cultural practices of individual and collective self-fashioning that seek to *prefigure* radical alternatives to the structural and subjective dimensions of colonial power identified earlier in the chapter. I call this a *resurgent politics of recognition* and take it up in more detail in my concluding chapter.

In chapters 2, 3, and 4, I set out to empirically demonstrate the largely theoretical insights that are derived from my applied use of Fanon's critique of Hegel's master/slave narrative through three case studies drawn from the post-1969 history of Indigenous–state relations in Canada. These case studies will also serve to flesh out in more detail a number of recent debates within the liberal recognition and identity politics literature, including those that have focused on the following cluster of issues and concerns.

The Left-Materialist Challenge

The ascendant status of "identity," "culture," and "recognition" in contemporary political struggles has not emerged without controversy. Critics on the left, for example, have long voiced concern over what they claim to be the excessively insular and divisive character of many culture-based, identity-related movements.[65] More specifically, they argue that the inherently parochial and particularistic orientation of recognition-based politics is serving (or worse, has already served) to undermine more egalitarian and universal aspirations, like those focused on class and directed toward a more equitable distribution of socioeconomic goods. As Brian Barry explains: "Pursuit of the multiculturalist [recognition] agenda makes the achievement of broadly based egalitarian policies difficult in two ways. At a minimum it diverts political effort away from universalistic goals. But a more serious problem is that multiculturalism may very well destroy the conditions for putting together a coalition in favour of across-the-board equalisation of opportunities and resources."[66] In such contexts it would indeed appear that "recognition struggles are serving less to supplement, complicate and enrich redistribution struggles than to marginalize, eclipse and displace them," as Nancy Fraser's work suggests.[67] In short, advocates of the left-materialist critique challenge the affirmative relationship drawn between recognition and freedom by many defenders of identity/difference politics on the grounds that such a politics has proven itself incapable of transforming the generative material conditions that so often work to foreclose the realization of self-determination in the lives of ordinary citizens.

Chapter 2 interrogates the above challenge through an examination of the cultural, political, and economic dynamics that informed the Dene Nation's struggle for national recognition and self-determination in the 1970s and early 1980s. During this period the Dene Nation was the main organization representing the political interests of the Dene peoples of the Northwest Territories, of which my own community is a part (the Yellowknives Dene First Nation). Although sensitive to certain concerns animating the left-materialist position, I argue that there is nothing intrinsic to the identity-related struggles of Indigenous peoples that predispose them to the cluster of charges noted above. To the contrary, I suggest that insofar as Indigenous cultural claims always involve demands for a more equitable distribution of land, political power, and economic resources, the left-materialist claim regarding the displacement of economic concerns by cultural ones is misplaced when applied to settler-colonial contexts.[68] However, if one takes a modified version of the displacement thesis and instead examines the relationship between Indigenous recognition claims and the distinction made by Nancy Fraser between "transformative" and "affirmative" forms of redistribution the criticism begins to hold more weight.[69] For Fraser, "transformative" models of redistribution are those that aspire to correct unjust distributions of power and resources *at their source*, whereas "affirmative" strategies, by contrast, strive to alter or modify the second-order effects of these first-order root causes. As we shall see with the example drawn from my community, the last forty years has witnessed a gradual erosion of this transformative vision within the mainstream Dene self-determination movement, which in the context of northern land claims and economic development has resulted in a partial decoupling of Indigenous "cultural" claims from the radical aspirations for social, political and economic change that once underpinned them. However, following my reading of Fanon, I argue that this gradual displacement of questions of Indigenous sovereignty and alternative political economies by narrowly conceived cultural claims within the Dene struggle is better understood as an *effect* of primitive accumulation via the hegemonization of the liberal discourse of recognition than due to some core deficiency with Indigenous cultural politics as such.

The Essentialism Challenge

The second constellation of criticisms frequently leveled against the recognition paradigm revolves around the "essentialist" articulations of individual and collective identity that sometimes anchor demands for cultural accommodation in theory and practice. In recent feminist, queer, and antiracist literature, the term "essentialism" is often used pejoratively to refer to those theories and social practices that treat identity categories such as gender, race, and class as "fixed, immutable and universal," instead of being constructed, contingent, and open to "cultural variation."[70] According to Ann Philips, when recognition-based models of cultural pluralism invoke essentialist articulations of identity they risk functioning "not as a cultural liberator but as a cultural straitjacket," forcing members of minority cultural groups "into a regime of authenticity, denying them the chance to cross cultural borders, borrow cultural influences, define and redefine themselves."[71] In order to avoid this potentially repressive feature of identity politics, we are told that the various expressions of identification and signification that underpin demands for recognition—such as "gender," "culture," "nationhood," and "tradition"—must remain open-ended and never immune from contestation or democratic deliberation. The anti-essentialist position thus poses yet another set of challenges to the affirmative relationship drawn between recognition and freedom by uncritical supporters of the politics of difference.

Chapter 3 unpacks some of the problems identified by the anti-essentialist challenge through a gendered analysis of the decade of Indigenous mega-constitutional politics spanning the patriation of Canada's Constitution Act, 1982 and the demise of the Charlottetown Accord in 1992. The Charlottetown Accord was a proposed agreement struck between the federal government, the provincial and territorial governments, and Aboriginal representatives on a proposed series of amendments to the Constitution Act, 1982. Among other things, the amendment sought to address issues concerning the recognition of Quebec's distinct status within confederation, the recognition of an Aboriginal right to self-government, and parliamentary reform.

Although I remain indebted to the critical insights offered by Frantz Fanon and activists within the Dene Nation regarding the entangled relationship among racism, state power, capitalism, and colonial dispossession, all paid insufficient attention to the role played by patriarchy in this corrosive configuration of power. Recent feminist analyses of the ten-year effort to constitutionally entrench an Aboriginal right to self-government provide a particularly illustrative corrective to this shortcoming. Specifically, these analyses have done an excellent job foregrounding the manner in which contemporary essentialist articulations of Indigenous culture have converged with the legacy of patriarchal misrecognition under the Indian Act to discursively inform our recent efforts to attain recognition of a right to self-government. However, even though I find much of this anti-essentialist-inspired analysis compelling, I nonetheless hope to illuminate two problems that arise when this form of criticism is uncritically wielded in the context of Indigenous peoples' struggles for recognition and self-determination. First, using recent feminist and deliberative democratic critiques of Indigenous recognition politics as a backdrop, I demonstrate how normative appropriations of social constructivism can undercut the liberatory aspirations of anti-essentialist criticism by failing to adequately address the complexity of interlocking social relations that serve to exasperate the types of exclusionary cultural practices that critics of essentialism find so disconcerting. Second, and perhaps more problematically, I show that when constructivist views of culture are posited as a universal feature of social life and then used as a means to evaluate the legitimacy of Indigenous claims for cultural recognition against the uncontested authority of the colonial state, it can serve to sanction the very forms of domination and inequality that anti-essentialist criticism ought to mitigate.

Chapter 4 examines the convergence of Indigenous recognition politics with the more recent transitional justice discourse of "reconciliation" that began to gain considerable attention in Canada following the publication of the *Report of the Royal Commission on Aboriginal Peoples* (RCAP) in 1996. RCAP was established by the federal government in 1991 in the wake of two national crises that unraveled the previous summer and fall: the failed Meech Lake Accord and the armed standoff between the Mohawks of Kanesatake, Quebec, and the Canadian military (popularly known as the "Oka Crisis"). The commission was established with a sixteen-point mandate to investigate the troubled relationship between Aboriginal peoples and the state, and to issue a series of comprehensive recommendations that might serve to facilitate a process of genuine "reconciliation." The last thirty years have witnessed a global proliferation of state institutional mechanisms that promote "forgiveness" and "reconciliation" as a means of resolving the adverse social impacts of various forms of intrastate violence and historical injustice. Originally, however, this approach to conflict resolution was developed in polities undergoing a formal "transition" from the violent history of openly authoritarian regimes to more democratic forms of rule. This chapter will explore the efficacy of transitional justice mechanisms—such as state apologies, commissions of inquiry, truth and reconciliation commissions, individual reparations, and so forth—when applied to the "nontransitional" context of the Canadian settler state.

In doing so, I argue that in settler-colonial contexts such as Canada—where there is no formal period marking an explicit transition from an authoritarian past to a democratic present—state-sanctioned approaches to reconciliation tend to ideologically fabricate such a transition by narrowly situating the abuses of settler colonization firmly *in the past*. In these situations, reconciliation itself becomes temporally framed as the process of individually and collectively *overcoming* the harmful "legacy" left in the wake of this past abuse, while leaving the *present* structure of colonial rule largely unscathed. In such a context, those who refuse to forgive or reconcile are typically represented in the policy literature as suffering from this legacy, unable or unwilling to "move on" because of their simmering anger and resentment. Drawing again on Frantz Fanon's work, I challenge the ways in which Canadian reconciliation politics tends to uncritically represent Indigenous expressions of anger and resentment as "negative" emotions that threaten to impede the realization of reconciliation in the lives of Indigenous people and communities on the one hand, and between Indigenous nations and Canada on the other. Although it is on occasion acknowledged that reactive emotions like anger and resentment can generate both positive and negative effects, more often than not defenders of reconciliation represent these emotional expressions in an unsympathetic light—as irrational, as physically and psychologically unhealthy, as reactionary, backward looking, and even as socially pathological. In contradistinction to this view, I argue that in the context of ongoing settler-colonial injustice, Indigenous peoples' anger and resentment can indicate a sign of moral protest and political outrage that we ought to at least take seriously, if not embrace as a sign of our critical consciousness.

By the end of chapter 4 it should be evident why Fanon did not attribute much emancipatory potential to either a Hegelian or liberal politics of recognition when applied to colonial situations; this did not lead Fanon to reject the recognition paradigm entirely, however. Instead, what Fanon's work does is redirect our attention to the host of *self-affirmative* cultural practices that colonized peoples often critically engage in to *empower themselves,* as opposed to relying too heavily on the subjectifying apparatus of the state or other dominant institutions of power to do this for them. In doing so, Fanon's position challenges colonized peoples to transcend the fantasy that the settler-state apparatus—as a structure of domination *predicated* on our ongoing dispossession—is somehow capable of producing liberatory effects.[72] The task of chapter 5 is to flesh out this self-affirmative thread in Fanon's thought and politics through a critical reading of his engagement with the work of Jean-Paul Sartre on the one hand, and the *negritude* movement on the other. Although negritude constituted a diverse body of inter- and postwar, francophone black artistic production and political activism, at its core the movement emphasized the need for colonized people and communities to purge themselves of the internalized effects of colonial racism through an affirmation of the worth of black difference. I argue that even though Fanon's critical appraisal of negritude clearly saw the revaluation of precolonial African cultural forms as a crucial means of momentarily freeing the colonized from the interpellative grasp of racist misrecognition, in the end it will be shown that he shared Sartre's unwillingness to acknowledge the transformative role that critically revived Indigenous cultural practices might play in the construction of alternatives to the colonial project of genocide and land dispossession. I thus conclude the chapter with the claim that, although insightful in many respects, Fanon's overly instrumental view of the relationship between culture and decolonization renders his theory inadequate as a framework for understanding contemporary Indigenous struggles for self-determination. Indigenous peoples tend to view their resurgent practices of cultural self-recognition and empowerment as *permanent* features of our decolonial political projects, not transitional ones.

The conclusion begins with a reiteration of the main line of argument defended in *Red Skin, White Masks*—that the liberal recognition-based approach to Indigenous self-determination in Canada that began to consolidate itself after the demise of the 1969 White Paper has not only failed, but now serves to reproduce the very forms of colonial power which our original demands for recognition sought to transcend. This argument will undoubtedly be controversial to many Indigenous scholars and Aboriginal organization leaders insofar as it suggests that much of our efforts over the last four decades to attain settler-state recognition of our rights to land and self-government have in fact encouraged the opposite—the continued dispossession of our homelands and the ongoing usurpation of our self-determining authority. I suggest that this conclusion demands that we begin to collectively redirect our struggles *away* from a politics that seeks to attain a conciliatory form of settler-state recognition for Indigenous nations toward a *resurgent politics of recognition* premised on self-actualization, direct action, and the resurgence of cultural practices that are attentive to the subjective and structural composition of settler-colonial power. I thus conclude my investigation in *Red Skin, White Masks* with "5 theses" on Indigenous politics that highlight the core features of this resurgent approach to Indigenous decolonization in light of the Idle No More movement that exploded onto the Canadian political scene in Canada in the late fall/early winter of 2012. What originally began in the fall of 2012 as an education campaign designed to inform Canadians about a particularly repugnant and undemocratic piece of legislation recently passed by the Canadian federal government—the Jobs and Growth Act, or Bill C-45, which threatens to erode Indigenous land and treaty rights as well as environmental protections for much of our waterways—had erupted by mid-January 2013 into a full-blown defense of Indigenous land and sovereignty. Idle No More offers a productive case study through which to explore what a resurgent Indigenous politics might look like on the ground.

1

The Politics of Recognition in Colonial Contexts

Humanity does not gradually progress from combat to combat until it arrives at universal reciprocity, where the rule of law finally replaces warfare. Humanity installs each of its violences in a system of rules and thus proceeds from domination to domination.

—MICHEL FOUCAULT, *"Nietzsche, Genealogy, History"*

For Hegel there is reciprocity; here the master laughs at the consciousness of the slave. What he wants from the slave is not recognition but work.

—FRANTZ FANON, *Black Skin, White Masks*

My introductory chapter began by making two broad claims: first, I claimed that since 1969 we have witnessed the modus operandi of colonial power relations in Canada shift from a more or less unconcealed structure of domination to a form of colonial governance that works through the medium of state recognition and accommodation; and second, I claimed that regardless of this shift Canadian settler-colonialism remains structurally oriented around achieving the same power effect it sought in the pre-1969 period: the dispossession of Indigenous peoples of their lands and self-determining authority. This chapter further develops my first claim by providing a theoretical account of *how* the politics of recognition has come to serve the interests of colonial power in the ways that it has. It is to this question, I claim, that Fanon provides a strikingly perceptive answer: in situations where colonial rule does not depend solely on the exercise of state violence, its reproduction instead rests on the ability to entice Indigenous peoples to *identify*, either implicitly or explicitly, with the profoundly *asymmetrical* and *nonreciprocal* forms of recognition either imposed on or granted to them by the settler state and society.

Fanon first developed this insight in his 1952 text, *Black Skin, White Masks*, where he persuasively challenges the applicability of Hegel's dialectic of recognition to colonial and racialized settings.[1] In contradistinction to what he viewed as Hegel's abstraction, Fanon argued that, in *actual* contexts of domination (such as colonialism), not only are the terms of recognition usually determined by and in the interests of the master (the colonizing state and society), but also over time slave populations (the colonized) tend to develop what he called "psycho-affective" attachments to these master-sanctioned forms of recognition, and that this attachment is essential in maintaining the economic and political structure of master/slave (colonizer/colonized) relations themselves.[2] By the end of this chapter it should be clear in theoretical terms that the contemporary politics of recognition is ill equipped to deal with the interrelated structural and psycho-affective dimensions of colonial power that Fanon implicated in the preservation of colonial hierarchies. Once this theoretical ground has been paved, I can then proceed in chapters 2, 3, and 4 to evaluate Fanon's critique against three empirical case studies drawn from the post-1969 history of Indigenous–state relations in Canada.

This chapter is organized into four sections. In the first section, I outline some of the underlying assumptions that inform the politics of recognition from Hegel's master/slave to the work of Charles Taylor. In the second section, I apply the insights of Fanon's critique of Hegel's dialectic of recognition to highlight a number of problems that appear to plague Taylor's politics of recognition when applied to colonial contexts. Although I tend to focus most of my attention on Taylor's work, it should be clear that the conclusions reached in this chapter are by no means limited to his contribution alone. In the third section, I hope to show that the processes of colonial subjection identified in the previous sections, although formidable, are not total. As Robert Young argues, Fanon himself spent much of his career as a psychiatrist investigating "the inner effects of colonialism" in order to establish "a means through which they could be resisted, turning the inculcation of inferiority into self-empowerment."[3] Here I argue that the self-affirmative logic underlying Fanon's writings on anticolonial agency and empowerment offer a potential means of evading the liberal politics of recognition's tendency to produce colonial subjects. The groundwork laid in section 3 will provide a launching point for my discussion in chapter 5 and my conclusion, where the theory and practice of Indigenous anticolonialism as a resurgent practice of cultural self-recognition will be taken up in more detail. And finally, in the last section, I address an important counterargument to my position through a critical engagement with the work of Anishinaabe political philosopher Dale Turner.

RECOGNITION FROM HEGEL'S MASTER-SLAVE TO CHARLES TAYLOR'S "POLITICS OF RECOGNITION"

It is now commonly acknowledged that one of Hegel's most enduring contributions to contemporary social and political thought has been his concept of "recognition." In the words of Nancy Fraser and Axel Honneth: "Whether the issue is indigenous land claims or women's carework, homosexual marriage or Muslim headscarves . . . the term 'recognition' [is increasingly used] to unpack the normative bases of [today's] political claims. . . . 'Recognition' has become a key word of our time."[4]

For my purposes here it will suffice to limit my discussion of Hegel's theory of recognition to his chapter "Lordship and Bondage" in the *Phenomenology of Spirit*.[5] This narrower approach can be justified on two grounds. First, although others have recognized the importance of Hegel's earlier and later writings on recognition, Fanon was primarily concerned, following Alexander Kojève and Jean-Paul Sartre,[6] with recognition as it appeared in the master/slave dialectic of the *Phenomenology of Spirit*. In this respect, it has been suggested that Fanon's work be read as an important, yet largely ignored, contribution to the so-called Hegel "renaissance" that occurred in France's intellectual scene after World War II.[7] The second justification is that this chapter is not about Hegel per se. Rather, it concerns the contemporary appropriation (whether implicit or explicit) of his theory of recognition by activists, political theorists, and policy makers working on issues pertaining to Indigenous self-determination in Canada. Only once I have teased out the logic of recognition at play in Hegel's master/slave narrative, can I begin to unpack and problematize this appropriation.

As suggested in the previous chapter, at its core, Hegel's master/slave narrative can be read in at least two ways that continue to inform contemporary recognition-based theories of liberal pluralism. On the first reading, Hegel's dialectic outlines a theory of identity formation that cuts against the classical liberal view of the subject insofar as it situates social relations at the fore of human subjectivity. On this account, relations of recognition are deemed "constitutive of subjectivity: one becomes an individual subject only in virtue of recognizing, and being recognized by another subject."[8] Our senses of self are thus dependent on and shaped through our complex relations with others. This insight into the intersubjective nature of identity formation underlies Hegel's often quoted assertion that "self-consciousness exists in and for itself when, and by the fact that, it so exists for another; that is, it exists only in being acknowledged."[9]

On the second reading, the dialectic moves beyond highlighting the relational nature of human subjectivity to elucidate what Hegel sees as the intersubjective conditions required for the *realization of human freedom*. From this perspective, the master/slave narrative can be read in a normative light in that it suggests that the realization of oneself as an essential, self-determining agent requires that one not only be recognized as self-determining, but that one be recognized by another self-consciousness that is also recognized as self-determining. It is through these reciprocal processes and exchanges of recognition that the condition of possibility for freedom emerges.[10] Hence Hegel's repeated insistence that relations of recognition be *mutual*. This point is driven home in the latter half of Hegel's section "Lordship and Bondage," when he discusses the ironic fate of the master in a context of asymmetrical recognition. After the "life-and-death struggle" between the two self-consciousnesses temporarily cashes out in the hierarchical master/slave relationship, Hegel goes on to depict a surprising turn of events in which the *master's* desire for recognition as an essential "being-for-itself" is thwarted by the fact that he or she is only recognized by the unessential and dependent consciousness of the slave,[11] and of course recognition by a slave hardly constitutes recognition at all. In this "onesided and unequal" relationship the master fails to gain certainty of "being-for-self as the truth of himself. On the contrary, his truth is in reality the unessential consciousness and its unessential action."[12] Meanwhile, as the master continues to wallow in his sluggish state of increased dependency, the slave, through his or her transformative labor, "becomes conscious of what he truly is" and "*qua* worker" comes to realize "his own independence."[13] Thus, in the end, the truth of independent consciousness and one's status as a self-determining actor is realized more through the praxis of the slave— through his or her transformative work in and on the world. However, here it is important to note that for Hegel, "the revolution of the slave is not simply to replace the master while maintaining the unequal hierarchical recognition." This, of course, would only temporarily invert the relation, and the slave would eventually meet the same fate as the master. Rather, as Robert Williams reminds us, Hegel's project was to move "*beyond* the patterns of domination [and] inequality" that typify asymmetrical relations of recognition as such.[14] It is also on this point that many contemporary theorists of recognition remain committed.

In *Bound by Recognition*, Patchen Markell suggests that one of the most significant differences between recognition in Hegel's master/slave and the "politics of recognition" today is that state institutions tend to play a fundamental role in mediating relations of recognition in the latter, but not the former.[15] For example, regarding policies aimed at preserving cultural diversity, Markell writes: "far from being simple face-to-face encounters between subjects, *à la* Hegel's stylized story in the *Phenomenology*," multiculturalism tends to "involve large-scale exchanges of recognition in which states typically play a crucial role."[16] Charles Taylor's "The Politics of Recognition" provides a particularly salient example of this. In this essay, Taylor draws on the insights of Hegel, among others, to mount a sustained critique of what he claims to be the increasingly "impracticable" nature of "difference-blind" liberalism when applied to culturally diverse polities such as the United States and Canada.[17] Alternatively, Taylor defends a variant of liberal thought that posits that, under certain circumstances, diverse states can indeed recognize and accommodate a range of group-specific claims without having to abandon their commitment to a core set of fundamental rights.[18] Furthermore, these types of claims can be defended on liberal grounds because it is within and against the horizon of one's cultural community that individuals come to develop their identities, and thus the capacity to make sense of their lives and life choices. In short, our identities provide the "background against which our tastes and desires and opinions and aspirations make sense. Without this orienting framework we would be unable to derive meaning from our lives—we would not know "who we are" or "where [we are] coming from." We would be "at sea," as Taylor puts it elsewhere.[19]

Thus, much like Hegel before him, Taylor argues that human actors do not develop their identities in "isolation," rather they are "formed" through "dialogue with others, in agreement or struggle with their recognition of us."[20] However, given that our identities are formed through these relations, it also follows that they can be significantly *deformed* when these processes go awry. This is what Taylor means when he asserts that identities are shaped not only by recognition, but also its *absence*, "often by the *mis*recognition of others. A person or a group of people can suffer real damage, real distortion, if the people or society around them mirror back to them a confining or demeaning or contemptible picture of themselves. Nonrecognition or misrecognition can inflict harm, can be a form of oppression, imprisoning one in a false, distorted, and reduced mode of being."[21] This idea that asymmetrical relations of recognition can impede human freedom by "imprisoning" someone in a distorted relation-to-self is asserted repeatedly in Taylor's essay. For instance, we are frequently told that disparaging forms of recognition can inflict "wounds" on their "victims," "saddling [them] with a crippling self-hatred"; or that withholding recognition can "inflict damage" on "those who are denied it."[22] And given that misrecognition has the capacity to "harm" others in this manner, it follows, according to Taylor, that it be considered "a form of oppression" on par with "injustices" such as "inequality" and "exploitation."[23] In Taylor, recognition is elevated to the status of a "vital human need."[24]

At this point the practical implications of Taylor's theory begin to reveal themselves. In his more prescriptive moments, Taylor suggests that, in Canada, both the Quebecois and Indigenous peoples exemplify the types of threatened minorities that ought to be considered eligible for some form of recognition capable of accommodating their cultural distinctiveness. For Indigenous peoples specifically, this might require the delegation of political and cultural "autonomy" to Native groups through the institutions of "self-government."[25] Elsewhere, Taylor suggests that this could mean "in practice allowing for a new form of jurisdiction in Canada, perhaps weaker than the provinces, but, unlike municipalities."[26] Accommodating the claims of First Nations in this way would ideally allow Native communities to "preserve their cultural integrity" and thus help stave off the psychological disorientation and resultant unfreedom associated with exposure to structured patterns of mis- or nonrecognition.[27] In this way, the institutionalization of a liberal regime of reciprocal recognition would better enable Indigenous peoples to realize their status as distinct and self-determining actors.

Although it is true that the normative dimension of Taylor's project represents an improvement over Canada's "past tactics of exclusion, genocide, and assimilation," in the following section I argue that the logic informing this dimension—where "recognition" is conceived as something that is ultimately "granted" or "accorded" a subaltern group or entity by a dominant group or entity—prefigures its failure to significantly modify, let alone transcend, the breadth of power at play in colonial relationships.[28] I also hope to show that Fanon, whose work Taylor relies on to delineate the relationship between misrecognition and the forms of unfreedom and subjection discussed above, anticipated this failure over fifty years ago.

Frantz Fanon's "Sociodiagnostic" Critique of Recognition Politics

In the second half of "The Politics of Recognition" Taylor identifies Fanon's classic *The Wretched of the Earth* as one of the first texts to elicit the role that misrecognition plays in propping up relations of domination.[29] By extension Fanon's analysis in *The Wretched of the Earth* is also used to support one of the central political arguments underlying Taylor's analysis, namely, his call for the cultural recognition of sub-state groups that have suffered at the hands of a hegemonic political power. Although Taylor acknowledges that Fanon advocated "violent" struggle as the primary means of overcoming the "psychoexistential" complexes instilled in colonial subjects by misrecognition, he nonetheless insists that Fanon's argument is applicable to contemporary debates surrounding the "politics of difference" more generally.[30] Below I want to challenge Taylor's use of Fanon in this context: not by disputing Taylor's assertion that Fanon's work constitutes an important theorization of the ways in which the subjectivities of the oppressed can be deformed by mis- or nonrecognition, but rather by contesting his assumption that a more accommodating, liberal regime of mutual recognition might be capable of addressing the power relations typical of those between Indigenous peoples and settler states. Interestingly, Fanon posed a similar challenge in his earlier work, *Black Skin, White Masks*.

Fanon's concern with the relationship between human freedom and equality in relations of recognition represents a central and reoccurring theme in *Black Skin, White Masks*.[31] As mentioned at the outset of this chapter, it was there that Fanon convincingly argued that the long-term stability of a colonial system of governance relies as much on the "internalization" of the forms of racist recognition imposed or bestowed on the Indigenous population by the colonial state and society as it does on brute force. For Fanon, then, the longevity of a colonial social formation depends, to a significant degree, on its capacity to transform the colonized population into *subjects* of imperial rule.

Here Fanon anticipates at least one aspect of the well-known work of French Marxist philosopher Louis Althusser, who would later argue that the reproduction of capitalist relations of production rests on the "recognition function" of ideology, namely, the ability of a state's "ideological apparatus" to "interpellate" individuals as subjects of class rule.[32] For Fanon, colonialism operates in a similarly dual-structured manner: it includes "not only the interrelations of *objective* historical conditions but also human *attitudes* to these conditions."[33] Fanon argued that it was the interplay between the structural/objective and recognitive/subjective features of colonialism that ensured its hegemony over time.

With respect to the subjective dimension, *Black Skin, White Masks* painstakingly outlines the myriad ways in which those "attitudes" conducive to colonial rule are cultivated among the colonized through the unequal exchange of institutionalized and interpersonal patterns of recognition between the colonial society and the Indigenous population. In effect, Fanon showed how, over time, colonized populations tend to internalize the derogatory images imposed on them by their colonial "masters," and how as a result of this process, these images, along with the structural relations with which they are entwined, come to be recognized (or at least endured) as more or less natural.[34] This point is made agonizingly clear in arguably the most famous passage from *Black Skin, White Masks* where Fanon shares an alienating encounter on the streets of Paris with a little white child. "Look, a Negro!" Fanon recalled the child saying, "Moma, see the Negro! I'm frightened! frightened!"[35] At that moment the imposition of the child's racist gaze "sealed" Fanon into a "crushing objecthood," fixing him like "a chemical solution is fixed by a dye."[36] He found himself temporarily *accepting* that he was indeed the subject of the child's call: "It was true, it amused me," thought Fanon.[37] But then "I subjected myself to an objective examination, I discovered my blackness, my ethnic characteristics; and I was battered down by tom-toms, cannibalism, intellectual deficiency, fetishism, racial defects."[38] Far from assuring Fanon's humanity, the other's recognition imprisoned him in an externally determined and devalued conception of himself. Instead of being acknowledged as a "man among men," he was reduced to "an object [among] other objects."[39]

Left as is, Fanon's insights into the ultimately subjectifying nature of colonial recognition appear to square nicely with Taylor's work. For example, although Fanon never uses the term himself, he appears to be mapping the debilitating effects associated with *mis*recognition in the sense that Taylor uses the term. Indeed, *Black Skin, White Masks* is littered with passages highlighting the innumerable ways in which the imposition of the settler's gaze can inflict damage on Indigenous societies at both the individual and collective levels. Taylor is more or less explicit about his debt to Fanon in this respect too. "Since 1492," he writes with *The Wretched of the Earth* in mind, "Europeans have projected an image of [the colonized] as somehow inferior, 'uncivilized,' and through the force of conquest have been able to impose this image on the conquered."[40] Even with these similarities, however, I believe that a close reading of *Black Skin, White Masks* renders problematic Taylor's approach in several interrelated and crucial respects.

The first problem has to do with its failure to adequately confront the dual structure of colonialism itself. Fanon insisted, for example, that a colonial configuration of power could be transformed only if attacked at both levels of operation: the objective and the subjective.[41] This point is made at the outset of *Black Skin, White Masks* and reverberates throughout all of Fanon's work. As indicated in his introduction, although a significant amount of *Black Skin, White Masks* would highlight and explore the "psychological" terrain of colonialism, this would not be done in a manner decoupled from an analysis of its structural or material foundations. Indeed, Fanon claimed that there "will be an authentic disalienation" of the colonized subject "only to the degree to which things, in the most materialistic meaning of the word, [are] returned to their proper places."[42] Hence the term "sociodiagnostic" for Fanon's project: "If there is an inferiority complex, it is the outcome of a double process . . . primarily economic; [and] subsequently the internalization . . . of his inferiority."[43] In Fanon, colonial-capitalist exploitation and domination is correctly situated alongside misrecognition and alienation as foundational sources of colonial injustice. "The Negro problem," writes Fanon, "does not resolve itself into the problem of Negroes living among white men but rather of Negroes being exploited, enslaved, despised by a colonialist, capitalist society that is only accidentally white."[44]

Fanon was enough of a Marxist to understand the role played by capitalism in exasperating hierarchical relations of recognition. However, he was also much more perceptive than many Marxists of his day in his insistence that the subjective realm of colonialism be the target of strategic transformation along with the socioeconomic structure. The colonized person "must wage war on both levels," insisted Fanon. "Since historically they influence each other, any unilateral liberation is incomplete, and the gravest mistake would be to believe in their automatic interdependence."[45] For Fanon, attacking colonial power on one front, in other words, would not guarantee the subversion of its effects on the other. "This is why a Marxist analysis should always be slightly stretched when it comes to addressing the colonial issue," Fanon would later write in *The Wretched of the Earth*.[46] Here, I would argue that Fanon's "stretching" of the Marxist paradigm constitutes one of the most innovative contributions to classical Marxist debates on ideology. Unlike the position of, say, Georg Lukacs, who boldly claimed in *History and Class Consciousness* that there is "no problem" and therefore "no solution" that does not ultimately lead back to the question of economic structure,[47] Fanon revealed the ways in which those axes of domination historically relegated in Marxism to the superstructural realm—such as racism and the effects it has on those subject to it—could substantively configure the character of social relations relatively autonomously from capitalist economics.

Lately a number of scholars have taken aim at the contribution of recognition theorists like Taylor on analogous grounds: that their work offers little insight into how to address the more overtly structural and/or economic features of social oppression.[48] We have also been told that this lack of insight has contributed to a shift in the terrain of contemporary political thought and practice more generally—from "redistribution to recognition," to use Nancy Fraser's formulation. According to Fraser, whereas proponents of redistribution tend to highlight and confront injustices in the economic sphere, advocates of the newer "politics of recognition" tend to focus on and attack injustices in the cultural realm. On the redistribution front, proposed remedies for injustice range between "affirmative" strategies, like the administration of welfare, to more "transformative" methods, like the transformation of the capitalist mode of production itself. In contrast, strategies aimed at injustices associated with misrecognition tend to focus on "cultural and symbolic change." Again, this could involve "affirmative" approaches, such as the recognition and reaffirmation of previously disparaged identities, or these strategies could adopt a more "transformative" form, such as the "deconstruction" of dominant "patterns of representation" in ways that would "change everyone's social identities."[49]

I think that Fanon's work, which anticipates the recognition/redistribution debate by half a century, highlights several key shortcomings in the approaches of both Taylor and Fraser. Taylor's approach is insufficient insofar as it tends to, at its best, address the political economy of colonialism in a strictly "affirmative" manner: through reformist state redistribution schemes like granting certain cultural rights and concessions to Aboriginal communities via self-government and land claims packages. Although this approach may alter the intensity of some of the effects of colonial-capitalist exploitation and domination, it does little to address their generative structures, in this case a capitalist economy constituted by racial and gender hierarchies and the colonial state. When his work is at its weakest, however, Taylor tends to focus on the recognition end of the spectrum too much, and as a result leaves uninterrogated colonialism's deep-seated structural features. Richard J. F. Day has succinctly framed the problem this way: "Although Taylor's recognition model allows for diversity of culture within a particular state by admitting the possibility of multiple national identifications," it is less "permissive with regard to polity and economy . . . in assuming that any subaltern group that is granted [recognition] will thereby acquire a *subordinate* articulation with a *capitalist state*."[50] Seen from this angle, Taylor's theory leaves one of the two operative levels of colonial power identified by Fanon untouched.

This line of criticism is well worn and can be traced back to at least the work of early Karl Marx. As such, I doubt that many would be surprised that Taylor's variant of liberalism *as liberalism* fails to confront the structural or economic aspects of colonialism at its generative roots. To my mind, however, this shortcoming in Taylor's approach is particularly surprising given the fact that, although many Indigenous leaders and communities today tend to instrumentally couch their claims in reformist terms, this has not always been the case: indeed, historically, Indigenous demands for *cultural recognition* have often been expressed in ways that have explicitly called into question the dominating nature of capitalist social relations and the state form.[51] And the same can be said of a growing number of today's most prominent Indigenous scholars and activists.[52] Mohawk political scientist Taiaiake Alfred, for example, has repeatedly argued that the goal of any traditionally rooted self-determination struggle ought to be to protect that which constitutes the "heart and soul of [I]ndigenous nations: a set of values that challenge the homogenizing force of Western liberalism and free-market capitalism; that honor the autonomy of individual conscience, non-coercive authority, and the deep interconnection between human beings and other elements of creation."[53] For Alfred, this vision is not only embodied in the practical philosophies and ethical systems of many of North America's Indigenous societies, but also flows from a "realization that capitalist economics and liberal delusions of progress" have historically served as the "engines of colonial aggression and injustice" itself.[54] My point here is that an approach that is explicitly oriented around dialog and listening ought to be more sensitive to the claims and challenges emanating from these dissenting Indigenous voices.[55]

However, if Taylor's account pays insufficient attention to the clearly structural and economic realm of domination, then Fraser's does so from the opposite angle. In order to avoid what she sees as the pitfalls associated with the politics of recognition's latent essentialism and displacement of questions of distributive justice, Fraser proposes a means of integrating struggles for recognition with those of redistribution without subordinating one to the other. To this end, Fraser suggests that instead of understanding recognition as the revaluation of cultural or group-specific identity, and misrecognition as the disparagement of such identity and its consequent effects on the subjectivities of minorities, recognition and misrecognition should be conceived of in terms of the "institutionalized patterns of value" that affect one's ability to participate *as a peer* in social life. "To view recognition" in this manner, writes Fraser, "is to treat it as an issue of *social status*."[56]

Although Fraser's status model allows her to curtail some of the problems she attributes to identity politics, it does so at the expense of addressing two of the most pertinent features of injustices related to mis- or nonrecognition in colonial contexts. First, when applied to Indigenous struggles for recognition, Fraser's status model rests on the problematic background assumption that the settler state constitutes a legitimate framework within which Indigenous peoples might be more justly included, or from which they could be further excluded. Here Fraser, like Taylor, leaves intact two features of colonial domination that Indigenous assertions of nationhood call into question: the legitimacy of the settler state's claim to sovereignty over Indigenous people and their territories on the one hand, and the normative status of the state-form as an appropriate mode of governance on the other.[57] Indeed, at one point in her well-known exchange with Axel Honneth, Fraser hints at her theory's weakness in this regard. While discussing the work of Will Kymlicka, Fraser admits that her status model may not be as suited to situations where claims for recognition contest a current distribution of state sovereignty. Where

Kymlicka's approach is tailored to demands for recognition in multinational societies, Fraser's project, we are told, seeks to address such demands in "poly-ethnic" polities like the United States.[58] The problem with this caveat, how-ever, is that it is premised on a misrecognition of its own: namely, that as a state founded on the dispossessed territories of previously self-determining but now colonized Indigenous nations, the United States is a multinational state in much the way that Canada is. My second concern is this: if many of today's most volatile political conflicts *do* include subjective or psychological dimensions to them in the way that Fraser admits (and Taylor and Fanon describe), then I fear her approach, which attempts to eschew a direct engage-ment with this aspect of social oppression, risks leaving an important con-tributing dynamic to identity-related forms of domination unchecked. By avoiding this "psychologizing" tendency within the politics of recognition, Fraser claims to have located what is wrong with misrecognition in "social relations" and not "individual or interpersonal psychology." This is preferable, we are told, because when misrecognition "is identified with internal distor-tions in the structure of the consciousness of the oppressed, it is but a short step to blaming the victim."[59] This does not have to be the case. Fanon, for example, was unambiguous with respect to locating the cause of the "inferior-ity complex" of colonized subjects in the colonial social structure.[60] The prob-lem, however, is that any psychological problems that ensue, although socially constituted, can take on a life of their own, and thus need to be dealt with independently and in accordance with their own specific logics. As mentioned previously, Fanon was insistent that a change in the social structure would not guarantee a change in the subjectivities of the oppressed. Stated simply, if Fanon's insight into the interdependent yet semi-autonomous nature of the two facets of colonial power is correct, then dumping all our efforts into alleviating the institutional or structural impediments to participatory parity (whether redistributive or recognitive) may not do anything to undercut the debilitating forms of unfreedom related to misrecognition in the traditional sense.[61]

This brings us to the second key problem with Taylor's theory when applied to colonial contexts. I have already suggested that Taylor's liberal-recognition approach is incapable of curbing the damages wrought within and against Indigenous communities by the structures of state and capital, but what about his theory of recognition? Does it suffer the same fate vis-à-vis the forms of power that it seeks to undercut? As noted in the previous section, underlying Taylor's theory is the assumption that the flourishing of Indigenous peoples as distinct and self-determining entities is significantly dependent on their being afforded cultural recognition and institutional accommodation by the settler state apparatus. What makes this approach both so intriguing and so problematic, however, is that Fanon, whom Taylor uses to make his case, argued against a similar presumption in the penultimate chapter of *Black Skin, White Masks*. Moreover, like Taylor, Fanon did so with reference to Hegel's master/slave parable. There Fanon argued that the dialectical progression to reciprocity in relations of recognition is frequently undermined in colonial situations by the fact that, unlike the subjugated slave in Hegel's *Phenomenology of Spirit*, many colonized societies no longer have to *struggle* for their freedom and independence. It is often negotiated, achieved through constitutional amendment, or simply "declared" by the settler state and bestowed upon the Indigenous population in the form of political rights. Whatever the method, in these circumstances the colonized, "steeped in the inessentiality of servitude," are "*set free by [the] master*."[62] "One day the White Master, *without conflict*, recognize[s] the Negro slave."[63] As such, they do not have to lay down their lives to *prove* their "certainty of being" in the way that Hegel insisted.[64] The "upheaval" of formal freedom and independence thus reaches the colonized "from without": "The black man [is] acted upon. Values that [are] not . . . created by his actions, values that [are] not . . . born of the systolic tide of his blood, [dance] in a hued whirl around him. The upheaval [does] not make a difference in the Negro. He [goes] from *one way of life to another, but not from one life to another*."[65] There are a number of important issues underlying Fanon's concern here. The first involves the relationship he draws between struggle and the disalienation of the colonized subject. For Fanon it is through struggle and conflict (and for the later Fanon, *violent* struggle and conflict) that imperial subjects come to be rid of the "arsenal of complexes" driven into the core of their being through the colonial process.[66] I will have more to say about this aspect of Fanon's thought below, but for now I simply want to flag the fact that struggle serves as the mediating force through which the colonized come to shed their colonial identities, thus restoring them to their "proper places."[67] In contexts where recognition is conferred without struggle or conflict, this fundamental self-transformation—or as Lou Turner has put it, this "inner differentiation" at the level of the colonized's being—cannot occur, thus foreclosing the realization of freedom. Hence Fanon's claim that the colonized simply go from "one way of life to another, but not from one life to another"; the structure of domination is modified, but the subject position of the colonized remains unchanged—they become "emancipated slaves."[68]

The second important point to note is that when Fanon speaks of a lack of struggle in the decolonization movements of his day, he does not mean to suggest that the colonized in these contexts simply remained passive recipients of colonial practices. He readily admits, for example, that "from time to time" the colonized may indeed fight "for Liberty and Justice." However, when this fight is carried out in a manner that does not pose a foundational "break" with the background structures of colonial power as such—which, for Fanon, will always invoke struggle and conflict—then the best the colonized can hope for is "white liberty and white justice; that is, values secreted by [their] masters."[69] Without conflict and struggle the terms of recognition tend to remain in the possession of those in power to bestow on their inferiors in ways that they deem appropriate.[70] Note the double level of subjection here: without transformative struggle constituting an integral aspect of anticolonial praxis the Indigenous population will not only remain subjects of imperial rule insofar as they have not gone through a process of purging the psycho-existential complexes battered into them over the course of their colonial experience—a process of strategic *desubjectification*—but they will also remain so in that the Indigenous society will tend to come to see the forms of structurally limited and constrained recognition conferred to them by their colonial "masters" *as their own*: that is, the colonized will begin to *identify* with "white liberty and white justice." As Fanon would later phrase it in *The Wretched of the Earth*, these values eventually "seep" into the colonized and subtly structure and limit the possibility of their freedom.[71] Either way, for Fanon, the colonized will have failed to reestablish themselves as truly self-determining: as creators of the terms, values, and conditions by which they are to be recognized.[72]

My third concern with Taylor's politics of recognition involves a misguided sociological assumption that undergirds his appropriation of Hegel's notion of mutual recognition. As noted in the previous section, at the heart of Hegel's master/slave dialectic is the idea that both parties engaged in the struggle for recognition are dependent on the other's acknowledgment for their freedom and self-worth. Moreover, Hegel asserts that this dependency is even more crucial for the master in the relationship, for unlike the slave he or she is unable to achieve independence and objective self-certainty through the object of his or her own labor. Mutual dependency thus appears to be the background condition that ensures the dialectic progress towards reciprocity. This is why Taylor claims, with reference to Hegel, that "the struggle for recognition can only find *one satisfactory solution, and that is a regime of reciprocal recognition among equals.*"[73] However, as Fanon's work reminds us, the problem with this formulation is that when applied to actual struggles for recognition between hegemonic and subaltern communities the mutual character of dependency rarely exists. This observation is made in a lengthy footnote in *Black Skin, White Masks* where Fanon claims to have shown how the colonial master "basically differs" from the master depicted in Hegel's *Phenomenology of Spirit.* "For Hegel there is reciprocity," but in the colonies "the master laughs at the consciousness of the slave. What he wants from the slave is *not recognition but work.*"[74] To my mind this is one of the most crucial passages in *Black Skin, White Masks* for it outlines in precise terms what is wrong with the recognition paradigm when abstracted from the face-to-face encounter in Hegel's dialectic and applied to colonial situations. Although the issue here is an obvious one, it has nonetheless been critically overlooked in the contemporary recognition literature: in relations of domination that exist between nation-states and the sub-state national groups that they "incorporate" into their territorial and jurisdictional boundaries, there is no mutual dependency in terms of a need or desire for recognition.[75] In these contexts, the "master"—that is, the colonial state and state society—does not require recognition from the previously self-determining communities upon which its territorial, economic, and social infrastructure is constituted. What it needs is land, labor, and resources.[76] Thus, rather than leading to a condition of reciprocity the dialectic either breaks down with the explicit *non*recognition of the equal status of the colonized population, or with the strategic "domestication" of the terms of recognition leaving the foundation of the colonial relationship relatively undisturbed.[77]

Anyone familiar with the power dynamics that structure the Aboriginal rights movement in Canada should immediately see the applicability of Fanon's insights here. Indeed, one need not expend much effort to elicit the countless ways in which the liberal discourse of recognition has been limited and constrained by the state, the courts, corporate interests, and policy makers in ways that have helped preserve the colonial status quo. With respect to the law, for example, over the last thirty years the Supreme Court of Canada has consistently refused to recognize Aboriginal peoples' equal and self-determining status based on its adherence to legal precedent founded on the white supremacist myth that Indigenous societies were too primitive to bear political rights when they first encountered European powers.[78] Thus, even though the courts have secured an unprecedented degree of protection for certain "cultural" practices within the state, they have nonetheless repeatedly refused to challenge the racist origin of Canada's assumed sovereign authority over Indigenous peoples and their territories.

The political and economic ramifications of recent Aboriginal rights jurisprudence have been clear-cut. In *Delgamuukw v. British Columbia* it was declared that any residual Aboriginal rights that may have survived the unilateral assertion of Crown sovereignty could be infringed upon by the federal and provincial governments so long as this action could be shown to further "a compelling and substantial legislative objective" that is "consistent with the special fiduciary relationship between the Crown and the [A]boriginal peoples." What substantial objectives might justify infringement? According to the court, virtually any exploitative economic venture, including the "development of agriculture, forestry, mining, and hydroelectric power, the general economic development of the interior of British Columbia, protection of the environment or endangered species, and the building of infrastructure and the settlement of foreign populations to support those aims."[79] So today it appears, much as it did in Fanon's day, that colonial powers will only recognize the collective rights and identities of Indigenous peoples insofar as this recognition does not throw into question the background legal, political, and economic framework of the colonial relationship itself.[80]

But the above examples confirm only one aspect of Fanon's insight into the problem of recognition in colonial contexts: namely, the limitations this approach runs up against when pitted against these overtly structural expressions of domination. Are his criticisms and concerns equally relevant to the subjective or psycho-affective features of contemporary colonial power?

With respect to the forms of racist recognition driven into the psyches of Indigenous peoples through the institutions of the state, church, schools, and media, and by racist individuals within the dominant society, the answer is clearly yes. Countless studies, novels, and autobiographical narratives have outlined, in painful detail, how these expressions have saddled individuals with low self-esteem, depression, alcohol and drug abuse, and violent behaviors directed both inward against the self and outward toward others.[81]

Similarly convincing arguments have been made concerning the limited forms of recognition and accommodation offered to Indigenous communities by the state. For example, Taiaiake Alfred's work unpacks the ways in which the state institutional and discursive fields within and against which Indigenous demands for recognition are made and adjudicated can come to shape the self-understandings of the Indigenous claimants involved. The problem for Alfred is that these fields are by no means neutral: they are profoundly hierarchical and as such have the ability to asymmetrically govern how Indigenous subjects think and act not only in relation to the recognition claim at hand, but also in relation to themselves, to others, and the land. This is what I take Alfred to mean when he suggests, echoing Fanon, that the dominance of the legal approach to self-determination has over time helped produce a class of Aboriginal "citizens" whose rights and identities have become defined more in relation to the colonial state and its legal apparatus than the history and traditions of Indigenous nations themselves. Similarly, strategies that have sought independence via capitalist economic development have already facilitated the creation of an emergent Aboriginal bourgeoisie whose thirst for profit has come to outweigh their ancestral obligations to the land and to others. Whatever the method, the point here is that these strategies threaten to erode the most egalitarian, nonauthoritarian, and sustainable characteristics of traditional Indigenous cultural practices and forms of social organization.[82]

Self-Recognition and Anticolonial Empowerment

The argument sketched to this point is bleak in its implications. Indeed, left as is, it would appear that recognition inevitably leads to subjection, and as such much of what Indigenous peoples have sought over the last forty years to secure their freedom has in practice cunningly assured its opposite. Interpreted this way, my line of argument appears to adhere to an outdated conception of power, one in which postcolonial critics, often reacting against the likes of Fanon and others, have worked so diligently to refute. The implication of this view is that Indigenous subjects are *always* being interpellated by recognition, being constructed by colonial discourse, or being assimilated by colonial power structures.[83] As a result, resistance to this totalizing power is often portrayed as an inherently reactionary, zero-sum project. To the degree that

Fanon can be implicated in espousing such a totalizing view of colonial power, it has been suggested that he was unable to escape the Manichean logic so essential in propping up relations of colonial domination to begin with.[84]

I want to defend Fanon, at least partially, from the charge that he advocated such a devastating view of power. However, in order to assess the degree to which Fanon anticipates and accounts for this general line of criticism, we must unpack his theory of anticolonial agency and empowerment.

As argued throughout the preceding pages, Fanon did not attribute much emancipatory potential to Hegel's politics of recognition when applied to colonial situations. Yet this is not to say that he rejected the recognition paradigm entirely. As we have seen, like Hegel and Taylor, Fanon ascribed to the notion that relations of recognition are constitutive of subjectivity and that, when unequal, they can foreclose the realization of human freedom. On the latter point, however, he was deeply skeptical as to whether the mutuality envisioned by Hegel was achievable in the conditions indicative of contemporary colonialism. But if Fanon did not see freedom as naturally emanating from the slave being granted recognition from his or her master, where, if at all, did it originate?[85]

In effect, Fanon claimed that the pathway to self-determination instead lay in a quasi-Nietzschean form of personal and collective *self*-affirmation.[86] Rather than remaining dependent on their oppressors for their freedom and self-worth, Fanon recognized that the colonized must instead struggle to work through their alienation/subjection against the objectifying gaze and assimilative lure of colonial recognition. According to Fanon, it is this self-initiated process that "triggers a change of fundamental importance in the colonized's psycho-affective equilibrium."[87] According to this view, the colonized must initiate the process of decolonization by first recognizing *themselves* as free, dignified, and distinct contributors to humanity. Unlike Nietzsche, however, Fanon equated this process of *self-recognition* with the praxis undertaken by the slave in Hegel's *Phenomenology of Spirit*, which Fanon saw as illustrating the necessity on the part of the oppressed to "turn away" from their other-oriented master-dependency, and to instead struggle for freedom on their own terms and in accordance with their own values.[88] I would also argue that this is why Fanon, although critical of the at times bourgeois and essentialist character of certain works within the *negritude* tradition, nonetheless saw the project as necessary.[89] Fanon was attuned to ways in which the individual and collective revaluation of black culture and identity could serve as a source of pride and empowerment, and if approached critically and directed appropriately, could help jolt the colonized into an "actional" existence, as opposed to a "reactional" one characterized by *ressentiment*.[90] As Robert Young notes in the context of Third World decolonization, it was this initial process of collective self-affirmation that led many colonized populations to develop a "distinctive postcolonial epistemology and ontology" which enabled them to begin to conceive of and construct alternatives to the colonial project itself.[91]

I would argue that Fanon's call in *Black Skin, White Masks* for a simultaneous turn inward and away from the master, far from espousing a rigidly binaristic Manichean view of power relations, instead reflects a profound understanding of the complexity involved in contests over recognition in colonial and racialized environments. Unlike Hegel's life-and-death struggle between two opposing forces, Fanon added a multidimensional racial/cultural aspect to the dialectic, thereby underscoring the multifarious web of recognition relations that are at work in constructing identities and establishing (or undermining) the conditions necessary for human freedom and flourishing. Fanon showed that the power dynamics in which identities are formed and deformed were nothing like the hegemon/subaltern binary depicted by Hegel. In an anticipatory way, then, Fanon's insight can also be said to challenge the overly negative and all-subjectifying view of interpellation that would plague Althusser's theory of ideology more than a decade later. For Althusser, the process of interpellation always took the form of "a fundamental misrecognition" that served to produce within individuals the "specific characteristics and desires that commit them to the very actions that are required of them by their [subordinate] class position."[92] Fanon's innovation was that he showed how similar recognitive processes worked to "call forth" and empower individuals within communities of resistance.[93]

This is not to say, of course, that Fanon was able to completely escape the "Manicheism delirium" that he was so astute at diagnosing.[94] Those familiar with the legacy of Fanon's later work, for example, know that the "actional" existence that he saw self-recognition initiating in *Black Skin, White Masks* would in *The Wretched of the Earth* take the form of a direct and violent engagement with the colonial society and its institutional structure. "At the very moment [the colonized come to] discover their humanity," wrote Fanon, they must "begin to sharpen their weapons *to secure its victory*."[95] In Fanon's later work, violence would come to serve as a "kind of psychotherapy of the oppressed," offering "a primary form of agency through which the subject moves from non-being to being, from object to subject."[96] In this sense, the practice of revolutionary violence, rather than the affirmative recognition of the other, offered the most effective means to transform the subjectivities of the colonized, as well as to topple the social structure that produced colonized subjects to begin with.

TURNING OUR BACKS ON COLONIAL POWER?

Before concluding this chapter, I want to briefly address an important counterargument to the position I am advocating here, especially regarding the call to selectively "turn away" from engaging the discourses and structures of settler-colonial power with the aim of transforming these sites from within. Dale Turner offers such an argument in his book *This Is Not a Peace Pipe: Towards a Critical Indigenous Philosophy*, in which he advances the claim that if Indigenous peoples want the relationship between themselves and the Canadian state to be informed by their distinct worldviews, then "they will have to engage the state's legal and political discourses in more effective ways."[97] Underlying Turner's theoretical intervention is the assumption that colonial relations of power operate primarily by *excluding* the perspectives of Indigenous peoples from the discursive and institutional sites that give their rights content. Assuming this is true, then it would indeed appear that "critically undermining colonialism" requires that Indigenous peoples find more effective ways of "participating in the Canadian legal and political practices that determine the meaning of Aboriginal rights."[98]

For Turner, one of the preconditions for establishing a "postcolonial" relationship is the development of an intellectual community of Indigenous "word warriors" capable of engaging the legal and political discourses of the state. According to Turner, because it is an unfortunate but unavoidable fact that the rights of Indigenous peoples will for the foreseeable future be largely interpreted by non-Indigenous judges and policy makers within non-Indigenous institutions, it is imperative that Indigenous communities develop the capacity to effectively *interject* our unique perspectives into the conceptual spaces where our rights are framed. It is on this last point that Turner claims to distinguish his approach from the work of Indigenous intellectuals like Patricia Monture and Taiaiake Alfred. Turner claims that the problem with the decolonial strategies developed by these scholars is that they fail to propose a means of

effecting positive change within the very legal and political structures that currently hold a monopoly on the power to determine the scope and content of
our rights. According to Turner, by focusing too heavily on tactics that would
see us "turn our backs" on the institutions of colonial power, these Indigenous
scholars do not provide the tools required to protect us against the unilateral
construction of our rights by settler-state institutions. For Turner, it is through
an ethics of participation that Indigenous peoples can better hope to "shape
the legal and political relationship so that it respects Indigenous world views."[99]

The efficacy of Turner's intervention rests on a crucial theoretical assumption reflected in his text's quasi-Foucauldian use of the term *discourse*. I say
quasi-*Foucauldian* because when he refers to the discursive practices of word
warriors he assumes that these pack the "power" necessary to transform the
legal and political discourses of the state into something more amenable to
Indigenous languages of political thought. Here Turner assumes that the coun-
terdiscourses that word warriors interject into the field of Canadian law and
politics have the capacity to shape and govern the ways in which Aboriginal rights are reasoned about and acted on. The problem, however, is that
Turner is less willing to attribute the same degree of power to the legal and
political *discourses of the state*. This is what I mean when I claim that his use of
the concept is *quasi*-Foucauldian. When Turner speaks of the legal and political discourses of the state, he spends little time discussing the assimilative
power that these potentially hold in relation to the word warriors that are to
engage them. Indeed, the only place he does briefly mention this is at the end
of his final chapter, when he writes:

> For an indigenous person the problem of assimilation is always close at hand.
> The anxiety generated by moving between intellectual cultures is real, and
> many indigenous intellectuals find it easier to become part of mainstream cul-
> ture. This kind of assimilation will always exist, and it may not always be a bad
> thing for indigenous peoples as a whole. It becomes dangerous when indige-
> nous intellectuals become subsumed or appropriated by the dominant culture
> yet continue to act as if they were word warriors.[100]

Here we reach a limit in Turner's argument: there is little discussion of how
Indigenous peoples might curb the risks of *interpellation* as they seek to *interpolate* the much more powerful discursive economy of the Canadian legal and

political system. Although Turner repeatedly suggests that part of the answer to this problem lies in the ability of word warriors to remain grounded in the thought and practices of their communities, in the end he spends little time discussing what this might entail in practice.

Further, while Turner is right to pay attention to discursive forms of power, his analysis eclipses the role that *non*discursive configurations play in reproducing colonial relations. My concern here is that the problem with the legal and political discourses of the state is not only that they enjoy hegemonic status vis-à-vis Indigenous discourses, but that they are also backed by and hopelessly entwined with the economic, political, and military might of the state itself. This means that Indigenous peoples must be able to account for these material relations as well, which would require an exploration of theories and practices that move beyond liberal and ideational forms of discursive transformation. While I recognize that this might be beyond the scope of Turner's investigation, I think that speaking to the diversity of forms of decolonial practice would have made his case more convincing.

One of the important insights of Fanon's critique of the politics of recognition is that it provides us with theoretical tools that enable us to determine the relative transformability of certain fields of colonial power over others. These tools subsequently put us in a better position to critically assess which strategies hold the most promise, and which others are more susceptible to failure.

Conclusion

In retrospect, Fanon appears to have overstated the "cleansing" value he attributed to anticolonial violence.[101] Indeed, one could argue that many Algerians have yet to fully recover from the legacy left from the eight years of carnage and brutality that constituted Algeria's war of independence with France. Nor was the Front de Libération Nationale's (FLN) revolutionary seizure of the Algerian state apparatus enough to stave off what Fanon would call "the curse of [national] independence": namely, the subjection of the newly "liberated" people and territories to the tyranny of the market and a postindependence class of bourgeois national elites.[102] But if Fanon ultimately overstated violence's role as the "perfect mediation" through which the colonized come to liberate themselves from both the structural and psycho-affective features of colonial domination that he identified so masterfully, then what is the relevance of his work here and now?[103]

In this chapter I have suggested that Fanon's insights into the subjectifying nature of colonial recognition are as applicable today to the liberal "politics of recognition" as they were when he first formulated his critique of Hegel's master/slave relation. I have also suggested that Fanon's dual-structured conception of colonial power still captures the subtle (and not so subtle) ways in which a system of settler-state domination that does not sustain itself exclusively by force is reproduced over time. As Taiaiake Alfred argues, under these "postmodern" imperial conditions "oppression has become increasingly invisible; [it is] no longer constituted in conventional terms of military occupation, onerous taxation burdens, blatant land thefts, etc.," but rather through a "fluid confluence of politics, economics, psychology and culture."[104] But if the dispersal and effects of colonial and state power are now so diffuse, how is one to transform or resist them? Here I believe that Fanon's work remains insightful. In that all important footnote in *Black Skin, White Masks* where Fanon claimed to show how the condition of the slave in the *Phenomenology of Spirit* differed from those in the colonies, he suggested that Hegel provided a partial answer: that those struggling against colonialism must "turn away" from the colonial state and society and instead find in their own *decolonial praxis* the source of their liberation. Today this process will and must continue to involve some form of critical individual and collective *self*-recognition on the part of Indigenous societies, not only in an instrumental sense like Fanon seemed to have envisioned it, but with the understanding that our cultural practices have much to offer regarding the establishment of relationships within and between peoples and the natural world built on principles of reciprocity and respectful coexistence. Also, the empowerment that is derived from this critically self-affirmative and self-transformative ethics of desubjectification must be cautiously directed *away* from the assimilative lure of the statist politics of recognition, and instead be fashioned toward our own on-the-ground struggles of freedom. As the feminist, antiracist theorist bell hooks explains, such a project would minimally require that we stop being so preoccupied with looking "to that Other for recognition"; instead we should be "recognizing ourselves and [then seeking to] make contact with all who would engage us in a constructive manner."[105] In my concluding chapter I flesh-out what such a politics might look like in the present; a politics that is less oriented around attaining a definitive form of affirmative recognition from the settler state and society, and more about critically reevaluating, reconstructing, and redeploying

Indigenous cultural forms in ways that seek to prefigure, alongside those with similar ethical commitments, radical alternatives to the structural and psycho-affective facets of colonial domination discussed above. However, before I can commence with this concluding part of my project, Fanon's critique of recognition must first be evaluated against the politics of recognition as it has played out in the empirical context of Indigenous–state relations in Canada. Providing such an evaluation will be my focus in the next three chapters.

2

For the Land

The Dene Nation's Struggle for
Self-Determination

[For] [t]hirty years, our nations have been co-opted into movements of "self-government" and "land claims settlements," which are goals defined by the colonial state and which are in stark opposition to our original objectives. . . . Our people were promised that they would be recognized as nations and that their lands would be returned, but instead of realizing these goals we are left with a nasty case of metastasizing governmentalism.

—TAIAIAKE ALFRED, Wasáse

To encourage 'cultural diversity' requires not the separation of culture and politics, but their marriage and to insist on that separation is to destroy, or attempt to destroy culture.

—DENE NATION, 1977

As suggested in my introduction and chapter 1, one of the problems most commonly associated with the politics of recognition has to do with the ways in which it has, at times, shown to be insufficiently informed by "a sociological understanding of power relations."[1] For self-proclaimed "historical materialist" critics Frances Widdowson and Albert Howard, the conflict at the heart of those power relations effaced by the liberal recognition paradigm is primarily economic in origin. "This conflict," Widdowson and Howard write, is "elaborated in all of Marx's writings [and] exists between the few who own the means of production and those who are the producers of all value."[2] Elsewhere, Widdowson and Howard make the absurdly reductionist claim that insofar as the politics of recognition "encourages the native population to identify in terms of *ethnicity* instead of *socioeconomic class*" it must be discarded as inherently "divisive and reactionary."[3] The authors then go on to tritely conclude that it is only by "eliminating this fundamental 'difference' [namely, *class* difference] that we can become a global tribe and the 'world can live as one.'"[4]

In this chapter, I examine further the left-materialist critique of identity/difference politics in light of the Dene Nation's struggle for recognition and self-determination in the 1970s and early 1980s. In doing so, I suggest that insofar as the identity-related claims of Indigenous peoples for recognition are always bound up with demands for a more equitable distribution of land, political power, and economic resources, the left-materialist concern regarding the effacement of political economy by questions of cultural recognition is misguided when applied to settler-state contexts. Indeed, following Ian Angus, I argue that, in contexts where "culture" is understood in an "inclusive anthropological sense" to "encompass both ideology and material conditions" the sharp distinction between base and superstructure that underwrites the left-materialist position appears "rather useless as a starting point for social philosophy and political criticism."[5] However, if one takes a modified version of the left-materialist challenge and instead examines the relationship between Indigenous recognition claims and the distinction made by Nancy Fraser between "transformative" and "affirmative" forms of redistribution, the criticism begins to hold more weight.[6] Recall that "transformative" models of redistribution are those that seek to correct unjust distributions of power and resources *at their source;* that is, they not only seek to alter "the *content* of current modes of domination and exploitation, but also the *forms* that give rise to them."[7] As we shall see below, the last thirty years we have witnessed a gradual erosion of this radical imaginary within the mainstream Dene recognition and self-determination movement, which in the context of land claims and economic development has resulted in a significant decoupling of Indigenous "cultural" claims from the transformative visions of social, political, and economic change that once constituted them. The purpose of this chapter is to elucidate in concrete terms how and why this has emerged as the case.

The argument presented below is broken into four sections and a conclusion. In the four sections I examine the process of primitive accumulation as experienced by the Dene peoples of the Northwest Territories, Canada. These sections are meant to illuminate in more practical terms the theoretical discussion I provided in the introduction and chapter 1. More specifically, in the first section, I examine the changing social, political, and economic context within and against which the Dene self-determination movement emerged in the 1970s and 1980s. In the second section I examine the place-based cultural foundation undergirding the Dene Nation's critique of capitalist imperialism as expressed at the public hearings of the Mackenzie Valley Pipeline Inquiry between 1975 and 1977. I call this place-based foundation *grounded normativity*. In the next two sections I show how a similar critique came to inform our demand for cultural recognition in the Dene Declaration of 1975, as well as the three subsequent land-claims proposals submitted by the Dene Nation to the federal government in 1976, 1977, and 1981. I argue that all four of these articulations of recognition were informed by a place-based ethics that fundamentally challenged the assumed legitimacy of colonial sovereignty over and capitalist social relations on Dene territories. And finally, in my conclusion, I examine some of the effects that the negotiation of land claims has had on this place-based ethics, and how these effects have in turn shaped the contemporary trajectory of Indigenous politics in northern Canada toward neocolonial ends. Although the last century has witnessed numerous attempts by the state to coercively integrate our land and communities into the fold of capitalist modernity, it was not until the negotiation of land-claims settlements in the 1970s and 1980s that this process began to significantly take hold. In this respect, it would appear, as my reading of Fanon suggests, that the process of primitive accumulation has been at least in part facilitated by the very mechanism of recognition that we hoped might shield our land and communities from it: the negotiation of a land settlement.

A Brief History of Denendeh

According to oral historical accounts, the Dene have occupied and governed themselves over the lands within and immediately surrounding what is now the Northwest Territories (NWT), Canada, since time immemorial. During the period under examination here, it was not uncommon for Dene to refer to this vast homeland as Denendeh, or "land of the people," which traditionally covered an area that spans over one million square kilometers from the mouth of the Mackenzie River (or Dehcho, as the Dene call it), southward to the northern tip of the provinces, and east to Hudson Bay. Today, however, the word "Denendeh" has come to represent much of the geographical area known as the present NWT (excluding, of course, Inuvialuit territory in the far north), thus distinguishing it from Nunavut (which, in 1999, was established as the publically governed territory of the Inuit). Non-Native accounts derived from recent archaeological and linguistic evidence, while imprecise and controversial, suggest that the first direct ancestors of the Dene migrated to our present location between two and three thousand years ago, although unspecified human population is thought to have occurred well before this time (anywhere between ten and twenty-eight thousand years ago).[8]

There are currently five Dene regions that fall within the political boundaries of the present NWT. The northernmost region is occupied by the Gwich'in Dene, whose comprehensive land-claim area, settled in 1992, borders the southernmost boundary of the Inuvialuit land-claim area, settled eight years before then.[9] Immediately to the south of the Gwich'in lie the territories of the Sahtu Dene (comprising the Hare, Mountain, and Bear Lake people), whose lands stretch west and north of Great Bear Lake, which in their own language is also referred to as Sahtu. In conjunction with the Métis of the region, the Sahtu Dene settled their comprehensive land claim in 1993.[10] Just south of the Sahtu claim area is the Dehcho region, occupied by Slavey-speaking Dene. Although their land claim has yet to be settled, Dehcho territory extends south beyond the Mackenzie River to the NWT/Alberta/British Columbia borders. Just north and to the west of the Dehcho region are the territories of the Tlicho Dene. Tlicho lands extend up from Great Slave Lake (or Tindee/Tucho, as the Dene refer to it) to the NWT/Nunavut border. The Tlicho are the most recent Dene group to settle their land-claim dispute, which in 2003 became law and includes the first Aboriginal self-government agreement in the NWT.[11] And finally, just south of Tlicho territory is the Akaitcho region, occupied by the Weledeh (or Yellowknives) and Chipewyan Dene. This region is my home territory and extends south of Great Slave Lake to the NWT/Albert/Saskatchewan borders and east to Nunavut. Unlike the other regions noted above, in 1999 our communities decided to pursue our land grievances (which have yet to be settled) via the specific claims process (through Treaty Land Entitlement, or TLE) instead of the comprehensive claims route.[12] Although vastly separated in terms of geography, all of the Dene nations occupying these regions speak related dialects of the Northern Athapaskan language family, and historically they shared many similarities in terms of spiritual beliefs, legal orders, forms of governance, and economic systems.

The 1950s and 60s witnessed several profound changes in the economic and political landscape of Denendeh, all of which would come to shape the character of Dene activism in the decades to follow. During this period, many

Dene individuals found themselves having to escalate their involvement in the cash economy of the emerging settler society due to an increase in the cost of trade goods and a decrease in the price of furs following World War II.[13] As a result, by the 1950s many families had to supplement income derived from hunting, trapping, and fishing with a combination of paid labor, welfare, and family allowance. Assuming that the fur trade would never recover from the postwar recession, the federal government began to initiate policies aimed at forcefully establishing permanent Dene communities, arguing that this would better facilitate the integration of adult workers into the wage economy, and at the same time provide a context conducive to educating Native children in the skills required for attaining menial employment in an emerging capitalist economy. Even with this being the case, by the late 1960s, the full effects of primitive accumulation had yet to take hold as a delicate balance was struck between a mode of life sustained by traditional land-based harvesting activities on the one hand, and income generated from state transfers and seasonal paid employment on the other.[14]

The fragile "articulation" struck in the 1950s and 60s between these two distinct ways of life—that of extractivist capitalism and Indigenous hunting/fishing/harvesting—was largely absent in the political sphere, however, where northern development was occurring in a far more asymmetrical manner.[15] The clearest example of this came in 1967, when Canada announced its plans to transfer the administrative center of the NWT from Ottawa to Yellowknife, without consulting the majority Native population. Before this, the sole political authority over issues concerning the NWT rested with the federal government in Ottawa. After the transfer, the size and power of both the Government of the Northwest Territories (GNWT) and its non-Native constituency increased dramatically. Between 1967 and 1979, for example, the GNWT grew from 75 to 2,845 employees, roughly 400 more than the number of federal employees employed in the region.[16] During the same period, the operating and capital budgets of the GNWT rose from $14,584,000 to $282,167,000—a near twenty-fold increase.[17] Not surprisingly, the influx of administrative staff and families significantly affected the area's general population, which jumped from roughly 29,000 to 35,000 between 1966 and 1971.[18] As the above numbers indicate, a significant percentage of this increase can be attributed to the newly formed northern bureaucracy. As the settler population continued to grow, many of the newcomers began to pressure the federal government to advance

northern economic initiatives, most notably in the form of nonrenewable resource development. As one might expect, all of this would generate feelings
of discontent and alienation within and among our communities, as we soon
found ourselves becoming a numerical minority in our homeland with little
influence over issues pertinent to the well-being of our land and way of life.
As the Dene Nation explained in 1984: "Although we [remained] the majority population in Denendeh [after 1967], we were finding ourselves to have
less say in the administration and laws of our land. Every year more mines
were discovered and opened, roads were built, parks proposed, oil and gas
wells drilled, without our consent or often our knowledge."[19]

From the position of the minority non-Native population, however, the
devolution of powers from Ottawa to Yellowknife seemed to reflect an attempt
to foster legitimate and responsible government north of 60 degrees. This was
the position advanced, for example, by the Advisory Commission on the
Development of Government in the Northwest Territories, also known as the
Carrothers Commission. In 1965 the federal government established the commission to investigate local preferences for political development in the NWT,
including the possibility of splitting the district into two geographical units.[20]
Over the following year, the commission documented the testimony of 3,039
residents in fifty-one communities across the region.[21] In 1966 the commission published its findings, which suggested that Canada keep the NWT intact,
but "locate the government of the Territories within the Territories, to decen-
tralize its operations as far as practicable, to transfer administrative functions
from the central to the territorial government in order that the latter may be
accountable on site for the administration of the public business, and to con-
centrate on economic development and opportunity for the residents of the
north."[22] The following year, Canada responded to the recommendations by
establishing Yellowknife as the territorial capital, and by committing to more
nonrenewable resource development in the area.

Not coincidentally, as the federal government prepared to establish a territorial bureaucracy in Yellowknife, excitement was mounting over the possibility of future petroleum discoveries off the northern shores of Canada and
the United States.[23] As it turned out, the excitement was well founded, and in
1968 a huge reservoir of oil and natural gas was discovered beneath Prudhoe
Bay, Alaska. Almost immediately, Canada started fielding plans from a con-
sortium of corporations to construct a multibillion-dollar pipeline that would

transport the gas via the Mackenzie River Valley to markets throughout southern Canada and the United States.[24] As the federal government stated in 1969: "From the first realization of the magnitude of the Prudhoe Bay find, it [had] been considered likely that . . . gas from the field would . . . find its way to markets in the USA by a pipeline through Canada."[25] At the time, the estimated cost of the Mackenzie Valley pipeline would have established it as the largest private sector development project in the history of Canada, and quite possibly the world.[26]

Unfortunately, for the Dene, Inuit, and Métis of the area, the proposed right-of-way for the pipeline—along with a massive infrastructure of roads, airstrips, camps, gravel pits, storage sites, stream/river crossings, and gas plants—would cut south across the entire western half of our homeland.[27] All of this meant little to the federal and territorial governments, both of which would at the time maintain their "tradition of ignoring native demands in the north."[28] Although the majority of Dene, Inuit, and Métis overwhelmingly rejected the idea of an imposed pipeline development from the outset, these communities were not initially provided with a means to formally voice their opposition. As Edgar Dosman put it, at the time "no channels existed for the articulation of [Native] concerns. They had no way of knowing what was going on, or what decisions had already been taken. Yet pipeline and resource decisions would change and probably destroy their traditions and way-of-life."[29]

The federal government's ability to completely ignore the voices of the North's Indigenous population would soon suffer a major setback, however. In 1969, when sixteen Dene chiefs convened at Fort Smith under the sponsorship of the Department of Indian Affairs and Northern Development, it was decided that the Dene needed a more independent and aggressive political body to represent their communities' concerns. It was at this meeting that leadership established the Indian Brotherhood of the Northwest Territories, or IB-NWT (renamed the Dene Nation in 1978). The Inuvialuit followed suit and established the Committee for Original Peoples' Entitlement, or COPE, in 1970. In 1971 the Inuit Tapirisat of Canada was formed to address the concerns of all Inuit in Canada, including those within the NWT. And finally, in 1972 the Metis Association of the Northwest Territories was set up to represent the interests of the Métis and nonstatus Dene population. Although each organization differed in its specific concerns and visions regarding the scope of northern development, all three would nonetheless mount a push to defend the interests of Indigenous peoples against the vision of economic and political expansion that state and industry began to aggressively impose the previous decade.[30]

For the Dene, making such a push would emerge as one of the IB-NWT's first major orders of business. This culminated in 1973, when Fort Smith chief François Paulette, along with fifteen other chiefs represented by the IB-NWT, filed a "caveat" with the Northwest Territories Registrar of Land Titles, claiming a Dene interest in more than one million square kilometers of the NWT.[31] The Crown responded by challenging the Dene right to file the caveat, but later that year Justice William G. Morrow of the Supreme Court of the Northwest Territories decided that they had "a potentially legitimate case and at least had a right to be heard."[32] In his subsequent decision, Justice Morrow ruled in favor of the Dene, claiming that the "indigenous people" had a definite interest in the land covered by the caveat, and that "they have what is known as aboriginal rights."[33] More importantly, however, Morrow concluded that historical evidence suggested that it was unlikely that the Dene had knowingly extinguished their title to the lands covered by Treaties 8 and 11, which they had negotiated with the Crown in 1900 and 1921, respectively.[34] Although the case was eventually appealed and subsequently thrown out on a technicality, the questions raised by Justice Morrow regarding the continued existence of Aboriginal title were never challenged at appeal.

Two major developments arose in the aftermath of this push of early 1970s Native activism. First, on August 8, 1973, the month before Justice Morrow rendered his decision in Re: Paulette, the federal government announced its new comprehensive land-claims policy.[35] This announcement, which emerged in the context of heightened Native concerns over the course of northern industrialization, widespread First Nations resistance to the federal government's 1969 "White Paper" on Indian policy, and the Supreme Court of Canada's 1973 Calder decision, essentially reversed the state's fifty-two-year policy of refusing to address Native land grievances where questions surrounding the existence of Aboriginal title remained open. Because the Dene had essentially asserted in filing their caveat that they had never extinguished their political rights or legal title to their traditional territories, despite having signed Treaties 8 and 11, the Crown proceeded with our claim under its new policy, which was set up to deal with cases "based on the assertion of continuing Aboriginal title to lands and resources." The thrust of the comprehensive claims policy, which was reaffirmed in 1981, is to "exchange the claims to undefined Aboriginal rights for a clearly defined package of rights and benefits set out in a settlement agreement."[36]

The second development was the establishment of the Mackenzie Valley Pipeline Inquiry, also known as the "Berger Inquiry." Realizing that it could no longer simply disregard the rights of northern Indigenous peoples, the Crown agreed to sponsor a "commission of inquiry" to investigate the environmental and social impacts potentially posed by the construction of the Mackenzie Valley project. Under political pressure from the New Democratic Party, the Trudeau administration somewhat reluctantly selected Justice Thomas Berger—an outspoken environmentalist and Native rights advocate—to head the investigation. Beginning in the summer of 1975, the commission traveled across Canada and the North, recording the statements, opinions and concerns of hundreds of expert witnesses and nearly a thousand individuals who would likely be affected by the proposed project, both Native and non-Native. After listening to twenty-one months of testimony, Berger released his two-volume report, *Northern Frontier, Northern Homeland*, which recommended that no pipeline ever be built along the north slope of the Yukon between Prudhoe Bay and the Mackenzie Delta, and that a ten-year moratorium be placed on the construction of the Mackenzie Valley project itself, which would ideally allow time for environmental and Native land claims issues to be resolved.[37] Ten years later, in reflecting on the importance of the Berger Inquiry for highlighting the struggles of Indigenous peoples, Frances Abele wrote: "Probably no royal commission or public inquiry has sustained such a large and diverse audience, or provoked, years after its conclusion, such strong emotional responses."[38]

"That Is Not Our Way":
Challenging Colonial Development

By the mid-1970s the Dene had developed a radical analysis of colonial development and effectively utilized both the IB-NWT and the Berger Inquiry to voice their position. As Peter Usher notes, this analysis amounted to a fundamental "critique of capitalism and industrialization."[39] At this point, I want to return to and further develop a claim I made in my introductory chapter regarding the difference between the normative foundation underwriting Indigenous anticolonialism and anticapitalism and that which underwrites similar sentiments within the Western radical tradition, most notably that of

Marxism. There I suggested that, when related back to the two pillars of Marx's primitive accumulation thesis—dispossession and proletarianization—it would appear that in Canada the history and experience of the former has structured the political relationship between Indigenous peoples and the state to a greater extent than the latter. I also suggested that the primary experience of dispossession is what also tends to fuel the most common modes of Indigenous resistance to and criticism of the colonial relationship itself: that is, Indigenous struggles against capitalist imperialism are best understood as struggles oriented around the question of *land*—struggles not only *for* land, but also deeply *informed* by what the land as a mode of reciprocal *relationship* (which is itself informed by place-based practices and associated form of knowledge) ought to teach us about living our lives in relation to one another and our surroundings in a respectful, nondominating and nonexploitative way. The ethical framework provided by these place-based practices and associated forms of knowledge is what I call "grounded normativity."

In his groundbreaking 1972 text, *God Is Red*, the late Lakota philosopher Vine Deloria Jr. argues that one of the most significant differences that exist between Indigenous and Western metaphysics revolves around the central importance of land to Indigenous modes of being, thought, and ethics.[40] When "ideology is divided according to American Indian and Western European [traditions]," writes Deloria, this "fundamental difference is one of great philosophical importance. American Indians hold their lands—*places*—as having the highest possible meaning, and all their statements are made with this reference point in mind."[41] Most Western societies, by contrast, tend to derive meaning from the world in historical/developmental terms, thereby placing *time* as the narrative of central importance.[42] Deloria then goes on to conclude: "When one group is concerned with the philosophical problem of space and the other with the philosophical problem of time, then the statements of either group do not make much sense when transferred from one context to the other without the proper consideration of what is taking place."[43]

In drawing our attention to the distinction between Indigenous place-based and Western time-oriented understandings of the world, Deloria does not simply intend to reiterate the rather obvious observation that most Indigenous societies hold a strong attachment to their homelands, but is instead attempting to explicate the position that land occupies as an ontological framework for understanding *relationships*. Seen in this light, it is a profound misunderstanding to think of land or place as simply some material object of profound importance to Indigenous cultures (although it is this too); instead, it ought to be understood as a field of "relationships of things to each other."[44] Place is a way of knowing, of experiencing and relating to the world and with others; and sometimes these relational practices and forms of knowledge guide forms of resistance against other rationalizations of the world that threaten to erase or destroy our senses of place.[45] This, I argue, is precisely the understanding of land that grounded our critique of colonialism and capitalism in the 1970s and early 1980s. In the Weledeh dialect of Dogrib (which is my community's language), for example, "land" (or dè) is translated in relational terms as that which encompasses not only the land (understood here as material), but also people and animals, rocks and trees, lakes and rivers, and so on.[46] Seen in this light, we are as much a part of the land as any other element. Furthermore, within this system of relations human beings are not the only constituent believed to embody spirit or agency. Ethically, this meant that humans held certain obligations to the land, animals, plants, and lakes in much the same way that we hold obligations to other people. And if these obligations were met, then the land, animals, plants, and lakes would reciprocate and meet their obligations to humans, thus ensuring the survival and well-being of all over time.[47] Consider, for example, the following story told by the late George Blondin, a respected Sahtu Dene elder. The tale recounts an experience his brother Edward had while hunting moose:

Edward was hunting near a small river when he heard a raven croaking, far off to his left. Ravens can't kill animals themselves, so they depend on hunters and wolves to kill food for them. Flying high in the sky, they spot animals too far away for hunters or wolves to see. They then fly to the hunter and attract his attention by croaking loudly, then fly back to where the animals are.

Edward stopped and watched the raven carefully. It made two trips back and forth in the same direction. Edward made a sharp turn and walked to where the raven was flying. There were no moose tracks, but he kept following the raven. When he got to the riverbank and looked down, Edward saw two big moose feeding on the bank. He shot them, skinned them, and covered the meat with their hides.

Before he left, Edward put some fat meat out on the snow for the raven. He knew that without the bird, he wouldn't have killed any meat that day.[48]

Notice how Blondin's narrative not only emphasizes the consciousness and individual agency of the raven, but also depicts the relationship between the hunter and the bird as mutually interdependent. The cooperation displayed between Edward and the raven provides a clear example of the ethic of reciprocity and sharing underlying Dene understandings of their relationship with land.

In the decades leading up to the Mackenzie Valley Pipeline Inquiry, it became apparent to many people within our communities that the organizational imperatives of capital accumulation signified an affront to our normative understanding of what constituted proper relationships—relationships between people, relationships between humans and their environment, and relationships between individuals and institutions of authority (whether economic or political). Even though by the mid-1970s this grounded normative framework had been worn by decades of colonial *displacement*, it was still functioning enough to frame both our critique of capitalist development and our ways of thinking about how we might establish political and economic relations both within our own communities and with Canada based on principles of reciprocity and mutual obligation. Not coincidentally, Peter Kulchyski highlights this spatial feature of Indigenous struggle well in his excellent book, *Like the Sound of a Drum: Aboriginal Cultural Politics in Denendeh and Nunavut*, when he writes: "It is possible to argue that precisely what distinguishes anti-colonial struggles from the classic Marxist accounts of the working class is that oppression for the colonized is registered in the spatial dimension—*as dispossession*—whereas for workers, oppression is measured as exploitation, as the theft of *time*."[49] I would simply add here that Indigenous ways of thinking about *nonoppressive* relations are often expressed with this spatial referent in mind as well.

Any cursory glance at the testimony made by Indigenous participants at the Berger Inquiry clearly demonstrates the significance of land in our critique of colonial development. One of the most profound statements of this sort was delivered by Philip Blake, a Dene from Fort McPherson. Notice the three interrelated meanings of "land" at play in his narrative: land-as-resource central to our material survival; land-as-identity, as constitutive of who we are as a people; and land-as-relationship:

> If our Indian nation is being destroyed so that poor people of the world might
> get a chance to share this world's riches, then as Indian people, I am sure that we

would seriously consider giving up our resources. But do you really expect us to give up our life and our lands so that those few people who are the richest and most powerful in the world today can maintain their own position of privilege?

That is not our way.

I strongly believe that we do have something to offer your nation, however, something other than our minerals. I believe it is in the self-interest of your own nation to allow the Indian nation to survive and develop in our own way, on our own land. For thousands of years we have lived with the land, we have taken care of the land, and the land has taken care of us. We did not believe that our society has to grow and expand and conquer new areas in order to fulfill our destiny as Indian people.

We have lived with the land, not tried to conquer of control it or rob it of its riches. We have not tried to get more and more riches and power, we have not tried to conquer new frontiers, or out do our parents or make sure that every year we are richer than the year before.

We have been satisfied to see our wealth as ourselves and the land we live with. It is our greatest wish to be able to pass on this land to succeeding generations in the same condition that our fathers have given it to us. We did not try to improve the land and we did not try to destroy it.

That is not our way.

I believe your nation might wish to see us, not as a relic from the past, but as a way of life, a system of values by which you may survive in the future. This we are willing to share.[50]

When Blake suggests in his testimony that as "Indian people" we must reject the pathological drive for accumulation that fuels capitalist expansion, he is basing this statement on a conception of Dene identity that locates us as an inseparable part of an expansive system of interdependent relations covering the land and animals, past and future generations, as well as other people and communities. For many Natives at the time of the Berger Inquiry, this relational conception of identity was nonnegotiable; it constituted a fundamental feature of what it meant to be Dene. Furthermore, it also demanded that we conduct ourselves in accordance with certain ethico-political norms, which stressed, among other things, the importance of sharing, egalitarianism, respecting the freedom and autonomy of both individuals and groups, and recognizing the obligations that one has not only to other people, but to the natural world as a whole.[51] I suggest that it was this place-based ethics that served as the foundation from which we critiqued the dual imperatives of colonial sovereignty and capitalist accumulation that came to dictate the course of northern development in the postwar period. In the following section, I show how the same foundation shaped the Dene Nation's demand for recognition and self-determination in the years to follow.

<h2 style="text-align:center">THE DENE DECLARATION:
UNDERSTANDING INDIGENOUS NATIONALISM</h2>

On July 19, 1975, at the second annual Joint General Assembly of the Indian Brotherhood of the NWT and the Metis and Non-Status Association of the NWT, more than three hundred Indigenous delegates unanimously voted to adopt what quickly became known as the Dene Declaration—a political manifesto demanding the full "recognition" of the Dene as a "self-determining" nation "within the country of Canada."[52] In his *Heeding the Voices of Our Ancestors*, Gerald Taiaiake Alfred provides a theory of Indigenous nationalism useful for developing an understanding of the politicized articulation of indigeniety called attention to in the Dene Declaration. According to Alfred, Indigenous expressions of nationhood are "best viewed as having both a relatively stable core which endures and peripheral elements that are easily adapted or manipulated to accommodate the demands of a particular political environment."[53] For Alfred, Indigenous political identities are not based on clearly delineated essences, nor are they merely "invented" to correspond with shifting political aspirations; rather, Indigenous articulations of nationhood are best understood as informed by a complex of cultural practices and traditions that have survived the onslaught of colonialism and continue to structure the form and content of Indigenous activism in the present.[54] Contrary to many other forms of nationalism, however, Alfred is quick to point out that most Indigenous movements do not seek recognition and self-determination "through the creation of a new state, but through the achievement of a cultural sovereignty and a political relationship based on group autonomy reflected in formal self-government arrangements."[55]

Dene nationalism during this period can be understood within a similar cultural frame—as a dynamic revival of Dene political concepts framed in a manner to meet the economic and political goals of contemporary Dene society. To this end, although our movement was firmly grounded in and motivated by political values and concepts rooted in the relational conception of land noted above, it also actively incorporated new social and political discourses to supplement these older traditions.[56]

A number of these discourses were drawn off to articulate our vision of a postcolonial political relationship with Canada, including, among others, Marxist political economy, world systems analysis, theories of development and underdevelopment, and Third World anticolonialism.[57] Although all of these conceptual tools helped shape, to varying degrees, our views on colonialism and self-determination, here I want to highlight one that remains particularly salient to this day: the Marxist concept "mode of production."[58] In its broadest articulation, "mode of production" can be said to encompass two interrelated social processes: the resources, technologies, and labor that a people deploy to produce what they need to materially sustain themselves over time, and the forms of thought, behavior, and social relationships that *both condition and are themselves conditioned by these productive forces.*[59] As the sum of these two interrelated processes, a "mode of production" can be interpreted, as Marx himself often did, as analogous to a way or "mode of life." A "mode of production must not be considered simply as being the production of the physical existence of individuals," write Marx and Engels in *The German Ideology*. "Rather it is a definite form of activity of these individuals, a definite form of *expressing their life*, a definite *mode of life* on their part."[60] I suggest that this broad understanding of mode of production as a *mode of life* accurately reflects what constituted "culture" in the sense that the Dene deployed the term, and which our claims for *cultural recognition* sought to secure through the negotiation of a land claim. Simply stated, in the three proposals examined below, our demand for recognition sought to protect the "intricately interconnected social totality" of a distinct *mode of life*;[61] a life on/with the land that stressed individual autonomy, collective responsibility, nonhierarchical authority, communal land tenure, and mutual aid,[62] and which sustained us "economically, spiritually, socially and politically."[63] As George Barnaby wrote in 1976: "The land claim is our fight to gain recognition as a different group of people—with our own way of seeing things, our own values, our own lifestyle, our own laws. . . . [It] is a fight for self-determination using our own system with which we have survived till now."[64]

Understanding "culture" as the interconnected social totality of distinct *mode of life* encompassing the economic, political, spiritual, and social is crucial for comprehending the state's response to the challenge posed by our land-claim proposals. As demonstrated in the following section, the state responded to this challenge, as Fanon himself might have predicted, by structurally circumscribing the terms and content of the recognition it was willing to make available to us through the negotiation of a land settlement. As noted previously, the reason the Crown agreed to get into the land-claims business in the first place was to "extinguish" the broad and undefined rights and title claims of First Nations in exchange for a limited set of rights and benefits set out in the text of the agreement itself. In the 1970s, Canada still required the explicit "cede, release and surrender" of Aboriginal rights and title prior to the resolution of a settlement, which from the Crown's perspective constituted the surest way to attain the political and economic "certainty" required to satisfy the state's interest in opening up Indigenous territories to further economic investment and capitalist development.[65] Although the state no longer requires the formal "extinguishment" of Aboriginal rights as a precondition to reaching an agreement, the purpose of the process has remained the same: to facilitate the "incorporation" of Indigenous people and territories into the capitalist mode of production and to ensure that alternative "socioeconomic visions" do not threaten the desired functioning of the market economy.[66] With this objective firmly in place, both Canada and the NWT insisted on negotiating a land settlement based on the following two principles: first, that a Dene political claim to self-determination was invalid; and second, that any settlement reached must attain "finality" through the extinguishment of what remained of Dene rights and title in exchange for the institutional recognition and protection of certain aspects of Dene "culture." However, for the state, recognizing and accommodating "the cultural" through the negotiation of land claims *would not* involve the recognition of alternative Indigenous economies and forms of political authority, as the mode of production/mode of life concept suggests; instead, the state insisted that any institutionalized accommodation of Indigenous cultural difference be reconcilable with *one* political formation—namely, colonial sovereignty—and *one* mode of production—namely, capitalism.

LAND CLAIMS AND THE
DOMESTICATION OF DENE NATIONHOOD

In his 1999 *Study on Treaties, Agreements and Other Constructive Arrangements between States and Indigenous Populations,* Special Rapporteur for the United

Nations Sub-Commission on the Prevention of Discrimination and Protection of Minorities Miguel Alfonso Martinez examines the myriad techniques
and rationales adopted by colonial settler regimes to "domesticate" the "international" status of Indigenous nations, thereby placing their claims squarely
under the "exclusive competence" of the "internal jurisdiction" of non-
Indigenous nation-states.[67] In the following analysis of the three land-claims
proposals submitted to the federal government by the Dene Nation between
1976 and 1981, it will be shown that, rather than recognize our right to self-
determination, both the GNWT and the Government of Canada defended
within the land-claims process a depoliticized discourse of Indigenous "cultural rights" that it used to rationalize the hegemony of non-Indigenous economic and political interests on Dene territory. In this way, it will be shown
that, from the state's perspective, the land-claims process constitutes a crucial
vehicle for the "domestication" of Indigenous claims to nationhood.

On October 25, 1976, the IB-NWT, under the leadership of Georges Erasmus, provided the federal government with a land-claim proposal designed to
accommodate the robust form of recognition expressed in the Dene Declaration. The proposal, titled "Agreement in Principle between the Dene Nation
and Her Majesty the Queen, in Right of Canada," called upon the federal government to negotiate with the Dene Nation in accordance with an expansive
list of principles, including the recognition of a Dene right to self-determination;
the right to retain ownership of a significant portion of our traditional territories; the right to exercise political jurisdiction over the territories in question;
the right to practice and preserve our languages, customs, traditions, and values; and the right to develop our own political and economic institutions. All
of these rights, we claimed, would be exercised "within Confederation" through
the establishment of a "Dene government" vested with political authority
over land and subject matters currently within the jurisdiction of the federal
and territorial governments.[68]

Essentially, the 1976 "Agreement in Principle" outlined in broad terms the
foundation for building a renewed relationship with the state that would secure
a degree of Indigenous political and economic autonomy unprecedented in
the history of land-claim settlements in Canada.[69] Although the specific *form*
this autonomy would take remained unspecified in the proposal, a number
of statements made and research reports produced by the Dene during this
period suggest that it would look radically different from the economic and

political institutions of the dominant society. In terms of political development, for example, the IB-NWT emphasized the need to construct contemporary political institutions on the traditional principle of popular sovereignty
and consensus decision-making, thus including as wide a spectrum of Dene
as possible in the formation of government policy.[70] This commitment to the
construction of alternative governance forms cashed out politically in 1976,
when the IB-NWT announced that it would officially boycott participating
in the territorial government, arguing that it was a "colonial institution" that
did not represent the perspectives of the Dene people, and that this was
reflected in the *style* and *structure* of government itself.[71] The boycott lasted
until 1979. George Barnaby, one of the two elected Dene officials to resign
from territorial politics in 1976 (the other being James Wah-Shee), explained
his motivation like this: "If we go through a whole Dene movement and we
end up with native people just giving orders to their own people, [then we will
not be] better off than now, when white people order us around." For Barnaby,
a "true [Dene] government" would be the "people themselves deciding what
they want" and then working together to achieve their desired goals.[72]

The principle of direct democracy was to apply to the economic sphere
as well. For instance, the proposal states that a noncolonial economy would
not only promote Dene self-sufficiency, but do so in a manner consistent with
our cultural values and "way of life." To this end, the claim outlines an economic vision that would develop a mode of production based on a combination of "continued renewable resource activities, such as hunting, fishing
and trapping," as well as "community-scale activities" designed "to meet our
needs in a more self-reliant fashion."[73] In the following years a number of these
"community-scale activities" were discussed and proposed, including a combination of locally operated manufacturing ventures, Native-run cooperatives,
and worker-controlled enterprises.[74]

At a 1974 Regional Co-Coordinators Workshop, the IB-NWT noted two
perspectives on development that it found compelling. The first was the example of "communal enterprise" and "development" exemplified in the postindependence struggle of Tanzania.[75] At one point, the IB-NWT was even in a
conversation with the Kahnawake Office of the Indians of Quebec Association about sending a delegation of Dene fieldworkers to learn from the Tanza-
nian experience.[76] The second was drawn from the following observation
made by Shuswap activist George Manuel and researcher Michael Posluns in

their book *The Fourth World*: "Real community development can never take place without economic development, but economic development without full local control is only another form of imperial conquest."[77] In the "Agreement in Principle," these economic models were pitched as culturally relevant alternatives to the "externally initiated economy" imposed on the Dene by the state. "True Dene development," the IB-NWT argued, "[must] entail political control, an adequate resource base, [and would not] permit a few to gain at the expense of the whole community." And finally, in keeping with our commitment to strengthening social relations premised on reciprocity, leadership proposed to structure our relationship with the non-Indigenous population according to the principle of *mutual self-determination*.[78] Subsequently, the IB-NWT agreed to uphold the political and existing property rights of all non-Native northerners. However, with regard to private property, the Dene Nation would only respect fee-simple title to lands acquired before October 15, 1975; after this date, land would be held in common in accordance with the values and principles set forth in the proposal.[79]

The Dene Declaration together with the proposed "Agreement in Principle" evoked a range of responses. On the one hand, our communities were greeted with an enormous display of support by progressive political organizations from across the country, including the Canadian Labor Congress, the Oil, Chemical and Atomic Workers International Union, Oxfam Canada, the United Steelworkers of America, and the New Democratic Party's "Waffle" movement, which was, at the time, known by many critics for its "strident socialism."[80]

At the same time, however, there were many that were openly hostile to the transformative message underlying our claim. The then minister of Indian Affairs, Judd Buchanan, for example, dismissed the Dene Declaration as "gobbledegook that a grade ten student could have written in fifteen minutes."[81] Even respected Cree leader Harold Cardinal blasted the declaration as an "intrusion of left-wing thinking that is perhaps much closer to the academic community in Toronto than it is to the Dene."[82] Much of the criticism leveled at the IB-NWT during this period expressed a similar sentiment, namely, that Dene leadership had been manipulated by white southern radicals and were therefore not acting in the interests of their own constituencies. As one *Edmonton Report* columnist wrote, "A bewildered Canada [is] gradually waking up to the fact that a radical socialist philosophy [has] taken hold of the native

peoples in the Mackenzie Valley. How is it that these territorial natives whose
politics up until now were generally considered non-existent should suddenly
emerge with such advanced left-wing inclinations?"[83] The public expressed a
similar point of view. As one gentleman stated to the Berger Inquiry: "Most of
[the] hollering . . . done by the Indian Brotherhood . . . [has been directed] by
whites, not the majority of Indians. . . . [The Dene] figured they made a real
good deal [with Treaty 11] and until the Indian Brotherhood with white backing started stirring things up, there wasn't any problem."[84] The Government of
the Northwest Territories added to the hysteria by suggesting that the Indian
Brotherhood "should be renamed the Radical Left."[85] At one point, there were
even rumors circulating across the North that some of our community members were being trained in tactics of "guerrilla warfare,"[86] and that the Royal
Canadian Mounted Police (RCMP) had employed "undercover operatives
to infiltrate the Brotherhood."[87] These racist, McCarthy-like accusations held
a great deal of currency for many non-Natives during the 1970s and into the
early 1980s.[88]

Aside from allegations of left-extremism, most government officials rejected
the Dene position based on the view that it violated the liberal value of equality
underwriting universal representation within Canadian political institutions.
Initially the most vocal proponent of this argument was the GNWT Legislative Assembly, which expressed its concerns in a position paper titled "Priorities of the North," submitted to the Department of Indian Affairs and Northern
Development in May of 1977.[89] The paper explicitly denounced the Dene
claim, arguing that it would amount to the establishment of an exclusionary,
indeed "race-based," jurisdiction in northern Canada. In the words of the legislative assembly: "This is why the 'native state' concept is, and always will be,
totally unacceptable to the people of the Northwest Territories"; because it
"lacks the necessary element of universality of participation in political institutions by any Canadian who chooses to live in the [Northwest] Territories."[90]

In response to the GNWT's repeated charge of racism, the IB-NWT submitted a second proposal to the federal government in July of 1977.[91] Like
its predecessor, the Metro Proposal stressed the importance of recognition
and self-determination for the Dene Nation. However, appreciating that many
people had "misinterpreted" our "Agreement in Principle" as discriminatory,
the IB-NWT sought to "make it clear" in the new claim that it was seeking
self-determination not only for the Dene, but for *all* citizens of the North, and

an "end to racial oppression" as such, whether it be the "oppression of Dene by non-Dene, or oppression of non-natives by Dene."[92]

To accommodate this vision, the Metro Proposal recommended that the North adopt a decentralized federative structure based on the following principles: that the NWT be divided into three geographical territories, "one where the Dene are a majority, one where the Inuit are a majority, and finally one where the non-native people are the majority"; that each of these three territories uphold the political rights of all of its citizens through the establishment of government institutions based on each group's respective traditions and in accordance with the desires and aspirations of their respective constituencies; that each territorial government divide powers and relate with the federal government in a manner similar to the current federal or provincial relationship; and that a "Metro" or "United Nations" governance structure be "organized by the three new governments to deal with matters, issues, and programs of common concern." Under this model, each newly established government would be responsible for sending "representatives" to negotiate "as equals" with those from the other governments "until an agreement was reached on any joint activity."[93] And finally, in accordance with Dene custom, economic relations within our proposed territory would not be dictated by the reign of capital; rather, all economic principles and values set forth in the previous Agreement in Principle would to apply to the new proposal as well.

It was at this point that the state began to counter our position with a depoliticized conception of Aboriginal "cultural" rights divorced from any substantive notion of Indigenous sovereignty or alternative political economies. In "Priorities of the North," for example, the GNWT argued that land claims ought to be used as a mechanism to secure the recognition and protection of Aboriginal "cultural" interests, but only if the state agreed to "separate" the negotiation of political rights to self-determination from the process. To this end, the Assembly proposed that a Native "Bill of Rights" be written into the constitution of the NWT. This would serve two purposes: first, it would "crystallize" the rights of Native people with respect to their traditional "use and enjoyment" of the land; and second, it would function to "preserve native languages and cultures in some form of immutable legislation."[94]

The federal government advanced a similar position its 1977 opinion paper, "Political Development in the Northwest Territories."[95] The "Political Development" paper was to serve as "detailed terms of reference" to guide the newly appointed Special Representative for Constitutional Development in the Northwest Territories, Charles (Bud) Drury.[96] Like the legislative assembly, the federal government stated that it would be willing to use land claims as a vehicle to "safeguard" Aboriginal "culture" and enable Aboriginal people and communities to pursue their "traditional" practices "to the extent that they may wish to do so."[97] Subsequently, Canada would agree to work closely with Native groups to develop programs within a number of areas, including education, housing, and economic development, as well as "the protection and promotion" of "other cultural interests," including "Indian and Inuit languages" and "rights to traditional activities such as hunting, fishing and trapping."[98] In securing these rights, however, the federal government insisted that it would not endorse a call for the establishment of political jurisdictions allocated "on grounds that differentiate between people on the basis of race."[99] Instead, Ottawa directed Drury to consider the "possible division of the Northwest Territories" on the basis of "functional" issues, "including economic, socio-cultural, and other relevant factors," but excluding "political divisions and structures" configured along Indigenous/non-Indigenous lines.[100] Thus, if the Dene wanted to participate in the constitutional development of the northern political apparatus, they would have to do so at a local and subordinate level within the common and presumably legitimate institutions of the NWT.[101] In short, for both the GNWT and the Government of Canada, cultural rights, not political rights, constituted the core issue to be resolved in the settlement of a Dene land claim.

In terms of political economy, both levels of government sought to tease apart the recognition of Indigenous cultural practices from any socioeconomic scheme that might potentially disrupt the further accumulation of capital through the development of the North's resource base. The GNWT, for example, simply asserted that the "long term economic development of the Northwest Territories will almost certainly depend on the further exploration and utilization of its natural resource[s]."[102] Recognizing the cultural claims of First Nations would be permitted, but only insofar as these claims could be reconciled with this "predominantly private enterprise mode of organization."[103] In a similar vein, the federal government suggested that while land claims would provide "native groups" with financial compensation for any infringement of their property rights, Canada's "national interest" dictated that the Crown "maintain its ownership and control of the potentially significant non-renewable resources in the Northwest Territories." And regarding the intensity of northern capitalist development, the Crown, like the Legislative Assembly, declared that business would continue unabated: "In view of the energy and other resource requirements that are now recognized as becoming increasingly urgent, the Government wishes to maintain some momentum in the exploration and development of northern non-renewable resource[s]." Land claims, according to the Crown, would better enable the Dene to "play a part" in this process, but in no way would they provide the economic and political infrastructure necessary to block or effectively cultivate a nonexploitative alternative to it.[104]

Instead of participating in Drury's investigation, the Dene Nation agreed to collaborate with the Metis Association of the NWT to construct a joint settlement claim that they provided the federal government in 1981. The proposal, titled *Public Government for the People of the North*, called for a transfer of power to a "province-like" jurisdiction named "Denendeh."[105] Although the Dene/ Métis refrained from invoking the explicit language of self-determination common to the previous two claims, the spirit of the document remains much the same. It demands, for instance, that sovereignty be distributed between Denendeh and the federal government in a manner similar to the current distribution of provincial and federal powers, although in some areas, such as fisheries, family relations, communications, and labor relations, Denendeh would require powers currently claimed by the federal government. The rationale here is that these areas are crucial for the protection and further development of the Dene "way of life."[106] It also calls for a significant return of the Dene peoples' traditional territory, which the Dene would retain the right to use, own, and manage collectively. Most remaining lands, with the exception of existing private property, would be allocated to the Government of Denendeh and remain under its jurisdictional authority.

Structurally speaking, Denendeh would be "province-like" and consist of two levels of government: a public territorial level, called the National Assembly of Denendeh, and regional governments at the community level.[107] Denendeh would be unlike provinces in other ways, however. For instance, the Dene again recommended that a direct democracy or "consensus" approach to political decision-making be instituted at both the local and territorial levels.[108] This was pitched as a culturally appropriate alternative to the "elitist" and adversarial form of government imposed on northerners from the South. Also, to protect the political rights and freedoms of Dene citizens in perpetuity, the Dene/Métis proposed that a "senate" be established as a second chamber of the public National Assembly with guaranteed Dene representation.[109] In order to protect the interests of everyone, however, the Dene/Métis proposed that a ten-year residency period be implemented, after which full political rights of all Denendeh citizens would be respected. But regardless of any residency requirement, the Government of Denendeh would be responsible for respecting the fundamental human rights and freedoms of all its citizens, particularly the rights outlined in sections 18, 19, 21, and 22 of the United Nations' International Covenant on Civil and Political Rights, of which Canada is a signatory.[110]

In terms of economic development, Denendeh would also operate unlike the provinces in a number of key ways. For example, the document suggests that all land and resource development adhere to standards set forth in a "Charter of Founding Principles," which would emphasize, among other things, maintaining a "harmonious relationship between the Dene and the physical environment."[111] Thus, the Dene/Métis stated that natural resource use would be determined "on the basis of a 'conserver society'" with a "firm commitment to renewables." Once again, building a contemporary economy committed to the traditional practice of harvesting and manufacturing renewable resources would form a significant aspect of economic development within the new territory. However, in circumstances where the exploration and development of Denendeh's nonrenewable resource base might be permitted to continue, this activity would only be allowed if it promised to ensure the "well-being of the people and resources of Denendeh" as a whole, "as opposed to the economic benefit of the developers." And to ensure economic self-sufficiency, the Dene/Métis proposed that 10 percent of all resource revenues derived in the territory be collected and paid into a "Dene Heritage Fund" managed by the Dene through the framework of the proposed senate. Remaining profits extracted through rents taken from nonrenewable resource outfits would be redirected back into programs aimed at bolstering the renewable resource sector, be used to cover the operating budgets of the Denendeh government at both the community and territorial levels, and to repay the federal government for its assistance in the delivery of unemployment insurance benefits, family allowances, and so on. Also like its predecessors, the proposal suggests that all private property rights be respected for lands acquired before the implementation of the agreement, although after this date, the Government of Denendeh would grant property titles solely through long-term leases and hold remaining lands in common for the benefit of all Denendeh citizens.[112]

Reaction to the Denendeh proposal varied. Some people were outraged at the proposed agreement, suggesting that it would provide too much protection for Dene rights and interests while ignoring those of the North's non-Native population.[113] One of the studies prepared for the federal government's Special Committee on Constitutional Development even suggested that the proposal's recommended restrictions on private property could be interpreted as violating what many northerners had come to consider an "inalienable right" to own property.[114] Others, however, viewed the proposal as a "unique opportunity to be a part of something exciting, a chance for all people of the north to join together and build a new style of government."[115]

CONCLUSION

In the end, the federal government remained one of the principal detractors of the Denendeh proposal. Unlike the position outlined in its own comprehensive claims policy, the Dene/Métis adamantly rejected the idea that Indigenous peoples must surrender or exchange their political rights and title as a prerequisite to reaching a land settlement. Maintaining this position caused negotiations to drag on until 1988, when, finally, a new "Agreement-in-Principle" (AIP) was reached between the Dene Nation, the Metis Association, and the Government of Canada. The new AIP offered the claimants "ownership of over 181,000 square kilometres of land, with subsurface rights for approximately 10,000 kilometres of it, and a payment of $500 million over fifteen years as compensation for lost land use in the past."[116] To reach the AIP stage, however, the Crown required two things. The first was that the recognition of Indigenous political rights be removed from the negotiation table. This essentially meant that the Dene Nation dropped its previous insistence, articulated in the Dene Declaration and the three claims examined above, that a substantive right to self-government form a fundamental component of any land deal. Second, the AIP required the Dene/Métis to agree to "cede, release and surrender" any residual Aboriginal rights and title to the remaining lands of the Northwest Territories. Negotiators for the Dene/Métis thus conceded that, if reached, a comprehensive claim would inevitably involve an "exchange" of Aboriginal "land rights" for a "clearly defined set of land-related and land based-rights."[117] At this point, however, those involved in the negotiations refused to see this as an extinguishment of their "political rights," which they would "continue to negotiate through other forums."[118]

On April 9, 1990, two years after community negotiators agreed to sign the new AIP, Indigenous representatives from across Denendeh convened at a special general assembly held in Fort Rae where they initialed a final agreement that included an extinguishment clause but excluded a self-government component. In July of the same year, a motion was passed at another general assembly, this time held in Dettah, to "have aboriginal and treaty rights affirmed, not extinguished, in the comprehensive claim agreement."[119] In the end, the majority of delegates voted to affirm the motion and in doing so rejected the Dene/Métis Final Agreement. No doubt frustrated with the non-negotiable nature of the Crown's position, Gwich'in representatives opposed the majority decision and formally withdrew from the general assembly. Following their lead, the Sahtu withdrew from the claim several weeks later. The Crown officially stopped funding the Dene Nation's claims secretariat after the withdrawal of the Gwich'in and Sahtu and instead offered to negotiate with these groups independently. In 1992 the Gwich'in, and in 1993 the Sahtu along with the Métis, extinguished their political rights and title by signing comprehensive agreements with Canada. These settlements signified the official end of an at times tenuous and fragile (but nonetheless unified) Dene national self-determination movement.[120]

Northern Indigenous perspectives on economic development began to shift significantly during this period as well. This shift was exemplified most clearly with the backing of diamond mega-mining projects by the Tlicho and Yellowknives Dene First Nation in the late 1990s, and again, in 2000, with the establishment of the Aboriginal Pipeline Group (APG), which represents the interests of most Dene regions in the NWT (excluding the Dehcho) and has since negotiated an agreement to purchase a one-third share in the newly proposed Mackenzie Gas Project (MGP). The MGP, like the proposed Mackenzie Valley Pipeline before it, promises to be one of the largest and costliest pipeline projects in the history of Canada.[121]

What is perhaps most interesting about the newest incarnation of the Mackenzie pipeline project is that many of the young Dene activists who opposed it in the 1970s are now either active supporters or founding members of the APG. Former Fort Good Hope chief Frank T'Seleie has explained his change in perspective like this:

You know, the world has changed a lot over the last 25 years. We're now masters of our own house in many ways. Many of us have settled our land claims and we have the power to make sure this pipeline is done the right way. Sure, I feel uneasy in some ways about promoting this. This gas is going to go south, maybe not today or tomorrow. But it is going to go, and I don't think we can afford to be left out.[122]

If primitive accumulation represents the process of dispossession through which noncapitalist social relations are transformed or integrated into market ones, then it would appear that this phenomenon has gained considerable momentum in the North over the last few decades. Although primitive accumulation no longer appears to require the openly violent dispossession of Indigenous communities and their entire land and resource base, it does demand that both remain open for exploitation and capitalist development. To my mind, a number of interrelated considerations have to be taken into account to figure out why this has emerged as the case in the North, and I would like to conclude by highlighting two of them. The first involves a significant transformation in the discourse of "sustainable development" over the last fifteen years. As Stuart Kirsch has argued, one of the most pressing challenges faced by Indigenous peoples has been the "speed with which capital now appropriates the terms of its critique."[123] Any visit to the North will unequivocally demonstrate the degree to which state and industry have been able to coopt the discourse of "sustainability" to push their shared vision of economic development. Unlike the discourse of sustainability underwriting the Dene claims examined above, which sought to establish political and economic relations that would foster the reciprocal well-being of people, communities and the land over time, sustainability now refers primarily to the *economic* sustainability of capital accumulation itself. The longer the projected lifespan of a proposed project—that is, the longer period that a project proposes to exploit a community's land, resources, and labor, the more "sustainable" it is said to be.

The second involves Fanon's concern regarding the ways in which the field of recognition politics can modify the subject positions of Indigenous people and communities over time. Aside from the inevitable debt trap that land claims lock many First Nations into, which can in turn compel these communities to open up their settlement lands to exploitation as an economic solution,[124] it appears that the land-claims process itself has also served to subtly shape how Indigenous peoples now think and act in relation to the land. As Paul Nadasdy suggests in his work with the Kluane First Nation in the Yukon, "to engage in the process of negotiating a land-claim agreement, First Nations people must translate their complex reciprocal relationship with the land into the equally complex but very different language of 'property.'"[125] I would suggest that one of the negative effects of this power-laden process of discursive translation has been a reorientation of the meaning of self-determination for many (but not all) Indigenous people in the North; a reorientation of Indigenous struggle from one that was once deeply *informed* by the land as a system of reciprocal relations and obligations (grounded normativity), which in turn informed our critique of capitalism in the period examined above, to a struggle that is now increasingly *for* land, understood now as material resource to be exploited in the capital accumulation process.

3

Essentialism and the Gendered Politics of Aboriginal Self-Government

[T]heorists who advocate a politics of difference, fluidity and hybridity
in order to challenge the binaries of essentialism . . . have been
outflanked by strategies of power.

— MICHAEL HARDT and ANTONIO NEGRI, *Empire*

In this chapter I explore in detail the second cluster of concerns often associated with the politics of recognition briefly identified in my introductory
chapter. These criticisms have tended to focus on the empirically problematic
and normatively suspect character of recognition claims based on "essentialist"
articulations of collective identity. According to social constructivist proponents of this line of critique, when claims for cultural accommodation are
grounded on essentialist expressions of group identity they can too easily be
deployed to justify repressive and authoritarian demands for group compliance
on the one hand, or sanction unjust practices of exclusion and marginalization on the other. Without certain guaranteed rights and state institutional
mechanisms in place to ensure that problematic cultural norms and practices
remain open to democratic deliberation and group contestation, it has been
argued that the self-determining status of subaltern individuals within minority
groups—especially women and children—will remain at risk.

Recognizing that social constructivist critiques of the politics of culture and
identity encompass a vast range of theoretical and disciplinary perspectives, in
this chapter I will focus more narrowly on the work of political theorist Seyla
Benhabib, whose contribution represents what I see as an important yet problematic attempt to bridge the gap between the insights afforded by social constructivist *theory* and what she views as the deliberative norms and processes
that ought to guide and frame democratic *practice*.[1] In doing so, I argue that
Benhabib's anti-essentialist critique works in concert with a statist feature of
her deliberative democratic theory, which functions to inadvertently sanction

colonial hierarchies. This argument can be broken into the following two claims. First, I contend that when examined through the lens of Indigenous peoples' struggles, Benhabib's social constructivist critique of the politics of recognition tends to not only overestimate the emancipatory potential of anti-essentialist criticism, but more importantly it also fails to address the full breadth of power relations that often serve to proliferate exclusionary and authoritarian community practices and articulations of identity to begin with. In this regard, I align my work with the growing number of scholars who have begun to critically interrogate anti-essentialist criticism when uniformly applied to a range of conceptually distinct and power-laden contexts.[2]

My second claim is directed more squarely at the statist character of Benhabib's deliberative democratic critique of the politics of recognition. Here I contend that when anti-essentialist theories of cultural identity are projected as a universal feature of social life and then employed as a justificatory measure for evaluating the legitimacy of claims for recognition within and against the uncontested authority of the *colonial state*, they can inadvertently sanction the very types of domination and inequality that both social constructivist and deliberative democratic projects ought to mitigate. This is especially the case with respect to Indigenous claims for recognition, which often throw into question, either implicitly or explicitly, the legitimacy of the state's assumed role as arbiter in contestations over recognition.

This chapter is organized into four sections. The first section provides a brief sketch of the constructivist critique of the politics of recognition Benhabib offers in *The Claims of Culture: Equality and Diversity in the Global Era*. As with my previous engagement with Charles Taylor in chapter 1, although I focus largely on Benhabib's work here, many of the conclusions reached in this section are by no means limited to her contribution alone. In the second section, I provide a history of Indigenous women's struggle against sexist provisions of the Indian Act and an examination of the ways in which this history of struggle informed an Indigenous feminist critique of the gendered dynamics underwriting the decade-long (1982–92) effort of mainstream Aboriginal organizations to secure a constitutional right to the self-government in Canada. In the next section, I argue that, although Benhabib is correct to highlight the ways in which preservationist claims to cultural recognition can and have been used by male segments of colonized societies to justify oppressive gender practices, her critique fails to adequately address the colonial context within which these practices have come to flourish. And finally, in the last section, I argue that insofar as Benhabib's theory uncritically positions the colonial state as a legitimate adjudicator of Indigenous recognition claims, her argument is itself ironically premised on the racist/essentialist assumption that Indigenous peoples were so uncivilized at the time of European contact that they did not constitute self-determining subjects in relation to the states that eventually asserted sovereignty over them.

SOCIAL CONSTRUCTIVISM AND DELIBERATIVE DEMOCRACY

Benhabib's *The Claims of Culture: Equality and Diversity in the Global Era* sets out to establish a model of deliberative democracy that is capable of accommodating universal demands for individual freedom and equality along with identity-specific demands for the recognition of cultural difference. According to Benhabib, the task of those who are simultaneously committed to a politics that values both cultural diversity *and* democratic equality should be "to create impartial institutions in the public sphere and civil society where [the] struggle for recognition of cultural differences and the contestation of cultural narratives can take place *without domination.*"[3] In order to accomplish this task, Benhabib insists that one reject claims for recognition founded on essentialist and therefore potentially authoritarian conceptualizations of culture and group identity: "Intercultural justice between human groups should be defended in the name of justice and freedom and not of an elusive preservation of cultures."[4] Identity movements that do seek to preserve the "purity or distinctiveness of cultures," Benhabib boldly asserts, are simply "irreconcilable with both democratic and more basic epistemic considerations."[5]

Benhabib opens her critique by challenging the empirical foundation upon which most contemporary theories of "mosaic multiculturalism" are based—what she terms the "reductionist sociology of culture."[6] Quoting the work of Terrance Turner, Benhabib contends that advocates of this form of multiculturalism often embrace a simplistic and sharply delineated conception of cultural identity, which, when institutionalized in the form of public policy risks "essentializing the idea of culture as the property of an ethnic group or race; it risks reifying cultures as separate entities by over emphasizing the internal homogeneity of cultures in terms that potentially legitimize repressive demands for communal conformity; and by treating cultures as badges of group identity, it tends to fetishize them in ways that put them beyond the reach of critical analysis."[7] Beyond potentially legitimizing these repressive practices, Ben-habib claims that the reductionist approach yields a number of other illiberal consequences, including "(1) the drawing of too rigid and firm boundaries around cultural identities; (2) the acceptance of the need to 'police' these boundaries to regulate internal membership and 'authentic' life-forms; (3) the privileging of the continuity and preservation of cultures over time as opposed to their reinvention, reappropriation, and even subversion; and (4) the legiti-mation of culture-controlling elites through a lack of open confrontation with their cultures' inegalitarian and exclusionary practices."[8]

In contradistinction to this reductionist approach, Benhabib draws on the work of Homi Bhabha and others to defend a constructivist view of identity in which all cultures constitute fluid systems of meaning and representation that are continually constructed and reconstructed through "complex dialogues and interactions with other cultures."[9] Cultures are thus "fluid, porous, and contested" phenomena, "which are internally riven by conflicting narratives."[10] Benhabib assures us, however, that this position is not meant to imply that cultures are unreal or fictional entities: "Cultural differences run very deep and are very real," insists Benhabib, the "imagined boundaries between [cultures] are not phantoms in deranged minds; [they] can guide human action and behaviour as well as any other cause of human action."[11]

Also unlike the reductionist perspective, Benhabib aligns justice in multi-cultural and multinational contexts not in terms of cultural preservation or autonomy, but rather with the "inclusion" of traditionally marginalized groups into a widening "democratic dialogue" with the citizenry, cultures, and institu-tions of the surrounding society. In order to facilitate this robust form of inclu-sion, Benhabib proposes a "dual track" model of deliberative democracy that stresses "maximal cultural contestation in the public sphere," as well as "the institutions and associations of civil society." So long as recognition-based claims adhere to the constructivist/inclusion paradigm and allow for the con-testability of cultural norms, practices, and boundaries in and through the institutional matrix of civil society and the state, then certain forms of "legal pluralism and institutional power sharing through regional and local parlia-ments" can and ought to be accommodated.[12] To ensure that pluralist insti-tutional arrangements meet this standard, Benhabib proposes a baseline of three "normative conditions" that ought to be met by any cultural group seek-ing recognition and accommodation. These conditions are:

egalitarian reciprocity. Members of cultural, religious, linguistic, and other minorities must not, in virtue of their membership status, be entitled to lesser
degrees of civil, political, economic, and cultural rights than the majority.

voluntary self-ascription. In consociationalist or federative multicultural societies,
an individual must not be automatically assigned to a cultural, religious, or linguistic group by virtue of his or her birth. An individual's group membership
must permit the most extensive form of self-ascription and self-identification
possible. There will be many cases when such self-identifications may be
contested, but the state should not simply grant the right to define and control membership to the group at the expense of the individual; it is desirable
at some point in their adult lives individuals be asked whether they accept
their continuing membership in their cultural communities of origin.

freedom of exit and association. The freedom of the individual to exit the ascrip-
tive group must be unrestricted, although exit may be accompanied by the
loss of certain kinds of formal and informal privileges. However, this wish
of individuals to remain group members, even while out marrying, must not
be rejected; accommodations must be found for inter-group marriages and
the children of such marriages.[13]

After outlining these normative requirements Benhabib concludes that,
although "cultural groups may not be able to survive as distinct entities under
these conditions," securing them is nonetheless "necessary if legal pluralism in
liberal-democratic states is to achieve the goals of cultural diversity as well as
democratic equality, without compromising the rights of women and children."[14] Under Benhabib's deliberative model, only demands for recognition
that adhere to the above standards and do not deny the contestability of cultural norms and practices can ensure the well-being of individual group members.[15] Here the cultural preservationist impulses of essentialism are clearly
portrayed as overly restrictive and rigid, while the inclusive domain of social
constructivism is cast as democratic and emancipatory.

Indigenous Women, Gender Discrimination, and Aboriginal Self-Government: A History

Before 1985 all federally registered First Nations women who married non-
Native men were forced to relinquish their Indian "status" under sexist provisions of the federal government's 1876 Indian Act.[16] Like many aspects of

Canadian Indian policy, the state's gendered criteria for determining who is eligible to claim Indian "status" under the law predates Canadian confederation. In 1850, definitions of status were generally broad in scope and included "any person of Indian birth or blood, any person reputed to belong to a particular group of Indians, and any person married to an Indian or adopted into an Indian family."[17] With respect to those individuals who acquired status through marriage, this early definition stated that any non-Aboriginal or non-status women who married a status male would herself acquire status, but the same was not true for non-Aboriginal men married to status women. Although the 1850 legislation did not yet lay out the terms under which a status woman could expect to lose her status for marrying a nonstatus man, it nonetheless established for the first time a definition of "Indian" that was tightly associated with patrilineal descent.[18]

In the years to follow, state-sanctioned gender discrimination within the field of Indian policy would escalate dramatically. For instance, under provisions of the 1869 Act for the Gradual Enfranchisement of Indians, status Indian women were legally excluded from the right to receive inheritances from their husbands, they were denied the right to vote and participate in formal band politics, and they could be declared enfranchised without consent upon the enfranchisement of their husbands; finally, Section 6 of the Gradual Enfranchisement Act stated that any status woman who married a nonstatus man would lose all rights and benefits commonly associated with membership in a federally recognized Indian community, including the rights to reside on reserve and receive housing there, federally subsidized health care, postsecondary education, and so on.[19] All of these sexist provisions were incorporated into Canada's Indian Act in 1876.

Although First Nations women have always resisted the state's attempt to dispossess them of their rights to land and community membership, it was not until the late 1960s and early 1970s that their efforts began to gain national coverage, if not success. This period witnessed the establishment of organizations such as Indian Rights for Indian Women (incorporated in 1970) and the Native Women's Association of Canada (incorporated in 1974), both of which would help advance the fight of Native women against the patriarchal structure of Indian legislation. In particular, these groups were instrumental in organizing enfranchised Native women around questions of gender equality and political empowerment at the local, national, and international levels.

Three foundational legal challenges emerged from this period of Indigenous women's activism: (1) *Lavell v. Canada* in 1971; (2) *Bédard v. Isaac* in 1972; and (3) *Lovelace v. Canada* in 1981.[20]

The first two legal challenges sought to force a repeal of the sexist provisions of the Indian Act by challenging in court their lack of conformity with Canada's 1960 Bill of Rights. In *Lavell v. Canada* this involved a challenge to Section 12 (1) (b) of the Indian Act—the provision containing the infamous "marrying out" clause. In his decision, Judge Grossberg of the Ontario County Court ruled against Lavell, arguing that in *losing* the limited rights and benefits associated with Indian status Lavell had *acquired* the full and equal rights of Canadian citizenship, thus rendering her charge of discrimination obsolete. In Grossberg's words: "In my view . . . the equality which should be sought and assured to the appellant upon her marriage is equality with all other Canadian married females. The appellant has such equality. The appellant has [therefore] not been deprived of any human rights or freedoms contemplated by the Canadian *Bill of Rights*."[21] The second case involved Yvonne Bédard, a Mohawk woman whose band sought to evict her and children from a house bestowed to her by her mother. Bédard argued in court that the only reason the band could legally claim the right to do so was because she had married a nonstatus man and thus lost her status and the associated right to live on reserve, which she claimed contravened the gender equality provisions outlined in the Bill of Rights. In the end, both Lavell and Bédard lost their cases at the federal level but were successful at gaining appeals, and their claims were eventually heard simultaneously by the Supreme Court of Canada.[22]

During the period leading up to the Supreme Court's decision, Lavell and Bédard were subject to ruthless criticism within First Nations communities and by mainstream First Nations political organizations. As Lenape scholar Joanne Barker notes, in making their stand both women were routinely accused of "being complicit and even conspiring" with the kinds of "colonialist, assimilationist, and racist ideologies" propagated by government bureaucrats and Department of Indian Affairs and Northern Development (DIAND) administrators.[23] In particular, the two women's appeals to baseline feminist norms regarding gender equality rights were often included as evidence of the culturally "inauthentic" character of their concerns. As Barker describes: "Demonizing an ideology of rights perceived to be based on selfish individualism and personal entitlement, and damned for being 'women's libbers' out to force bands into compliance with this ideology, the women and their concerns and experiences of discriminatory and violent sexist practices within their communities were dismissed as embodying all things not only non- but anti-Indian. Indian women's experiences, perspectives, and political agendas for reform were perceived as not only irrelevant but dangerous to Indian sovereignty movements."[24] The perceived culture clash between the individual rights of Native women and the collective rights of First Nations communities to recognition and self-determination led organizations like the National Indian Brotherhood (renamed the Assembly of First Nations in 1982) to intervene against Lavell and Bédard in their cases, arguing with the Attorney General of Canada that the Indian Act ought to supersede subsequent legislation, including the gender equality stipulations outlined in the Canadian Bill of Rights.[25]

In March of 1973 the Supreme Court of Canada ruled against Lavell and Bédard in a 5–4 decision, and in doing so upheld the patriarchal criterion for determining Indian status under Section 12 (1) (b) of the Indian Act. Among the numerous points made in his majority decision, Justice Ritchie argued "that equality before the law under the *Bill of Rights* means equality of treatment in the enforcement and application of the laws of Canada before the enforcement authorities and the ordinary Courts of the land," and that "*no such inequality is necessarily entailed* in the construction and application of s. 12 (1) (b)."[26] On this point, Justice Ritchie concurred with the lower court decision of Judge Grossberg, whom we recall argued that Lavell's charge of discrimination was unsubstantiated given that in losing her Indian status she had acquired the full and equal benefits of Canadian citizenship. The second significant point made in the decision was that the Bill of Rights should not be allowed to "render inoperative" the federal government's constitutional authority to legislate with respect to "Indian and lands reserved for Indians" as dictated by Section 91 (24) of the BNA Act of 1867.[27]

Sandra Lovelace, a Maliseet woman from the reserve community of Tobique, New Brunswick, mounted the next major legal intervention, but this time at the international level. Lovelace's efforts initially began in the 1970s as part of a community-wide struggle to address her reserve's escalating housing and homelessness crisis.[28] At issue during this period were the ways in which the Tobique band council had interpreted Indian Act legislation to exclude community women from acquiring property on reserve.[29] Over time, however, the intolerable living conditions experienced by the women of Tobique coalesced into a movement to change the Indian Act itself.[30] Because Lovelace had lost her status after marrying a nonstatus man, when she returned to the reserve with her children after her divorce the band was unwilling to provide her with access to housing. Women in the community began to mobilize around the Lovelace case, which in the winter of 1977 was brought to the United Nations Human Rights Committee.[31] In her complaint, Lovelace argued that Section 12 (1) (b) of the Indian Act was noncompliant with Article 27 of the International Covenant on Civil and Political Rights, which stipulates that in "those States in which ethnic, religious or linguistic minorities exist, persons belonging to such minorities shall not be denied the right to live in community with the other members of their group, to enjoy their own culture, to profess and practice their own religion, or to use their own language."[32]

While the United Nations Human Rights Committee was deliberating the case, the women and Tobique and their supporters initiated another strategy to force attention to the issues faced by Native women in Canada. In July of 1979, the women organized a hundred-mile walk from Oka, Quebec, to Parliament Hill in Ottawa. The direct action attracted significant national press coverage, and upon arrival the women staged a major protest and were able to secure a meeting with the prime minister and several cabinet members. The protest resulted in the federal government committing $300,000 toward women's reserve housing in Tobique, although some have questioned whether the money ever reached those most in need.[33] Finally, on July 30, 1981, the Committee rendered a decision in favour of Lovelace, ruling that Section 12 (1) (b) indeed violated Article 27 on the grounds that it denied Lovelace the right to live in her community of culture.[34]

The timing of the United Nations' decision in *Lovelace v. Canada* did not reflect well on the Canadian state. At the time, Canada was immersed in the process of repatriating its Constitution from England, and the proposed repatriation package was to include a Canadian Charter of Rights and Freedoms that would constitutionally entrench, among other things, gender equality rights. This eventually led the federal government to repeal the provision of the Indian Act dealing with outmarriages in 1985. This legislative initiative, known as Bill C-31, coincided with the three-year grace period within which Canada had to amend all legislation shown to contravene its newly minted charter. Importantly, the Bill C-31 amendment also states that bands have the right to create their own membership codes, although this clause requires that any membership rules established by a First Nation may not deprive current band members or those eligible to have their band membership reinstated for reasons that occurred before new membership rules were adopted. Following the Bill C-31 amendment, thousands of enfranchised First Nations women and their children applied to have their Indian status reinstated. Since the implementation of Bill C-31, however, several First Nations communities have challenged the right of reinstated women to access to the benefits associated with band citizenship. As political scientist Joyce Green explains:

> Following the 1985 C-31 revisions to the Indian Act, a number of Indian bands drafted membership codes, pursuant to the revised Indian Act. Some of the codes are racist and sexist in their effect, and some seem to resurrect the discriminatory formula of the pre-1985 Indian Act, now presumed as "custom." Yet, the 1982 Constitution prohibits discrimination and guarantees aboriginal and treaty rights equally to men and women. In order to prevent exited women and their children from being reinstated to their bands of origin, several bands initiated a legal action arguing that Aboriginal tradition legitimates the exclusion of women where they married anyone other than a band member, and that this tradition was itself protected by the constitutional recognition of aboriginal and treaty rights.[35]

Similar to the ways in which the efforts of Lavell and Bédard were constructed as traitorous to Indigenous traditions and sovereignty struggles discussed above, here again we see how the gender equality claims and individual rights of reinstated women and children are pitted against the collective right of First Nations to determine their own membership. The result, as Green notes, has been a dismissal of Native women's concerns as "untraditional and, by extension, as deleterious to indigenous liberation."[36]

The next major cycle of Native women's struggles occurred during the post-1982 debates regarding the application of gender equality rights to the context of Aboriginal self-government. With the Constitution Act, 1982 came the recognition of "existing aboriginal and treaty rights" under Section 35 (1). Part 37 of the Constitution Act, 1982 further stipulated that within a year a constitutional conference would be held to define the scope of these newly recognized rights, and that Aboriginal peoples as well as representatives of the Northwest Territories and Yukon would officially join provincial leaders as part of the negotiation process. There ended up being four of these confer-ences held between 1983 and 1987. The first conference, which took place in March of 1983, resulted in the first amendment to the Constitution Act, 1982. The amendment expanded the definition of "existing aboriginal and treaty rights" to include constitutional recognition to those rights and benefits secured through the negotiation of land claims agreements under Section 35 (3) and to ensure that constitutional recognition of Aboriginal rights applied equally "to male and female persons" under Section 35 (4).

The gender equality provision enshrined in the 1983 amendment did not come about easily. There were two reasons for this. First, the meeting that resulted in the amendment, as well as the three constitutional conferences that followed, formally excluded Aboriginal women's organizations from par-ticipating at the negotiating table.[37] And second, among the four Aboriginal organizations invited to participate in the conference (the Assembly of First Nations, the Métis National Council, the Inuit Tapirisat of Canada, and the Native Council of Canada), the largest and most powerful, the Assembly of First Nations, initially refused to endorse the amendment, arguing that it would unduly infringe on the authority of First Nations to "determine mem-bership criteria in light of their own perceptions of the traditions and needs of Indian people." By the end of the conference's second day, however, the AFN modified its position, likely because it did not want to be perceived as promoting another agenda with gender discriminatory implications. Subse-quently, on the final day of meetings, the AFN conceded that it would accept the sexual equality clause on the condition that "the issue of citizenship be left for further discussions."[38]

The marginalization of Native women and organizations from the 1983–87 constitutional conferences on Aboriginal rights would continue well into the era of attempted mega-constitutional amendments, particularly those that ended in the failed Charlottetown Accord of 1992.[39] The proposed Charlotte-town Accord emerged in the ashes of its 1987 predecessor, the Meech Lake Accord, which was a failed constitutional amendment package negotiated by the then prime minister of Canada, Brian Mulroney, and the ten provincial premiers. As I discuss in the following chapter, the Meech Lake Accord repre-sented the federal government's attempt to bring Quebec "back in" to the constitutional fold in the wake of the province's refusal to recognize the legiti-macy of the newly repatriated Constitution Act, 1982. First Nations leaders overwhelmingly opposed the Meech Lake deal because it failed to recognize the political interests of First Nations. The failure to include Aboriginal perspectives on a major constitutional overhaul ultimately helped tank the deal. The Charlottetown Accord picked up where Meech Lake left off, although with an attempt to make the process more inclusive. After a series of lengthy and intense negotiations, a proposed agreement was struck on August 28, 1992, between the federal government, the provincial and territorial governments, and Aboriginal representatives on a proposed series of amendments to the Constitution Act, 1982. Among other things, the amendment sought to address issues concerning the "distinct status" of Quebec within the confederation, the right of Aboriginal peoples to self-government, and parliamentary reform. In order to curb ongoing public concerns regarding the elitist and exclusionary character of negotiating major constitutional changes, the terms of the Charlottetown Accord were put to a national referendum on October 26, 1992, where they were ultimately rejected by a majority of Canadian voters.

During the negotiation process it became clear that many Aboriginal leaders and organizations wanted their communities vested with powers of self-government largely unencumbered by Canada, including its Charter of Rights and Freedoms. Although the negotiations leading up to the Charlottetown Accord made it clear that Aboriginal governments would not receive the degree of unfettered autonomy that many leaders had demanded during the process, in the end a compromise was reached whereby Aboriginal governments would, like their federal and provincial counterparts, be granted access to Section 33 of the Constitution Act, 1982, otherwise known as "the notwithstanding clause." Access to the "notwithstanding clause" would provide Aboriginal governments the power to "opt-out" of or suspend those provisions of the charter deemed impediments to self-rule. This led many supporters of the Native Women's Association of Canada to reject the Charlottetown deal, fearing that some Aboriginal governments might try to call on Section 33 as a means of undercutting the gender equality provisions outlined in the charter. As the Native Women's Association of Canada explained in 1991:

> We are human beings and we have rights that cannot be denied or removed at the whim of any government. That is how fundamental these individual Charter rights are. These views are in conflict with many First Nations and legal theoreticians who advocate for recognition by Canada of sovereignty, self-government

and collective rights. It is their unwavering view that the "collective" comes first, and that it will decide the rights of individuals. . . .

We recognize that there is a clash between collective rights of sovereign First Nations and individual rights of women. Stripped of equality by patriarchal laws which created "male privilege" as the norm on reserve lands, First Nations women have had a tremendous struggle to regain their social position. We want the Canadian Charter of Rights and Freedoms to apply to Aboriginal governments.[40]

Considering that Native women's organizations were excluded from participating in the constitutional negotiations that resulted in the Charlottetown Accord, and that several First Nations band councils had openly admitted that they were looking for ways to circumvent the obligations placed on their governments by Bill C-31, including through the invocation of essentialist arguments based on male-dominated interpretations of "culture" and "tradition," the concerns expressed by the Native Women's Association of Canada were not without merit. The result, unfortunately, has been a zero-sum contest pitting the individual human right of Indigenous women to sex equality against the collective human right of Indigenous peoples to self-determination.

SOCIAL CONSTRUCTIVISM AND
SETTLER-COLONIAL PATRIARCHY

As the brief history depicted above indicates, those communities that have argued against the integration of reinstated First Nations women under Bill C-31 and/or the protection of gender equality provisions in the context of Aboriginal self-government have tended to rationalize their positions with reference to interrelated arguments grounded on claims to Indigenous sovereignty and cultural incommensurability. According to the sovereignty position, the exclusion of First Nations women reinstated under Bill C-31 is justified on the grounds that First Nations governments, not the colonial settler state, have the fundamental right to determine in accordance with their own cultures and political traditions regulations that govern membership in Indigenous communities. At face value, the sovereignty argument holds significant weight. In contexts such as Canada, where the legitimacy of Canadian sovereignty has been shown to rest on the problematic assumption that its claimed land base was *terra nullius* at the time of acquisition (discussed further below), it would indeed appear that First Nations ought to retain authority over the rules governing membership in their communities. In practice, however, the sovereignty argument has been indelibly shaped by the sexist grammar of state Indian legislation over time. As Mi'kmaq scholar Bonita Lawrence explains: "Indian legislation in the Indian Act has functioned so completely—and yet so apparently invisibly—along gendered lines that at present the rewriting of Indian identity under Bill C-31 in ways that target men as well as women are viewed as intense violations of sovereignty, while the gendered violations of sovereignty that occurred in successive Indian Acts since 1869 have been virtually normalized as the problems of individual women."[41] According to Lawrence's analysis, if the sovereignty argument were taken seriously by First Nations communities, it would compel such communities to critically inter-rogate the sexist attack on Indigenous self-determination that has resulted in the historical dispossession of thousands of Indigenous women and their off-spring through the Indian Act's outmarriage clause, instead of selectively lim-iting one's critique to the imposition of Bill C-31 in 1985.

The cultural incommensurability position is the one that has fallen under the most scrutiny of social constructivist critics. It claims that respecting the gender equality rights of individual First Nations women, as stipulated, for example, under Section 15 of the Charter of Rights and Freedoms and Sec-tion 35 (4) of the Constitution Act, 1982, clashes with the fundamentally "collectivist" orientation of Indigenous cultures and political traditions. As the Assembly of First Nations stated to the standing committee on Aboriginal Affairs in 1982:

> As Indian people we cannot afford to have individual rights override collective rights. Our societies have never been structured that way, unlike yours, and that is where the clash comes. If you isolate the individual rights from the collective rights, then you are heading down another path that is ever more discrimina-tory. The Charter of Rights is based on equality. In other words, everybody is the same across the country . . . so the Charter of Rights automatically is in conflict with our philosophy and culture and organization of collective rights.[42]

Under Benhabib's model, the situation described above is clearly unaccept-able. In fact, one could argue that it provides a textbook example of why preser-vationist demands for collective recognition should not outweigh the univer-sal rights of individual group members. Further, it also appears to demonstrate how the institutional accommodation of essentialist articulations of cultural identity through the allocation of unhampered self-government rights can facilitate the further exclusion and marginalization of a community's less-powerful members, especially when this form of accommodation is not subject to the norms that guide deliberative democratic practice or adhere to baseline conditions such as egalitarian reciprocity, voluntary self-ascription, and freedom of exit and association.[43] In particular, the reliance by many First Nation leaders and organizations on arguments stressing the incommensurability of liberal democratic and Indigenous cultural conceptions of citizenship seems to lend credence to these concerns. However, although I agree with Benhabib's condemnation of these exclusionary practices as unjust, I nonetheless must challenge both her identification of the source as well as her prescriptive gestures toward a solution to these practices. I simply fail to see how developing a deliberative order that calls on the state to institutionally police a more open-ended, fluid, and contestable understanding of cultural identity through democratic deliberation can subvert the deeply entrenched relations of power at play here.

Benhabib's anti-essentialist criticism includes two dimensions: it claims to be grounded on, first, an *empirical* understanding about the constructed nature of cultural identities, which she then, second, deploys in a *normative* argument in defense of gender justice for Aboriginal women and other marginalized members of cultural minorities.[44] Indeed, I would argue that recognizing the social *fact* of cultural contestability is a necessary (although insufficient) condition for cultivating what most deliberative democrats posit as a just democratic order. In other words, what is convenient about the social constructivist position to the deliberative democratic project is that it justifies subjecting "the cultural" to the norms that guide deliberative conceptions of "the political": that is, it renders cultural forms and practices subject "to appropriate processes of public deliberation by free and equal citizens."[45] When viewed from this angle, it would appear that the very possibility of cultivating a truly democratic and emancipatory multicultural or multinational politics hinges on culture's so-called fluid and therefore democratically negotiable nature.[46] However, as such scholars as Michael Hardt and Antonio Negri argue, the problem with this formulation is that it assumes that the oppressive relations of power under scrutiny operate in a very precise manner.[47] In short, the efficacy of anti-essentialist interventions such as Benhabib's rests on the assumption that unjust configurations of power are produced and maintained primarily through the production and naturalization of hierarchically ordered binary oppositions based on what appear to be fixed or nonnegotiable differences; differences between, say, male and female, black and white, gay and straight, colonizer and colonized. And indeed, in contexts where oppressive hierarchies *are* primarily sustained through these naturalized divisions, the affirmation of "hybridity and [the] ambivalences of our cultures ... seem to challenge the binary logic of Self and Other that stands behind colonialist, sexist, and racist constructions."[48] But what does this strategic intervention have to say about situations where relations of dominance and subordination are neither primarily produced nor sustained through these essentialized binary oppositions?

I ask, because in the context of Indigenous women's struggle for community citizenship rights, the binary logic that ought to be at the source of their marginalization is not readily apparent. There is no doubt that certain segments of the male Native elite have problematically seized the language of cultural incommensurability, tradition, and self-preservation to justify the asymmetrical privileges that they have inherited from the subjectifying regime of sexist misrecognition under successive pieces of Indian legislation since 1869, but the reification and misuse of culture in this case cannot be understood without reference to the colonial context within which it continues to flourish. "This constructivist viewpoint, while in some respects very useful," writes Bonita Lawrence, "is also deeply troubling to many Native people."[49] For Lawrence, what is lacking in too many constructivist analyses of supposed Indigenous cultural essentialisms is a deep understanding of the complex web of oppressive social relations that anchor the Canadian state's relationship with Indigenous nations, of which the gendered production and maintenance of essentialist identity formations constitutes only one. As a result of this relationship, adverse social indicators such as poverty, unemployment, substandard housing conditions, infant mortality, morbidity, youth suicide, incarceration, women as victims of abuse and sexual violence, and child prostitution are much more common in Indigenous communities than they are in any other segment of Canadian society, whereas educational success and retention, acceptable health and housing conditions, and access to social services and economic opportunity are generally far lower.[50] These state-sanctioned conditions have made it difficult for some First Nations governments to provide an adequate system of support for the members they have now, let alone thousands of reinstated women and children. In fact, by thrusting these disadvantaged members into the hands of the communities without rectifying the profound inequalities that structure the relationship *between* Indigenous peoples and the state, the federal government has simply served to aggravate the problem *within* these communities even further.[51]

The essentialist defense of certain First Nations' gender exclusionary practices also cannot be understood outside of the context of the eliminatory logic of the state's historical approach to dealing with its so-called "Indian Problem." This logic is perhaps most forcefully exemplified in the federal government's proposed *Statement of the Government of Canada on Indian Policy* in 1969— also known as the White Paper. As Peter Kulchyski's recent work argues, the White Paper explicitly deployed a human rights framework of individual equality in an effort to do away with the collective Aboriginal and treaty rights of Indigenous nations.[52] In this case, formal legal equality was used by the state as a wrecking ball that threatened to undermine Aboriginal and treaty rights by unilaterally enfranchising First Nations individuals as Canadian citizens under the law while proposing to transfer reserve lands to First Nations communities as fee-simple holdings subject to Canadian property laws and the pressures of the capitalist market. This all to say that, when the Assembly of First Nations expressed concern over the threat of "individual rights overriding collective rights" during self-government negotiations in the 1980s and 1990s,[53] this was not *solely* an expression of internalized sexism articulated in a patriarchal defense of custom and tradition, although for some it was unfortunately this too; it was also a conditioned response to the very real state proposal to eliminate First Nations as such.

It is also important to recall that the human right to equal treatment under the law was the rationale used to undermine the gendered violation of Indigenous sovereignty that resulted in the court challenges of Lavell and Bédard in the 1970s. Both court decisions used individual equality, as exemplified by the rights of Canadian citizenship enshrined in the 1960 Bill of Rights, to rule against the plaintiffs' charge of gender discrimination via the Indian Act. Here I suggest that the emergent liberal rights apparatus of the Canadian Bill of Rights provided the plaintiffs with a legal *incentive* to address their concerns in a manner that was ultimately ill-suited to the task of both gender justice for Indigenous women and self-determination for Indigenous nations.

In such contexts, I simply do not see how deliberatively policing hybrid cultural forms can subvert the colonial context within which these gendered practices flourish. Even if we were to provide institutional spaces within which one might deconstruct and expose the Native elite's sexist misuse of culture as a means of maintaining patriarchal privilege, we would still leave intact the host of other social relations that work in concert with patriarchy to inform the misuse to begin with. In effect, we would be locked in a vicious circle of essentialist claims-making and identity deconstruction, having to repeatedly deliberate over and unpack problematic identity claims and practices only to have them resurface in another place and context because we have failed to undermine the full conditions of their production.

This assessment of Benhabib's constructivist position should not be interpreted as rehashing some reductionist model of oppression where patriarchy is simplistically cast as some second-order, epiphenomenal "effect" of the more "foundational" problem of settler-colonialism. What I am suggesting here is quite different: that the oppression faced by Indigenous women in Canada cannot be adequately understood when separated from the other axes of oppression that have converged to sustain it over time. In the settler-colonial context of Canada, these power relations of course include patriarchy, but also white supremacy, capitalism, and state domination. By focusing too narrowly on the gendered character of essentialist cultural claims, Benhabib failed to take into consideration the multiplicity of ways in which these other dynamics have served to inform, indeed proliferate, these sexist practices.

SOCIAL CONSTRUCTIVISM, COLONIAL DOMINATION, AND THE STATE

In the previous section I suggested that Benhabib's anti-essentialist critique of the politics of recognition represents both a sociological statement about the hybrid nature of cultural identities, as well as a normative project aimed at progressive social change. However, unlike more explicitly poststructuralist-inspired theorists who tend to view anti-essentialist criticism as a potentially transformative practice in its own right, Benhabib moves beyond the realm of deconstructive critique and applies what she sees as the best insights of social constructivist thought to the development of a deliberative project capable of accommodating justifiable demands for cultural recognition without violating individual claims to equality.[54] In doing so, I claim she makes a very problematic move: once she establishes the constructedness of cultural identities as a definitive feature of social life, she then proceeds to ground her normative position on what a political order ought to look like based on this universal depiction.[55] What form ought this political order take? As noted previously, for Benhabib it should comprise "impartial institutions in the public sphere and civil society where [the] struggle for recognition of cultural differences and the contestation of cultural narratives can take place without domination."[56] If group demands for cultural recognition meet this deliberative standard, there is no reason why the state should not provide legal and institutional accommodation for the group in question.[57] This, again, is quite different from the standard poststructuralist position, which tends to view the institutionalization of any claim to universality with suspicion.[58]

Now, thus far my critique has been directed fairly broadly at the colonial implications of what I have characterized as an uncritical normative privileging of cultural contestability in Benhabib's social constructivism. Seen from this angle, Benhabib's deliberative approach appears problematic only insofar as it has appropriated this uncritical strand of constructivist thought. In this section, I want to flip the gaze around. That is, I want to examine more closely a colonial implication of Benhabib's statist model of deliberative democracy, and in doing so show how her social constructivist commitments work in concert with this statism to reinforce a colonial structure of dominance.

My concern here is that by employing the so-called social fact of cultural contestability as a standard against which democratic theorists, judges, policy makers, and the state ought to assess the legitimacy of claims for recognition, Benhabib's theory potentially sanctions the very forms of power and domination that anti-essentialist democratic projects ought to mitigate. First, by placing the burden squarely on the shoulders of claimants of recognition to prove that their identity movements do not deny the contestability of cultural practices before they are eligible for institutional accommodation, Benhabib's model potentially renders rectifying forms of recognition and redistribution unattainable for Indigenous groups whose cultural expressions do not adhere to this excessively fluid form. Second, and more problematically, *even if* Indigenous claims for recognition do manage to meet these criteria, her theory leaves uninterrupted the colonial social and political structure that is assigned the adjudicative role in assessing recognition claims and enforcing postdeliberative claim decisions. Political theorist Duncan Ivison perceptively refers to this second problem as the "legitimacy" crisis faced by most deliberative approaches when applied to colonial contexts.[59] I will now discuss these two problems in turn.

First, in many cases Indigenous peoples' struggles for recognition and self-determination simply defy all protocols associated with social constructivist criticism. As Arif Dirlik has commented: "Not only do [they] affirm the possibility of a 'real' native identity, but [they] also assert for the basis of such an identity a native subjectivity that has survived, depending on location, as many as five centuries of colonialism and cultural disorientation. Not only [do they] believe in the possibility of recapturing the essence of precolonial indigenous culture, but [they] also base this belief on a spirituality that exists outside of historical time. . . . In all of these different ways, indigenous ideology would seem to provide a textbook case of 'self-Orientalization.'"[60]

Dirlik does not end his observations here, however; in other works he goes on to discuss the ways that Indigenous scholars and activists defend what would appear to be essentialist notions of indigeneity in their attempts to provide radical alternatives to "the challenge of modern political organization—in particular the nation-state—and [which] offer possibilities that need to be considered seriously in any place-based democratic alternatives" to the hegemony of state and capitalist forms of domination.[61] Our discussion of the place-based alternatives to colonial economic and political development articulated by the Dene Nation in the previous chapter provides an excellent example of such a project.

Benhabib's intervention, however, focuses solely on the exclusionary features of essentialist identity formations, and this understanding is subsequently reflected in her deliberative approach. The potential problem here, of course, is that by theoretically and institutionally privileging recognition claims that adhere to an infinitely negotiable conception of culture, it is unclear what Indigenous claims Benhabib's deliberative model would be willing and able to accommodate. For one, almost every Indigenous demand for recognition that I can think of is couched, at least in part, in the vernacular of "cultural survival" and "autonomy"—and rightfully so, given the history of genocidal state assimilation policies that Indigenous people and communities have been forced to endure. Thus, as Arif Dirlik and Roxann Prazniak caution, even when the emancipatory potential of seemingly essentialist Indigenous claims are not readily apparent, it is crucial to "distinguish between claims to identity of the powerful and the powerless, because the powerless may face such threats, including on occasion the threat of extinction, that is intellectually, politically, and morally irresponsible to encompass within one notion of 'essentialism.'"[62]

In the concluding chapter of *The Claims of Culture* Benhabib recognizes the challenge that Indigenous claims to self-determination present her position. "These peoples," she writes, "are seeking not to preserve their language, customs, and culture alone but to attain the integrity of ways of life greatly at odds with modernity."[63] She continues:

> While being greatly skeptical about the chances for survival of these cultural groups, I think that from the standpoint of deliberative democracy, we need to create institutions through which members of these communities can negotiate and debate the future of their own conditions of existence.... As I have suggested ... the self-determination rights of many of these groups clash with gender equality norms of the majority culture. [However, if] self-determination is viewed not simply as the right to be left alone in governing one's affairs, but is also understood as the right to participate in the larger community, then the negotiation of these ways of life to accommodate more egalitarian gender norms becomes possible.[64]

Although Benhabib recognizes the limits of her approach in colonial contexts, in the end she is still unrelenting in her commitment to a conception of democratic governance that views justice for Indigenous communities in terms of their greater inclusion into the institutional matrix of the larger settler state and society. Indeed, her whole approach suggests that this inclusion is *necessary* so that Indigenous peoples' nonliberal, nonmodern cultural norms and practices remain open to contestation and group deliberation. Indigenous peoples, in other words, require access to the deliberative mechanisms and democratic institutions of the enlightened colonial society *for the well-being of their own citizens*. The assumption here being that the colonial imposition of patriarchal governance structures in First Nations communities has so damaged customary gender roles that the colonial state apparatus is now required to intervene in the political life of First Nations communities to ensure that Indigenous women's rights are honored and upheld. Here, the legitimacy of a substantive right to Indigenous autonomy and self-determination is perversely undercut by the very success of the colonial project itself. The adverse effects of colonization demand more colonial intervention.

Second, although these proposals may avoid some of the effects associated with essentialist group practices, they nonetheless leave unscathed the presumption that the colonial state constitutes a legitimate authority to determine which demands for Indigenous recognition ought to be accommodated and which ought to be denied. Ironically, however, the state's assumed position in these struggles is itself what is contested by many Indigenous claims for cultural recognition. What is also ironic is the fact that that the state's assumed authority in these matters is premised on the profoundly essentialist, indeed *racist*, understanding that Indigenous peoples were too uncivilized to constitute equal and self-determining nations when European powers unilaterally asserted their sovereignty over Native North America.

When the first Europeans arrived in what is now Canada, survival required that they immediately enter into political and economic relationships with the diverse, sovereign, and self-governing Indigenous nations that they encountered. Over the ensuing four centuries the relationship between Indigenous nations and the growing settler society would undergo substantial changes, shifting from "mutually beneficial associations . . . between equal nations to the coercive imposition of a structure of domination." As the settler society grew in numbers and strength, their dependence on the technologies and knowledge of Indigenous peoples began to wane, and the relationship shifted from one premised on peaceful coexistence and relative equality between peoples to a colonial relationship "in which Aboriginal peoples and their cultures were treated as unequal and inferior."[65] Over the last decade, numerous scholars have convincingly shown how the conceptualization of Indigenous societies as politically and culturally inferior continues to inform Canada's presumed authority over Indigenous lands and people.[66] Because Indigenous societies were considered so low on the natural scale of social and cultural evolution, settler authorities felt justified in claiming North America legally vacant, or *terra nullius*, and sovereignty was acquired by the mere act of settlement itself. As Michael Asch's work has pointed out, the Supreme Court of Canada still implicitly and consistently invokes the racist *terra nullius* thesis to justify the unequal distribution of sovereignty that structures the relationship between Indigenous peoples and Canada.[67]

The colonial state is not only a racial structure, however; it is also fundamentally *patriarchal* in character. To date, one of the best analyses of the patriarchal nature of settler-state power has come from one the most persistent and thoughtful critics of *Charter* protection for Indigenous women: the late Mohawk legal scholar Patricia Monture. As an unrelenting advocate of both Indigenous nationalist struggles *and* emancipation for Indigenous women, Monture's work embodies among the best of contemporary Indigenous feminist theory and practice, even though she did not identify her work in these terms.[68] What Monture's work adds to the intersectionality of Indigenous feminist approaches to decolonization is a critical analysis of the colonial state as manifestation of male power, which she claims renders its legal apparatus very problematic as a site of emancipation for Indigenous women. "The Canadian state is the invisible male perpetrator who unlike Aboriginal men does *not* have a victim face," asserts Monture in her pathbreaking book, *Thunder in My Soul*. "And at the feet of the state I can lay my anger to rest."[69]

I think that Monture's concern with the legalist approach to seeking gender justice for Native women adopted by organizations like The Native Women's Association of Canada is that such an approach implicitly assumes that the colonial state is ultimately a *gender-neutral* apparatus that only *historically* adopted a patriarchal logic to frame Indian legislation, instead of understanding male dominance as a constitutive feature of state power as such. What are the implications of turning to the state as a protector of Indigenous women's rights if the state itself constitutes the material embodiment of masculinist, patriarchal power? Here I suggest that Monture's insights coalesce productively with those of political theorist Wendy Brown. For Brown, gender emancipation strategies that rely on the state apparatus in this way have deeply contradictory implications given that "domination, dependence, discipline, and protection, the terms marking the itinerary of women's subordination in vastly different cultures and epochs, are also characteristic effects of state power."[70] Subsequently, when women turn to the state apparatus in their struggles for gender justice they risk reiterating rather than transforming the subjective and material conditions of their own oppression. At the very least, Monture's Indigenous feminist critique of the colonial state provides us with a tool to critically reflect on the contradictory impulses associated with seeking emancipation from the adverse gendered and racist effects of state power by means of law. This does not require that Indigenous peoples vacate the legal field entirely, however. As

Kwakwaka'waka scholar Sarah Hunt writes, "Surely we must engage with this powerful system, but appealing to the law alone will not stop the violence."[71] For Hunt, as with Monture, this system must be used very cautiously and strategically, so as to not "reproduce the systems and ideologies that colonialism has produced."[72] And, as Anishinaabe feminist Dory Nason suggests, these strategic engagements must be supplemented, if not eventually replaced, by "those values, practices and traditions that are the core of Indigenous women's power and authority—concepts that have been, and remain under attack, and which strike at the core of a settler-colonial misogyny that refuses to acknowledge the ways in which it targets Indigenous women for destruction."[73]

Here we have arrived at a paradox. If, as I have argued, Benhabib's use of social constructivism represents not only an empirical statement about the nature of cultural identities, but also a means of undercutting those forms of domination that she views as being legitimized through the reification of essentialist and nonnegotiable cultural forms, then her theory has failed to serve its purpose in the colonial context. In fact, by treating the state as a natural and uncontested arbiter in struggles for recognition—or, as Richard J. F. Day has put it, by assuming that "the state somehow 'inherently' occupies a pole of universality, [providing an] appropriate ground for dialogue between [Indigenous peoples,] ethnic groups, regions, and so on"—Benhabib's model has firmly imbedded Indigenous nations within the racialized and patriarchal structure of colonial domination that their claims for cultural recognition posit as unjust and illegitimate.[74] According to Arif Dirlik it is precisely through this double maneuver—the uncritical and premature positing of cultural "in-betweenness" as both a universal and normative aspect of "the human condition"—that anti-essentialist democratic projects abandon their transformative potential and crystallize into a "new kind of determinism from which there is no escape."[75]

Conclusion

To avoid some of the problems that have come to the fore in the preceding sections, I think it is crucial that advocates of anti-essentialist criticism begin to acknowledge that, as *discourses*, both constructivist and essentialist articulations of identity can aid in either the maintenance or subversion of oppressive configurations of power. Here I employ "discourse" in a Foucauldian manner to refer to the myriad ways in which the objects of our knowledge are defined and produced through the languages we employ in our engagement with the world and with others. Discursive formations, in other words, are not neutral; they "construct" the topic and objects of our knowledge; they govern "the way that a topic can be meaningfully talked about and reasoned about." They also influence how ideas are "put into practice and used to regulate the conduct of others." Just as a discursive formation can legitimize certain ways of thinking and acting, they can also profoundly limit and constrain "other ways of talking and conducting ourselves in relation to the topic or constructing knowledge about it."[76] And it is precisely on this last point where I believe constructivist-inspired projects such as Benhabib's have failed: in their a priori attack on all essentialist claims-making they have refused to acknowledge the repressive ways in which their own discursive interventions have effectively undermined certain forms of subaltern resistance, and have thus unduly constrained the field of legitimate action for Indigenous peoples in their national liberation struggles.

The same can be also be said about the ways in which the discourse of "culture" has been used by certain segments within the Indigenous community to further exclude and marginalize the status of Native women. What is needed in this case is an explicit acknowledgment of the manner in which the Indian Act has itself come to discursively shape, regulate, and govern how many of us have come to think about Indigenous identity and community belonging. As a result, we have to be cautious that our appeals to "culture" and "tradition" in our contemporary struggles for recognition do not replicate the racist and sexist misrecognitions of the Indian Act and in the process unwittingly reproduce the structure of dispossession we originally set out to challenge.

In sum, then, no discourse on identity should be prematurely cast as either inherently productive or repressive prior to an engaged consideration of the historical, political, and socioeconomic contexts and actors involved. To my mind, paying closer attention to context when studying the underlying dynamics of identity-related struggle might better enable critics, especially those writing from positions of privilege and power, to distinguish between "discourses that naturalize *oppression* and discourses that naturalize *resistance*."[77] This is particularly relevant from the perspective of Indigenous peoples' struggles, where activists may sometimes employ what appear to outsiders as essentialist notions of culture and tradition in their efforts to transcend, not reinforce, oppressive structures and practices.

4

Seeing Red

Reconciliation and Resentment

Our greatest critics and commentators are men and women of
resentment. . . . Our revolutionaries are men and women of resentment.
In an age deprived of passion . . . they alone have the one dependable
emotional motive, constant and obsessive, slow-burning but totally
dependable. Through resentment, they get things done.

—ROBERT SOLOMON, *Living with Nietzsche*

The person who most forcefully expressed the discourse of resentment
is Frantz Fanon.

—MARC FERRO, *Resentment in History*

On June 11, 2008, the Conservative prime minister of Canada, Stephen J.
Harper, issued an official apology on behalf of the Canadian state to
Indigenous survivors of the Indian residential school system.[1] Characterized as
the inauguration of a "new chapter" in the history of Aboriginal–non-Aboriginal
relations in the country, the residential school apology was a highly anticipated
and emotionally loaded event. Across the country, Native and non-Native
people alike gathered in living rooms, band offices, churches, and community
halls to witness and pay homage to this so-called "historic" occasion. Although
there was a great deal of Native skepticism toward the apology in the days
leading up to it, in its immediate aftermath it appeared that many, if not most,
observers felt that Harper's apology was a genuine and necessary "first step"
on the long road to forgiveness and reconciliation.[2]

The benefit of the doubt that was originally afforded the authenticity of the
prime minister's apology has since dissipated. Public distrust began to escalate
following a well-scrutinized address by Harper at a gathering of the G20 in
Pittsburgh, Pennsylvania, on September 25, 2009. It was there that Harper made
the somewhat astonishing (but typically arrogant and self-congratulatory)

claim that Canadians had "no history of colonialism." Harper continued: "We have all of the things that many people admire about the great powers but none of the things that threaten or bother them."[3] On October 1, 2009, the National Chief of the Assembly of First Nations, Shawn Atleo, responded to the prime minister's claim: "The Prime Minister's statement speaks to the need for greater public education about First Nations and Canadian history. . . . The future cannot be built without due regard to the past, without reconciling the incredible harm and injustice with a genuine commitment to move forward in truth and respect."[4] In this chapter, I explore some of the issues raised by these two seemingly contradictory events—the residential school apology and call for forgiveness and reconciliation on the one hand, and the selective amnesia of Harper's G20 address on the other—and how they speak to the current entanglement of settler coloniality with the politics of reconciliation that began to gain traction in Canada during the 1990s.

Over the last three decades, a global industry has emerged promoting the issuing of official apologies advocating "forgiveness" and "reconciliation" as an important precondition for resolving the deleterious social impacts of intrastate violence, mass atrocity, and historical injustice.[5] Originally, this industry was developed in state contexts that sought to undergo a formal "transition" from the violent history of openly authoritarian regimes to more democratic forms of rule—known in the literature as "transitional justice"—but more recently has been imported by somewhat stable, liberal-democratic settler polities like Canada and Australia.[6] In Canada, we have witnessed this relatively recent "reconciliation politics" converge with a slightly older "politics of recognition," advocating the institutional recognition and accommodation of Indigenous cultural difference as an important means of reconciling the colonial relationship between Indigenous peoples and the state. Political theorist Andrew Schaap explains the convergence of these two discourses well: "In societies divided by a history of political violence, political reconciliation depends on transforming a relation of enmity into one of civic friendship. In such contexts the discourse of *recognition* provides a ready frame in terms of which reconciliation might be conceived."[7]

In Canada "reconciliation" tends to be invoked in three distinct yet interrelated ways when deployed in the context of Indigenous peoples' struggles for self-determination. First, "reconciliation" is frequently used to refer to the diversity of individual or collective practices that Indigenous people undertake to reestablish a positive "relation-to-self" in situations where this relation has been damaged or distorted by some form of symbolic or structural violence. Acquiring or being afforded due "recognition" by another subject (or subjects) is often said to play a fundamental role in facilitating reconciliation in this first sense.[8] Second, "reconciliation" is also commonly referred to as the act of restoring estranged or damaged social and political relationships. It is frequently inferred by proponents of political reconciliation that restoring these relationships requires that individuals and groups work to overcome the debilitating pain, anger, and resentment that frequently persist in the wake of being injured or harmed by a perceived or real injustice.[9] In settler-state contexts, "truth and reconciliation" commissions, coupled with state arrangements that claim to recognize and accommodate Indigenous identity-related differences, are viewed as important institutional means to facilitate reconciliation in these first two senses.[10] These institutional mechanisms are also seen as a crucial way to help evade the cycles of violence that can occur when societal cultural differences are suppressed and when so-called "negative" emotions such as anger and resentment are left to fester within and between disparate social groups.[11] The third notion of "reconciliation" commonly invoked in the Canadian context refers to the process by which things are brought "to agreement, concord, or harmony; the fact of being made consistent or compatible."[12] As Anishinaabe political philosopher Dale Turner's recent work reminds us, this third form of reconciliation—the act of rendering things *consistent*—is the one that lies at the core of Canada's legal and political understanding of term: namely, rendering consistent Indigenous assertions of nationhood with the state's unilateral assertion of sovereignty over Native peoples' lands and populations. It is the state's attempt to impose this third understanding of reconciliation on the institutional and discursive field of Indigenous–non-Indigenous relations that is effectively undermining the realization of the previous two forms of reconciliation.

Thomas Brudholm's recent book, *Resentment's Virtue: Jean Améry and the Refusal to Forgive*, offers an important critique of the global turn to reconciliation politics that has emerged in the last thirty years. Specifically, Brudholm's study provides a much-needed "counterpoint" to the "near-hegemonic status" afforded "the logic of forgiveness in the literatures on transitional justice and reconciliation."[13] Focusing on the Truth and Reconciliation Commission of South Africa, Brudholm shows how advocates of transitional justice often base their normative assumptions about the presumed "good" of forgiveness and reconciliation on a number of uncritical assumptions about the supposed "bad" of harboring reactive emotions like anger and resentment: that these feelings are physically and mentally unhealthy, irrational, retrograde, and, when collectively expressed, prone to producing increased social instability and political violence. Brudholm challenges these assumptions through a fascinating engagement with the writings of essayist and holocaust survivor Jean Améry, whose own work challenges the scathing and very influential portrayal of *ressentiment* as an irredeemably vengeful, reactionary, and backward-looking force by Friedrich Nietzsche in *On the Genealogy of Morals* (1887).[14] According to Brudholm, Améry's work forces us to consider that under certain conditions a disciplined maintenance of resentment in the wake of historical injustice can signify "the reflex expression of a moral protest" that is as "permissible and admirable as the posture of forgiveness."[15]

In this chapter, I undertake a similar line of argumentation, although with two significant differences. First, as a critique of the field and practice of *transitional justice*, Brudholm's study is "limited to the *aftermath* of mass atrocities" and to the "*time after* the violence has been brought to an end."[16] In the following pages, the political import of Indigenous peoples' emotional responses to settler colonization is instead explored against the "nontransitional" backdrop of the state's approach to reconciliation that began to explicitly inform government policy following the release of the *Report of the Royal Commission on Aboriginal Peoples* (RCAP) in 1996.[17] I show that in settler-colonial contexts— where there is no period marking a clear or formal transition from an authoritarian past to a democratic present—state-sanctioned approaches to reconciliation must ideologically manufacture such a transition by allocating the abuses of settler colonization to the dustbins of history, and/or purposely disentangle processes of reconciliation from questions of settler-coloniality as such. Once either or both of these conceptual obfuscations have been accomplished, holding the contradictory position that Canada has "no history of colonialism" following an official government apology to Indigenous survivors of one of the state's most notoriously brutal colonial institutions begins to make sense; indeed, one could argue that this form of conceptual revisionism is *required* of an approach that attempts to apply transitional justice mechanisms to nontransitional circumstances. In such conditions, reconciliation takes on a temporal character as the individual and collective process of overcoming the subsequent *legacy* of past abuse, not the abusive colonial structure itself. And what are we to make of those who refuse to forgive and/or reconcile in these situations? They are typically cast as being saddled by the damaging psychological residue of this legacy, of which anger and resentment are frequently highlighted.

The second difference is that I use the work of Frantz Fanon as my central theoretical referent instead of that of Jean Améry. As Améry himself perceptively noted in an important 1969 essay, Fanon held a very nuanced perspective on both the potentially transformative and retrograde aspects of colonized peoples' "hatred, contempt and resentment" when expressed within and against the subjective and structural features of colonial power.[18] This chapter builds on Fanon's insights to demonstrate two things. First, far from being a largely disempowering and unhealthy affliction, I show that under certain conditions Indigenous peoples' individual and collective expressions of anger and resentment can help prompt the very forms of self-affirmative praxis that generate rehabilitated Indigenous subjectivities and decolonized forms of life in ways that the combined politics of recognition and reconciliation has so far proven itself incapable of doing. And second, in light of Canada's failure to deliver on its emancipatory promise of postcolonial reconciliation, I suggest that what implicitly gets interpreted by the state as Indigenous peoples' *ressentiment*—understood as an incapacitating inability or unwillingness to get over the past—is actually an entirely appropriate manifestation of our *resentment:* a politicized expression of Indigenous anger and outrage directed at a structural and symbolic violence that still structures our lives, our relations with others, and our relationships with land.

I develop this argument in three sections and a conclusion. In the first section, I discuss the ways in which "negative emotions" like anger and resentment get taken up in the literature on forgiveness and reconciliation in Canada. In the next section, I provide a reading of Fanon's theories of internalized colonialism and decolonization in order to counter the largely unsympathetic interpretation of Indigenous peoples' negative emotional responses to settler-colonial rule in the Canadian discourse on reconciliation. This section will also provide a historical account of the transformative role played by Indigenous peoples' anger and resentment in generating self-affirmative acts of resistance

and Indigenous direct action that prompted the state to respond with pacifying gestures of recognition and reconciliation. And finally, I provide an analysis of the "turn to reconciliation" in Aboriginal policy following the release of
the RCAP report in 1996. Here I develop my claim that Indigenous peoples'
resentment represents a legitimate response to the neocolonial politics of reconciliation that emerged in the wake of RCAP.

DWELLING ON THE NEGATIVE:
RESENTMENT AND RECONCILIATION

In common usage, "resentment" is usually referenced negatively to indicate a
feeling closely associated with anger.[19] However, where one can be *angry* with
any number of things, resentment is typically reserved for and directed against
instances of perceived wrongdoing. The *Oxford English Dictionary*, for example, defines resentment as a feeling of "bitter indignation at having been
treated *unfairly*."[20] One could argue, then, that resentment, unlike anger, has
an in-built *political* component to it, given that it is often expressed in response
to an alleged slight, instance of maltreatment, or injustice. Seen from this
angle, resentment can be understood as a particularly virulent expression of
politicized anger.[21]

   The political dimension of resentment has not gone unnoticed within
the Western philosophical tradition; philosophers such as Adam Smith, John
Rawls, Robert Solomon, Jeffrie Murphy, Alice MacLachlan, and Thomas Brudholm (to name only a few) have all written extensively on the "moral" significance of emotions like resentment.[22] In *A Theory of Justice*, for example, Rawls
writes that "resentment is a moral feeling. If we resent our having less than
others, it must be because we think that their being better off is the result
of unjust institutions, or wrongful conduct on their part."[23] In a similar vein,
Jeffrie Murphy argues that resentment can be both a legitimate and valuable
expression of anger in response to the unjust abrogation of one's rights; it is
an affective indicator of our sense of self-worth or self-respect.[24] And Alice
MacLachlan writes: "In emphasizing the moral function of resentment as one
kind of anger . . . philosophers have offered an important service to angry
victims of political violence, who are often voiceless except in their ability to
articulate and express resentment."[25] Thomas Brudholm notes that, although
these theorists vary regarding "the conditions and circumstances under which

anger or resentment is appropriate," they nonetheless all draw an important "distinction between excessive and pathological forms of anger and resentment, on the one hand, and appropriate and valuable forms, on the other hand."[26]

Discussions within the field of recognition and reconciliation politics, however, rarely treat reactive emotions like anger and resentment even-handedly. Indeed, in such contexts, anger and resentment are more likely to be seen as pathologies that need to be overcome. However, given the genealogical association of feelings like resentment with political and moral protest, why have they received such bad press in the literature on reconciliation? I think there are at least two reasons to consider here. First, as several scholars have noted, in the transitional justice and reconciliation literature our understanding of resentment has been deeply shaded by Nietzsche's profoundly influential characterization of *ressentiment* in *On the Genealogy of Morals*.[27] There, *ressentiment* is portrayed as a reactive, backward, and passive orientation to the world, which, for Nietzsche, signifies the abnegation of freedom as self-valorizing, life-affirming action. To be saddled with *ressentiment* is to be irrationally preoccupied with and incapacitated by offences suffered in the past. "*Ressentiment*," writes Jean Améry, "nails" its victims to "the past," it "blocks the exit . . . to the future" and "twists" the "time-sense" of those trapped in it.[28] This theme is taken up again in *Thus Spoke Zarathustra*, where Nietzsche describes the so-called "man of *ressentiment*" as an "angry *spectator* of everything past."[29] For Nietzsche, *ressentiment* is an expression of one's "impotence" against "that which *has been*."[30] For the resenting subject, "memory" is a "festering wound."[31] In Nietzsche's view, to wallow in resentment is to deny one's capacity to actively "forget," to "let go," to *get on with life*.[32] In the third section below I show how state reconciliation policy in Canada is deeply invested in the view that Indigenous peoples suffer from *ressentiment* in a way not entirely unlike Nietzsche describes.

The second reason why negative emotions like anger and resentment find few defenders in the field of reconciliation politics is because they sometimes *can* manifest themselves in unhealthy and disempowering ways. My argument here does not deny this. Individual narratives highlighting the perils associated with clinging to one's anger and resentment appear too frequently in the Canadian reconciliation literature to do so. Consider, for example, the following account by Ojibwe author Richard Wagamese, which speaks to the

personal necessity of overcoming anger and resentment as a precondition in
his own healing journey:

> For years I carried simmering anger and resentment. The more I learned about
> the implementation of [Indian residential school] policy and how it affected
> Aboriginal people across the country, the more anger I felt. I ascribed all my
> pain to residential schools and those responsible. . . . But when I was in my late
> forties, I had enough of the anger. I was tired of being drunk and blaming the
> residential schools and those responsible. . . . My life was slipping away on me
> and I did not want to become an older person still clinging to [such] disempow-
> ering emotion[s].[33]

Taken together, these are all very serious concerns. It makes no sense at all to
affirm the worth of resentment over a politics of recognition and reconciliation if doing so increases the likelihood of reproducing internalized forms of
violence. Nor could one possibly affirm the political significance of Nietzschean *ressentiment* if doing so means irrationally chaining ourselves "to the
past." While I recognize that Indigenous peoples' negative emotional responses
to settler colonization can play out in some of these problematic ways, it is
important to recognize that they do not always do so. As we shall see in the
next section, these affective reactions can also lead to forms of anticolonial
resistance grounded on transformed Indigenous political subjectivities. I suggest that the transformative potential of these emotions is also why Frantz
Fanon refused to dismiss or condemn them; instead he demanded that they
be *understood*, that their transformative potential be *harnessed*, and that their
structural referent be *identified* and *uprooted*.

The Resentment of the Colonized and the Rise of Reconciliation Politics in Canada

Understanding Fanon's views regarding the political significance of what he
calls "emotional factors" in the formation of anticolonial subjectivities and
decolonizing practices requires that we briefly revisit his theory of internalized colonialism.[34] Recall from chapter 1 that, for Fanon, in contexts where the
reproduction of colonial rule does not rely solely on force, it requires the production of "colonial subjects" that acquiesce to the forms of power that have
been imposed on them. "Internalization" thus occurs when the social relations

of colonialism, along with the forms of recognition and representation that serve to legitimate them, come to be seen as "true" or "natural" to the colonized themselves. "The status of 'native' is a neurosis," explains Sartre in his preface to *The Wretched of the Earth*, "introduced and maintained by the colonist in the colonized *with their consent*."[35] Similar to how the Italian Marxist theorist Antonio Gramsci viewed the reproduction of class dominance in situations absent ongoing state violence, colonial hegemony is maintained through a combination of coercion and consent.[36] Under such conditions, colonial domination appears "more subtle, less bloody," to use Fanon's words.[37]

For Fanon, this "psychological-economic structure" is what produces the condition of stagnancy and inertia that characterizes the colonial world.[38] *The Wretched of the Earth*, for example, is littered with passages that highlight the fundamentally passive and lethargic condition that the colonial situation produces. The "colonial world," writes Fanon, is "compartmentalized, Manichaean and *petrified*"; it is a world in which the "colonial subject" is "penned in," lies "coiled and robbed," taught "to remain in his place and not overstep his limits."[39] In *Black Skin, White Masks*, Fanon describes this Manichaean relation as "locked" or "fixed" by the assumptions of racial and cultural inferiority and superiority held by the colonized and colonizer, respectively.[40] Unlike racist arguments that attribute the supposed inertia of colonized societies to the cultural and technological underdevelopment of the colonized themselves, Fanon identifies the colonial social structure as the source of this immobility.[41]

Although the internalized negative energy produced by this "hostile" situation will first express itself against the colonized's "own people"—"This is the period when black turns on black," writes Fanon, when colonial violence "assumes a black or Arab face"—over time, it begins to incite a negative *reaction* in the colonial subject.[42] It is my claim that this reaction indicates a breakdown of the psychological structure of internalized colonialism. The colonized subject, degraded, impoverished, and abused, begins to look at the colonist's world of "lights and paved roads" with envy, contempt, and resentment.[43] The colonized begin to *desire* what has been denied them: land, freedom, and dignity. They begin dreaming of revenge, of taking their oppressor's place:

> The gaze that the colonized subject casts at the colonist's sector is a look of lust, a look of envy. Dreams of possession. Every type of possession: at sitting at the colonist's table and sleeping in his bed, preferably with his wife. The colonized

man is an envious man. The colonist is aware of this as he catches the furtive glance, and constantly on his guard, realizes bitterly that: "They want to take our place." And it is true that there is not one colonized subject who at least once a day does not dream of taking the place of the colonist.[44]

Although Fanon is quick to insist that the "legitimate desire for revenge" borne of the colonized subject's nascent "hatred" and "resentment" toward the colonist cannot alone "nurture a war of liberation," I suggest that these negative emotions nonetheless mark an important turning point in the individual and collective coming-to-consciousness of the colonized.[45] More specifically, I think that they represent the *externalization* of that which was previously *internalized*: a purging, if you will, of the so-called "inferiority complex" of the colonized subject. In the context of internalized colonialism, the material conditions of poverty and violence that condition the colonial situation appear muted to the colonized because they are understood to be the product of one's own cultural deficiencies. In such a context, the formation of a colonial "enemy"—that is, a source external to ourselves that we come to associate with "our misfortunes"—signifies a collapse of this internalized colonial psychic structure.[46] For Fanon, only once this rupture has occurred—or, to use Jean Améry's phrase, once these "sterile" emotions "come to recognize themselves" for "what they really are . . . consequences of social repression"[47]— can the colonized then cast their "exasperated hatred and rage in this new direction."[48]

Importantly, Fanon insists that these reactive emotions can also prompt the colonized to revalue and affirm Indigenous cultural traditions and social practices that are systematically denigrated yet never fully destroyed in situations of colonial rule. After years of dehumanization the colonized begin to resent the assumed "supremacy of white values" that has served to ideologically justify their continued exploitation and domination. "In the period of decolonization," writes Fanon, "the colonized masses thumb their noses at these very values, shower them with insults and vomit them up."[49] Eventually, this newfound resentment of colonial values prompts the colonized to affirm the worth of their own traditions, of their own civilizations, which in turn generates feelings of pride and self-certainty unknown in the colonial period. For Fanon, this "anti-racist racism" or "the determination to defends one's skin" is "characteristic of the colonized's response to colonial oppression" and provides them with the motivating "reason the join the struggle."[50] Although Fanon ultimately saw this example of Indigenous cultural self-recognition as an expression akin to Nietzschean *ressentiment*—that is, as a limited and retrograde "reaction" to colonial power—he nonetheless claimed it as necessary for the same reason he affirmed the transformative potential of emotional factors like anger and resentment: they signify an important "break" in the forms of colonial subjection that have hitherto kept the colonized "in their place."[51] In the following chapters, I delve further into what I claim to be Fanon's overly "instrumental" view of culture's value vis-à-vis decolonization in light of the more substantive position held by contemporary theorists and activists of Indigenous resurgence.

In the context of internalized colonialism, then, it would appear that the emergence of reactive emotions like anger and resentment can indicate a breakdown of colonial subjection and thus open up the possibility of developing alternative subjectivities and anticolonial practices. Indeed, if we look at the historical context that informed the coupling of recognition with reconciliation politics following Canada's launch of RCAP in 1991, we see a remarkably similar process taking place. Let us now turn briefly to this important history of struggle.

Managing the Crisis: Reconciliation and the Royal Commission on Aboriginal Peoples

The federal government was forced to establish RCAP in the wake of two national crises that erupted in the tumultuous "Indian summer" of 1990. The first involved the legislative stonewalling of the Meech Lake Accord by Cree Manitoba Member of the Legislative Assembly (MLA) Elijah Harper. The Meech Lake Accord was a failed constitutional amendment package negotiated in 1987 by the then prime minister of Canada, Brian Mulroney, and the ten provincial premiers. The process was the federal government's attempt to bring Quebec "back in" to the constitutional fold in the wake of the province's refusal to accept the constitutional repatriation deal of 1981, which formed the basis of the the Constitution Act, 1982. Indigenous opposition to Meech Lake was staunch and vocal, in large part due to the fact that the process failed to recognize the political concerns and aspirations of First Nations.[52] In a disruptive act of legislative protest, Elijah Harper was able to prevent the province from endorsing the package within the three-year ratification deadline stipulated in the Constitution Act. The agreement subsequently tanked because it failed to gain the required ratification of all ten provinces, which is required of all proposed constitutional amendments.[53]

The second crisis involved a seventy-eight-day armed "standoff" beginning on July 11, 1990, between the Mohawk nation of Kanesatake, the Quebec provincial police (Sûreté du Québec, or SQ), and the Canadian armed forces near the town of Oka, Quebec. On June 30, 1990, the municipality of Oka was granted a court injunction to dismantle a peaceful barricade erected by the people of Kanesatake in an effort to defend their sacred lands from further encroachment by non-Native developers. The territory in question was slotted for development by a local golf course, which planned on extending nine holes onto land the Mohawks had been fighting to have recognized as their own for almost three hundred years.[54] Eleven days later, on July 11, one hundred heavily armed members of the SQ stormed the community. The police invasion culminated in a twenty-four-second exchange of gunfire that killed SQ Corporal Marcel Lemay.[55] In a display of solidarity, the neighboring Mohawk nation of Kahnawake set up their own barricades, including one that blocked the Mercier Bridge leading into the greater Montreal area. Galvanized by the Mohawk resistance, Indigenous peoples from across the continent followed suit, engaging in a diverse array of solidarity actions that ranged from information leafleting to the establishment of peace encampments to the erection of blockades on several major Canadian transport corridors, both road and rail. Although polls conducted during the standoff showed some support by non-Native Canadians outside of Quebec for the Mohawk cause,[56] most received their information about the so-called "Oka Crisis" through the corporate media, which overwhelmingly represented the event as a "law and order" issue fundamentally undermined by Indigenous peoples' uncontrollable anger and resentment.[57]

For many Indigenous people and their supporters, however, these two national crises were seen as the inevitable culmination of a near decade-long escalation of Native frustration with a colonial state that steadfastly refused to uphold the rights that had been recently "recognized and affirmed" in section 35 (1) of the Constitution Act, 1982. By the late 1980s this frustration was clearly boiling over, resulting in a marked rise in First Nations' militancy and land-based direct action.[58] The following are some of the better-documented examples from the time:

1. The Innu occupation and blockade of the Canadian Air Force/NATO base at Goose Bay in present-day Labrador. The occupation was led largely by Innu women to challenge the further dispossession of their territories and subsequent destruction of their land-based way of life by the military industrial complex's encroachment onto their homeland of Nitassinan.[59]

2. The Lubicon Cree struggle against oil and gas development on their traditional territories in present-day Alberta. The Lubicon Cree have been struggling to protect a way of life threatened by intensified nonrenewable development on their homelands since at least 1939, when they first learned that they were left out of the negotiations that led to the signing of Treaty 8 in 1899. In defending their continued right to the land, the community has engaged in a number of very public protests, including a well-publicized boycott of the 1988 Calgary Winter Olympics and the associated Glenbow Museum exhibit, *The Spirit Sings*.[60]

3. First Nations blockades in British Columbia. Through the 1980s First Nations in present-day British Columbia grew extremely frustrated with the painfully slow pace of the federal government's comprehensive land claims process and the province's racist refusal to recognize Aboriginal title within its claimed borders. The result was a decade's worth of very disruptive and publicized blockades, which at their height in 1990 were such a common occurrence that Vancouver newspapers felt the need to publish traffic advisories identifying delays caused by First Nation roadblocks in the province's interior. Many of the blockades were able to halt resource extraction on Native land for protracted periods of time.[61]

4. The Algonquins of Barriere Lake. By 1989 the Algonquins of Barrier Lake were embroiled in a struggle to protect their way of life by resisting clear-cut logging operations within their traditional territories in present-day Quebec. Under the leadership of customary chief Jean-Maurice Matchewan, the community used blockades to successfully impede clear-cutting activities adversely affecting their lands and community.[62]

5. The Temagami First Nation blockades of 1988 and 1989 in present-day Ontario. The Temagami blockades were set up to protect their nation's homeland from further encroachment by non-Native development. The blockades of 1988–89 were the most recent assertions of Temagami sovereignty in over a century-long struggle to protect the community's right to land and freedom from colonial settlement and proliferating economic development.[63]

From the vantage point of the colonial state, by the time the seventy-eight-day standoff at Kanesatake started, things were already out of control in Indian Country. If settler-state stability and authority is required to ensure "certainty" over Indigenous lands and resources to create an investment climate friendly for expanded capitalist accumulation, then the barrage of Indigenous practices of disruptive countersovereignty that emerged with increased frequency in the 1980s was an embarrassing demonstration that Canada no longer had its shit together with respect to managing the so-called "Indian Problem." On top of this, the material form that these expressions of Indigenous sovereignty took on the ground—*the blockade*, explicitly erected to impede the power of state and capital from entering and leaving Indigenous territories respectively— must have been particularly troubling to the settler-colonial establishment. All of this activity was an indication that Indigenous people and communities were no longer willing to wait for Canada (or even their own leaders) to negotiate a just relationship with them in good faith. In Fanon's terms, Indigenous peoples were no longer willing to "remain in their place."[64] There was also growing concern that Indigenous youth in particular were no longer willing to play by Canada's rules—especially regarding the potential use of violence—when it came to advancing their communities' rights and interests. As Georges Erasmus, then national chief of the Assembly of First Nations, warned in 1988: "Canada, if you do not deal with this generation of leaders, then we cannot promise that you are going to like the kind of violent political action that we can just about guarantee the next generation is going to bring to you." Consider this "a warning," Erasmus continued: "We want to let you know that you're playing with fire. We may be the last generation of leaders that are prepared to sit down and peacefully negotiate our concerns with you."[65] Erasmus's warning was ignored, and the siege at Kanasatake occurred two years later.

In the wake of having to engage in one of the largest and costliest military operations since the Korean War, the federal government announced on August 23, 1991, that a royal commission would be established with a sprawling sixteen-point mandate to investigate the abusive relationship that had clearly developed between Indigenous peoples and the state.[66] Published two years behind schedule in November 1996, the $58-million, five-volume, approximately four-thousand-page *Report of the Royal Commission on Aboriginal Peoples* offers a vision of reconciliation between Aboriginal peoples and

Canada based on the core principles of "mutual recognition, mutual respect, sharing and mutual responsibility."[67] Of the 440 recommendations made by RCAP, the following are some of the more noteworthy:

Legislation, including issuing a new Royal Proclamation, stating Canada's commitment to a new relationship with companion legislation establishing a new treaty process and recognition of Aboriginal Nations' governments;

Recognition of an Aboriginal order of government, subject to the Charter of Rights and Freedoms, with authority over matters relating to the good government and welfare of Aboriginal peoples and their territories;

Replacement of the federal Department of Indian Affairs with two departments, one to implement the new relationship with Aboriginal nations and one to provide services to non-self-governing communities;

Creation of an Aboriginal parliament;

Expansion of the Aboriginal land and resource base;

Recognition of Metis self-government, provision of a land base, and recognition of Metis rights to hunt and fish on Crown land;

Initiatives to address social, education, health, and housing needs, including the training of ten thousand health professionals over a ten-year period, the establishment of an Aboriginal peoples' university, and recognition of Aboriginal peoples' authority over child welfare.[68]

RCAP's vision of a reconciled relationship premised on mutual recognition is not without flaw—indeed, many critics have convincingly argued that its vision still ultimately situates Indigenous lands and political authority in a subordinate position within the political and economic framework of Canadian sovereignty.[69] However, RCAP still offers the most comprehensive set of recommendations, informed by five years of research involving 178 days of public hearings in 96 communities across Canada, aimed at reforming the relationship between Indigenous peoples and the state to date. The extensive public consultations employed by RCAP subsequently produced a set of recommendations with a significant degree of democratic legitimacy to them, especially to those Indigenous people and communities who would be most affected by RCAP's proposals. At the very least, then, the RCAP report provides a potentially productive point of entry into the much more challenging conversation that we need to collectively have about what it will take to truly decolonize the relationship between Indigenous and non-Indigenous peoples in Canada. This conversation has yet to happen.

The decade of heightened First Nations militancy that culminated in the resistance at Kanesatake created the political and cultural context that RCAP's call for recognition and reconciliation sought to mitigate—namely, the simmering anger and resentment of the colonized transformed into a resurgent affirmation of Indigenous difference that threatened to disrupt settler-colonialism's sovereign claim over Indigenous peoples and our lands. In light of this, to suggest that we replace these emotions by a more a conciliatory and constructive attitude like "forgiveness" seems misplaced to me.[70] Of course, individual and collective expressions of anticolonial anger and resentment can be destructive and harmful to relationships; but these emotional forces are rarely, if ever, as destructive and violent as the colonial relationship they critically call into question. "The responsibility for violence," argues Taiaiake Alfred, "begins and ends with the state, not with the people who are challenging the inherent injustices perpetrated by the state."[71] Yet, as the history of First Nations' struggle that led to RCAP demonstrates, these emotions can also play an important role in generating practices of resistance and cultural resurgence, both of which are required to build a more just relationship with non-Indigenous peoples on and in relation to the lands that we now share. I return to this discussion in my concluding chapter.

Righteous Resentment? The Failure of Reconciliation from Gathering Strength to Canada's Residential School Apology

The critical importance of Indigenous peoples' emotional reactions to settler colonization appears even more pronounced in light of Canada's problematic approach to conceptualizing and implementing reconciliation in the wake of the RCAP report. There have been two broad criticisms of the federal government's approach to reconciling its relationship with Indigenous peoples: the first involves the state's rigid historical temporalization of the problem in need of reconciling (colonial injustice), which in turn leads to, second, the current politics of reconciliation's inability to adequately transform the structure of dispossession that continues to frame Indigenous peoples' relationship with the state.[72] Stephanie Irlbacher-Fox captures these concerns well when she writes that "by conflating specific unjust events, policies, and laws with 'history,' what is unjust becomes temporally separate from the present, unchangeable. This narrows options for restitution: we cannot change the past."[73] In such a context, I argue that Indigenous peoples' anger and resentment represents an entirely understandable—and, in Fanon's words, "legitimate"—response to our settler-colonial present.[74]

The federal government officially responded to the recommendations of RCAP in January of 1998 with *Gathering Strength: Canada's Aboriginal Action Plan*.[75] Claiming to "build on" RCAP's core principles of "mutual respect, mutual recognition, mutual responsibility, and sharing," *Gathering Strength* begins with a "Statement of Reconciliation" in which the Government of Canada recognizes "the mistakes and injustices of the past" in order "to set a new course in its policies for Aboriginal peoples."[76] This is the first policy statement by the federal government that explicitly applies the conceptual language typically associated with "transitional justice" to the nontransitional context of a formally liberal democratic settler state. The result, I suggest, is an approach to reconciliation that goes out of its way to fabricate a sharp divide between Canada's unscrupulous "past" and the unfortunate "legacy" this past has produced for Indigenous people and communities in the present.

The policy implications of the state's historical framing of colonialism are troubling. If there is no colonial present, as *Gathering Strength* insists, but only a colonial past that continues to have adverse effects on Indigenous people and communities, then the federal government need not undertake the actions required to transform the current institutional and social relationships that have been shown to produce the suffering we currently see reverberating at pandemic levels within and across Indigenous communities today.[77] Rather than addressing these structural issues, state policy has instead focused its reconciliation efforts on repairing the psychologically injured or damaged status of Indigenous people themselves. Sam McKegney links this policy orientation to the increased public interest placed on the "discourse of healing" in the 1990s, which positioned Aboriginal *people* as the "primary objects of study rather than the system of acculturative violence."[78] Hence, the only concrete monetary commitment made in *Gathering Strength* includes a one-time grant payment of $350 million allocated "for community-based healing as a first step to deal with the legacy of physical and sexual abuse at residential schools."[79] The grant was used to establish the Aboriginal Healing Foundation in March of 1998.[80] The Conservative government of Canada announced in

2010 that additional funding for the Aboriginal Healing Foundation would not be provided.

According to Taiaiake Alfred, Canada's approach to reconciliation has clearly failed to implement the "massive restitution, including land, financial transfers, and other forms of assistance to compensate for past and continuing injustices against our peoples."[81] The state's lack of commitment in this regard is particularly evident in *Gathering Strength*'s stated position on Canada's land claims and self-government policies. Rather than affirm Aboriginal title and substantially redistribute lands and resources to Indigenous communities through a renewed treaty process, or recognize Indigenous autonomy and redistribute political authority from the state to Indigenous nations based on the principle of Indigenous self-determination, *Gathering Strength* essentially reiterates, more or less unmodified, its present policy position as evidence of the essentially just nature of the current relationship between Indigenous peoples and the state.

For example, regarding the comprehensive claims process, although *Gathering Strength* states Canada's "willingness to discuss its current approach with Aboriginal, provincial, and territorial partners in order to respond to concerns about the existing policy," the "alternatives" that have since been pursued are even more restrictive than was the original policy.[82] At the time of *Gathering Strength*'s publication in 1998, the "concerns" alluded to by the federal government involved more than two decades' worth of First Nations' criticisms regarding the comprehensive claims policy's "extinguishment" provisions, which at the time explicitly required Aboriginal peoples to "cede, release and surrender" all undefined Aboriginal rights and title in exchange for the benefits clearly delineated in the text of the settlement itself. The state has pursued two alternatives to formal extinguishment: the so-called "modified" rights approach developed during negotiations over the Nisga'a Final Agreement (2000), and the "nonassertion" approach developed during negotiations over the Tlicho Agreement (2003).

With respect to the former, Aboriginal rights and title are no longer formally "extinguished" in the settlement but rather "modified" to include *only* those rights and benefits outlined in the claim package. The provisions detailed in the settlement are the only legally binding rights that the signatory First Nation can claim after the agreement has been ratified. Regarding the latter, in order to reach a settlement a First Nation must legally agree to not "assert" or "claim" any Aboriginal rights that are not already detailed in the text of the agreement. Again, the provisions specified in the settlement exhaust all claimable Aboriginal rights. Although the semantics of the comprehensive claims policy have changed, the legal and political outcomes remain the same.[83] Peter Kulchyski suggests that these alternative approaches to formal extinguishment may be even worse than the original policy, given that the latter at least left open the possibility of making a claim for an Aboriginal right that was originally unforeseen at the time of signing an extinguishment agreement. "Leave it to the state," Kulchyski concludes, "to find a way to replace one of its oldest, most outdated, ineffective and unjust policies—the extinguishment clause—with something worse."[84]

A similar colonial trend can be seen in *Gathering Strength*'s stated commitment to implementing an Aboriginal right to self-government. Here the federal government simply reaffirms its previous 1995 policy position on the matter, which claims to "recognize" the "inherent right of self-government for Aboriginal people as an existing Aboriginal right within section 35 of the *Constitution Act, 1982*." The use of the term "inherent" here is nonsense when considered in light of the scope of the policy, as there is really nothing "inherent" about the limited range of rights that Canada claims to recognize. The stated purpose of the federal government's position is to clearly establish the terms under which Aboriginal governments might negotiate "practical" governing arrangements in relation to their own communities and with other governments and jurisdictions. In setting out these terms, however, the state unilaterally curtails the jurisdictional authority made available to Aboriginal nations through the so-called "negotiation" process. As a result, Indigenous sovereignty and the right of self-determination based on the principle of equality between peoples is explicitly rejected as a foundation for negotiations: "The inherent right of self-government *does not* include a right of sovereignty in the international law sense." Instead, what the state grants is recognition of an Aboriginal right "to govern themselves in relation to matters that are *internal to their communities, integral to their unique cultures, identities, traditions, languages and institutions*."[85]

One should recognize a familiar pattern here. Instead of proceeding with negotiations based on the principle of Indigenous self-determination, Canada's policy framework is grounded in the assumption that Aboriginal rights are subordinately positioned within the ultimate sovereign authority of the Crown. On this point, Michael Asch has suggested that the policy clearly takes its cues from recent Aboriginal rights jurisprudence: "All court decisions rest on the presumption that, while it must be quite careful to protect Aboriginal rights, Parliament has the ultimate legislative authority to act with respect to any of them."[86] This restrictive premise coincides with the Supreme Court of Canada's own articulation of the meaning and purpose of "reconciliation" outlined in *R. v. Van der Peet* in 1996. As the court states, "what s. 35(1) does is provide the constitutional framework through which the fact that aboriginals lived on the land in distinctive societies, with their own practices, traditions and cultures, is acknowledged and reconciled with the Crown. The substantive rights that fall within the provision must be defined in light of this purpose; the aboriginal rights recognized and affirmed by s. 35(1) must be directed towards reconciliation of the pre-existence of Aboriginal societies with the sovereignty of the Crown."[87] And how, might we ask, does the court propose to "reconcile" the "pre-existence of Aboriginal societies with the sovereignty of the Crown"? Or, stated slightly differently, how does the court propose to *render consistent* Indigenous nationhood with state sovereignty? By refusing that the "aboriginal societies" in question had anything akin to sovereignty worth recognizing to begin with. Instead, what the court offers up is an interpretation of Aboriginal rights as narrowly construed "cultural" rights that can be "infringed" on by the state for any number of legislative reasons—ranging from conservation to settlement, to capitalist nonrenewable resource development, and even to protect white interests from the potential economic fallout of recognizing Aboriginal rights to land and water-based economic pursuits. Like all Aboriginal rights in Canada, then, the right of self-government is not absolute; even if such a right is found to be constitutionally protected, it can be transgressed in accordance with the justifiable infringement test laid out in *R. v. Sparrow* in 1990 and later expanded on in decisions like *R. v. Gladstone* in 1996, *Delgamuukw v. British Columbia* in 1997 and *R. v. Marshall (No. 2)* in 1999.[88] When all of these considerations are taken into account it becomes clear that there is nothing "inherent" about the right to self-government recognized in Canada's "Inherent Right" policy.

At least in *Gathering Strength* the federal government acknowledges that Canada has a colonial past. The same cannot be said about the state's next major gesture of reconciliation: the federal government's official 2008 "apology" to Indigenous survivors of the Indian residential school system. Informed by a similarly restrictive temporal frame, the 2008 "apology" focuses exclusively on the tragedy of residential schools, the last of which officially closed its doors in 1996. There is no recognition of a colonial past or present, nor is there any mention of the much broader system of land dispossession, political domination, and cultural genocide of which the residential school system formed only a part. Harper's apology is thus able, like *Gathering Strength* before it, to comfortably frame reconciliation in terms of overcoming a "sad chapter" in our shared history. "Forgiveness" and "reconciliation" are posited as a fundamental step in transcending the painful "legacy" that has hampered our collective efforts to "move on"; they are necessary to "begin anew" so that Indigenous peoples can start to build "new partnerships" together with non-Indigenous peoples on what is now unapologetically declared to be "our land."[89]

Thus, insofar as the above two examples even implicitly address the problem of settler-colonialism, they do so, to borrow Patrick Wolfe's useful formulation, as an "event" and not "a structure": that is, as a temporally situated experience which occurred at some relatively fixed period in history but which unfortunately continues to have negative consequences for our communities in the present.[90] By Wolfe's definition, however, there is nothing "historical" about the character of settler colonization in the sense just described. Settler-colonial formations are *territorially acquisitive in perpetuity*. As Wolfe explains, "settler colonialism has both negative and positive dimensions. Negatively, it strives for the dissolution of native societies. Positively, it erects a new colonial society on the expropriated land base—as I put it, settler colonizers come to stay: invasion is a structure not an event. In its positive aspect, elimination is an organizing principle of settler-colonial society rather than a one-off (and superseded) occurrence."[91] In the specific context of Canadian settler-colonialism, although the *means* by which the colonial state has sought to eliminate Indigenous peoples in order to gain access to our lands and resources have modified over the last two centuries—ranging from violent dispossession to the legislative elimination of First Nations legal status under sexist and racist provisions of the Indian Act to the "negotiation" of what are still essentially land surrenders under the present comprehensive land claims policy—the *ends* have always remained the same: to shore up continued access to Indigenous peoples' territories for the purposes of state formation, settlement, and capitalist development.

Identifying the persistent character of settler-colonialism allows us to better interrogate the repeated insinuation made in both *Gathering Strength* and the

federal government's 2008 apology about how the "legacy" of Canada's troubled history has injured Indigenous subjects so deeply that many of us are
now unable or unwilling to put the events of the past behind us. This returns
us to our previous discussion of *ressentiment*. If *ressentiment* is characterized by
a pathological inability to "get over the past," then according to the state-
sanctioned discourse of reconciliation, Indigenous peoples would appear to
suffer from *ressentiment* writ large. We just cannot seem to get over it. However, for most critics what makes *ressentiment* so problematic is that it is also
an *irrational* attitude. "*Ressentiment*, by definition, is an irrational and base passion," writes Jeffrie Murphy, "It thus makes no sense to speak of rational or
justified or honourable *ressentiment*."[92] This has led moral philosophers like
Murphy and Brudholm to distinguish between irrational expressions of *ressentiment*, on the one hand, and more righteous expressions of "resentment,"
on the other. This distinction is useful for our present purposes. In the context
of Canadian settler-colonialism, I contend that what gets implicitly represented by the state as a form of Indigenous *ressentiment*—namely, Indigenous
peoples' seemingly pathological inability to get over harms inflicted in the
past—is actually a manifestation of our *righteous resentment*: that is, our bitter
indignation and persistent anger at being treated unjustly by a colonial state
both historically and in the present. In other words, what is treated in the
Canadian discourse of reconciliation as an unhealthy and debilitating incapacity to forgive and move on is actually a sign of our *critical consciousness*, of
our sense of justice and injustice, and of our awareness of and unwillingness
to *reconcile* ourselves with a structural and symbolic violence that is still very
much present in our lives. Viewed in this light, I suggest that Indigenous
peoples' individual and collective resentment—expressed as an angry and
vigilant *unwillingness to forgive*—ought to be seen as an affective indication
that we care deeply about ourselves, about our land and cultural communities,
and about the rights and obligations we hold as First Peoples.

CONCLUSION

Prime Minister Harper's 2008 "apology" on behalf of the Government of
Canada to Indian survivors of the residential school system was delivered
under the shadow of the 2007 Indian Residential School Settlement Agreement. The settlement agreement was negotiated in response to more than
twelve thousand abuse cases and more than seventy thousand former students

represented in numerous class-action lawsuits against the federal government and church organizations that ran the schools. The settlement, which is currently being implemented under court supervision, includes money allocated for "common experience" payments to students who attended residential schools; a compensation process for students who can demonstrate that they suffered sexual or serious physical and/or mental abuse while attending a residential school; a health support system for survivors and their families; a residential school commemoration project; and the creation of a Truth and Reconciliation Commission to research, document and preserve the testimony and experiences of residential school survivors.[93]

The specific commemorative and educational goals outlined in the Truth and Reconciliation Commission of Canada's (TRC) mandate are important and admirable. However, many of the shortcomings that plagued both *Gathering Strength* and the 2008 apology also plague the mandate's terms of reference. In particular, the TRC temporally situates the harms of settler-colonialism in the past and focuses the bulk of its reconciliatory efforts on repairing the injurious legacy left in the wake of this history. Indigenous subjects are the primary object of repair, not the colonial relationship. These shortcomings have produced many critics of the TRC. Taiaiake Alfred, for example, warns that genuine reconciliation is impossible without recognizing Indigenous peoples' right to freedom and self-determination, instituting restitution by returning enough of our lands so that we can regain economic self-sufficiency, and honoring our treaty relationships. Without these commitments reconciliation will remain a "pacifying discourse" that functions to assuage settler guilt, on the one hand, and absolve the federal government's responsibility to transform the colonial relationship between Canada and Indigenous nations, on the other.[94]

If this were not enough to raise concern, since negotiating the 2007 Residential School Settlement Agreement and offering the 2008 apology, the federal government has intensified its colonial approach to dealing with Indigenous peoples in practice. This intensification is most evident in the federal government's recently passed omnibus Bill C-45, otherwise known as the Jobs and Growth Act. Bill C-45 is a nearly 450-page budget implementation bill that makes significant changes to Canada's Navigable Water Act, the Indian Act, and the Environmental Assessment Act, among other pieces of federal legislation. Of concern to Indigenous people and communities in particular are the ways that Bill C-45 unilaterally undermines Aboriginal and treaty rights by making it easier for First Nations' band councils to lease out reserve lands with minimal community input or support, by gutting environmental protection for lakes and rivers, and by reducing the number of resource development projects that would have required environmental assessment under previous legislation.

Bill C-45 thus represents the latest installment of Canada's longstanding policy of colonial dispossession. This has led Indigenous people from all sectors of Indian Country to organize and resist under the mantra that we are "Idle No More!" Through social media, the Idle No More movement emerged with force in December 2012 as a result of the initial educational work of four women from the prairies—Nina Wilson, Sylvia McAdam, Jessica Gordon, and Sheelah McLean. Then, on December 11, Chief Theresa Spence of the Attawapiskat Cree Nation began a hunger strike to protest the deplorable living conditions on her reserve in northern Ontario, which she argued was the result of Canada's failure to live up to the "spirit and intent" of Treaty No. 9 (signed in 1905). Building on the inspirational work of these women, what originally began as an education campaign against a repugnant piece of federal legislation has since transformed into a grassroots struggle to transform the colonial relationship itself.

Drawing off the insights of Fanon, I have argued two points in this chapter. First, I claimed that Indigenous peoples' anger and resentment can generate forms of decolonized subjectivity and anticolonial practice that we ought to critically affirm rather than denigrate in our premature efforts to promote forgiveness and reconciliation on terms still largely dictated by the colonial state. And second, in light of the failure of Canada's approach to implement reconciliation in the wake of RCAP, I suggest that critically holding on to our anger and resentment can serve as an important emotional reminder that settler-colonialism is still very much alive and well in Canada, despite the state's repeated assertions otherwise.

In the next chapter I return to Fanon, although in a more critical light. I argue that although Fanon saw colonized people's anger and resentment as an important catalyst for change he nevertheless remained skeptical as to whether the rehabilitated forms of Indigenous subjectivity constructed out of this anger and resentment ought to inform our collective efforts to reconstruct decolonized relationships and communities. In contradistinction to Fanon,

I argue that insofar as these reactive emotions result in the affirmation and resurgence of Indigenous knowledge and cultural practices, they ought to be seen as providing the substantive foundation required to reconstruct relationships of reciprocity and peaceful coexistence within and against the psycho-affective and structural apparatus of settler-colonial power. In my concluding chapter I defend this claim in light of the recent Idle No More movement.

5

The Plunge into the
Chasm of the Past

Fanon, Self-Recognition, and Decolonization

Negritude is for destroying itself, it is a passage and not an outcome,
a means and not an ultimate end.

—JEAN-PAUL SARTRE, "Black Orpheus"

In no way do I have to dedicate myself to reviving a black civilization
unjustly ignored. I will not make myself the man of any past. I do not
want to sing the past to the detriment of my present and my future.

—FRANTZ FANON, *Black Skin, White Masks*

This chapter begins to sketch out in more detail the alternative politics of recognition briefly introduced at the end of chapter 1. As suggested there, far from evading the recognition paradigm entirely, Fanon instead turns our attention to the cultural practices of critical individual and collective *self-recognition* that colonized populations often engage in to empower themselves, instead of relying too heavily on the colonial state and society to do this for them. This is the realm of self-affirmative cultural, artistic, and political activity that Fanon associated largely but not exclusively with *negritude*. The negritude movement first emerged in France during the late 1930s as a response to anti-black racism. Although negritude constituted a diverse body of work and activism, at its core the movement emphasized the need for colonized people and communities to purge themselves of the internalized effects of systemic racism and colonial violence by rejecting assimilation and instead affirming the worth of their own identity-related differences. In this sense, it has been argued that negritude represents an important precursor to contemporary "identity politics" in the United States and elsewhere.[1]

However, despite the extensive commentary that Fanon's relationship to negritude has generated, no clear consensus has been reached regarding the

131

extent to which he ought to be read as a critic or supporter of the movement's claims and achievements. For example, some commentators, such as David Caute, Irene Grendzier and David Macey, have suggested that where Fanon can be read in his early work (particularly *Black Skin, White Masks*) as more sympathetic to certain aspects of negritude's objectives, over time he eventually came to stress the movement's limitations, either seeing it as representing, at best, a "transitional" stage in the dialectic of decolonization (following the position of Jean-Paul Sartre discussed below), or worse, as having little substantive value whatsoever.[2] Other critics, however, have advanced a near-opposite reading. As Jock McCullock writes with reference to Caute and Grendzier: "If the substance of these critiques are examined in detail, it is apparent that Fanon became *more* rather than *less* sympathetic to negritude with the passing of time."[3] And yet other commentators have refused to draw a sharp distinction between early and late Fanon's views on negritude altogether, instead arguing that, although the specifics of Fanon's complex views altered as his analysis moved from the Antilles to the Algerian contexts, he nevertheless always remained simultaneously a rigorous critic and critical advocate of certain features (and certain proponents) of the negritude movement.[4]

The interpretation advanced below is indebted to this third reading of Fanon. I demonstrate that although Fanon always questioned the specifics of negritude based on its, at times, essentialist and bourgeois character, he nevertheless viewed the associated practices of individual and collective self-recognition through the revaluation of black culture, history, and identity as a potentially crucial feature of the broader struggle for freedom against colonial domination. This potential hinged, however, entirely on negritude's ability to transcend what Fanon saw as its retrograde orientation towards a *subjective* affirmation of a precolonial *past* by grounding itself in the peoples' struggle against the *material* structure of colonial rule *in the present*.

Although Fanon saw the critical revaluation of Indigenous cultural forms as an important means of temporarily breaking the colonized free from the incapacitating effects of being exposed to structured patterns of colonial misrecognition, he was decidedly less willing to explore the role that these forms and practices might play in the construction of *alternatives* to the oppressive social relations that produce colonized subjects in the first place. This has led Katherine Gines to correctly conclude that while Fanon recognized the importance of affirming cultural difference as a form of individual and collective self-empowerment, he was less clear as to whether these differences ought to be substantively retained in the course of decolonization.[5] In this specific sense, then, it will be shown that Fanon clearly shared Sartre's view that negritude's emphasis on cultural self-affirmation constituted an important "means" but "not an ultimate end" of anticolonial struggle, even though both authors arrived at this analogous conclusion via different paths.

This chapter is organized into two sections and a conclusion. In the first section, I sketch the theory of intersubjective recognition that Sartre develops in *Being and Nothingness*, *Anti-Semite and Jew*, and "Black Orpheus." As Sonia Kruks and others have noted, Fanon's work was "for better and for worse" deeply influenced by Sartre's philosophical and political writings, particularly as these writings pertain to issues of recognition, reciprocity, and freedom.[6] Thus, to fully understand what I characterize as the limited *transitional* function that Fanon attributes to practices of self-recognition and cultural empowerment in the course of anticolonial struggle, we must first unpack Sartre's earlier views on these and similar matters. In the next section, I examine the instrumental relationship Fanon draws in his work between cultural self-recognition and projects of decolonization. This discussion will pave the way for the argument I lay out in my concluding chapter, which examines the substantive relationship forged between self-affirmative practices of cultural regeneration and decolonization by theorists and activists of Indigenous *resurgence* working in the settler-colonial context of Canada.

FROM THE PARTICULAR TO THE UNIVERSAL: JEAN-PAUL SARTRE, IDENTITY POLITICS, AND THE COLONIAL DIALECTIC

Sartre's *Anti-Semite and Jew* provides an analysis of the nature of French anti-Semitism in the wake of World War II.[7] Although many scholars have since criticized Sartre's hyper-constructivist account of Judaism and Jewish identity as a mere *effect* of anti-Semitism—reflected in Sartre's famous assertion that it is the anti-Semite "who creates the Jew"[8]—in the following section I want to bracket these well-warranted criticisms. Instead I want to focus on the logic underwriting Sartre's argument in order to demonstrate the transitional role he attributes to the recognition and self-affirmation of identity or difference in the struggle for freedom and equality on the one hand, and the ways in which Fanon simultaneously adapts and critiques this position in his writings on decolonization on the other.

Sartre's project in *Anti-Semite and Jew* is best read as a practical reworking of his prior engagement with Hegel's dialectic of recognition in *Being and Nothingness*, only this time cast, like Fanon's later intervention in *Black Skin, White Masks* through the lens of European racism. In stark contrast to Hegel's "optimistic" portrayal of intersubjective recognition in the *Phenomenology of Spirit*,[9] Sartre's rendition of the master/slave relation in *Being and Nothingness* denies the possibility of reciprocal relations of affirmative recognition. Although Sartre, like Hegel, acknowledges the role played by recognition in constituting subjectivity, unlike Hegel, Sartre portrays this constitution as a theft, as objectification, and as such the "death of [one's] possibilities."[10] For Sartre recognition constitutes a form of enslavement, of being "fixed" by "the look" of another.[11] As Sonia Kruks observes, "the Other," in Sartre's account, "is always a threat to my own experience of self, having the power to objectify me and to cause me to flee into self-objectification."[12] According to Sartre, the only way out of this situation is for the objectified to make the other into the object of *one's own look*, to "turn back" the gaze, thereby reversing the process of objectification.[13] At the heart of Sartre's theory of intersubjectivity, then, is the notion that recognition is forever mired in a power struggle, "a constant unending conflict between subjects who seek to make each other objects of the gaze as the precondition of reclaiming their inner freedom."[14] Conflict thus constitutes the core of Sartre's account of "being-for-others."[15]

However, when applied to the concrete situation of the Jew in an anti-Semitic society, the option of reversing the gaze and thus one's objectified status is denied by Sartre. This is because the Jew is not only objectified in the ontological sense of "being-for-others"—as the condition of his or her "fundamental relation" to others—but also *as a Jew*. This is what Sartre means when he states that the Jew "is overdetermined."[16] Overdetermination fundamentally undermines the Jew's ability to cast the gaze back. Anti-Semitism thus constitutes a relationship in which the gaze works unilaterally between the one who objectifies (the anti-Semite) and the one who is objectified (the Jew).

What, then, are the options available to the Jew in the context of anti-Semitic racism? Here Sartre introduces two concepts fundamental to his existentialism: authenticity and inauthenticity. The most common response explored in *Anti-Semite and Jew* is represented by the actions of the *inauthentic* Jew. According to Sartre, the inauthentic Jew is one who chooses to *flee* from his or her *situation as a Jew*. For Sartre, the Jew's *situation* is the "ensemble of limits and restrictions"—social, economic, political, cultural—that "forms [the Jew] and determines his possibilities." Yet the Jew's situation is also given meaning through the choices he or she makes "within and by it."[17] In short, the Jew's situation is the inherited field within which he or she must act, make choices, and derive meaning—and this context is, whether one likes it or not, an anti-Semitic one. Sartre suggests that, when faced with the painful burden of living in this situation, the inauthentic Jew will choose to "run away" from it, to "deny it, or choose to deny their responsibilities" to positively act within it.[18] Sartre equates inauthenticity here with assimilation, the process whereby the Jew, suffering from an "inferiority complex,"[19] seeks to reject her or his particularity by either appealing to abstract universal principles (what today we might call "difference-blind" equality), or by trying to eradicate her or his particularity as such (through religious conversion, secularization, intermar-riage, and so on).[20] Although Sartre's portrait of the inauthentic Jew is not meant to cast "moral blame" on the Jew for his or her evasive actions, Sartre is nonetheless quick to suggest that these actions serve to double back and rein-force the anti-Semitic propaganda that prompted the evasive conduct in the first place.[21] In short, the inauthentic Jew "has allowed himself to be persuaded by the anti-Semites; he is the first victim of their propaganda. He admits with them that, *if there is a Jew*, he must have the characteristics with which popular malevolence endows him."[22]

Sartre then contrasts the conduct of the inauthentic Jew with the actions of the Jew who acts authentically in their situation. Faced with this situation the authentic Jew actively commits to *affirming* his or her Jewish identity against the objectifying gaze of the anti-Semite. The authentic Jew refuses to let the racist propaganda of the anti-Semite determine from the outside her or his actions, his or her being. Instead "he stakes everything on human grandeur [and in accepting] the obligation to live in a situation that is defined precisely by the fact that it is unliveable . . . he derives pride from his humiliation."[23] It is through this gesture of self-affirmation that the Jew strips anti-Semitism of its discursive power and virulence. As Sartre explains: "The inauthentic Jew flees Jewish reality, and the anti-Semite makes him a Jew in spite of himself; but the authentic Jew *makes himself a Jew*, in the face of all and against all. He accepts all, even martyrdom, and the anti-Semite, deprived of his weapon, must be content to yelp at the Jew as he goes by, and can no longer touch him. At one stroke the Jew, like any authentic man, *escapes description*."[24] For Sartre, then, authentic self-affirmation provides an important weapon in the Jew's fight against the objectifying and alienating effects of anti-Semitic overdetermination. But given that anti-Semitism is a *socially constituted* phenomenon, Sartre is quick to point out that, while authenticity may serve as an important means through which to work over the individualized effects of objectification, on its own it will do little to undercut the *social relations* constitutive of anti-Semitism as such. "The choice of authenticity *is not a solution* of the social aspect of the Jewish problem," writes Sartre.[25] Rather, it "appears to be a *moral* decision, bringing certainty to the Jew on the ethical [or subjective] level but in no way serving as a solution on the social or political level."[26] For Sartre, the transformative potential of affirming one's difference will always be limited insofar as it leaves intact the generative conditions that serve to reproduce anti-Semitic conduct on the one hand, and the effects that this conduct has in shaping the subjectivity of Jews on the other. Ending anti-Semitism thus requires that existential self-affirmation be cashed out in a transformative engagement with these generative conditions; it requires that the Jew's *situation* be transformed "from the bottom up."[27] For the increasingly Marxist Sartre of the mid-1940s, the generative structures identified as most important in the fight against anti-Semitic racism were those associated with capitalism and class conflict. In Sartre's (overly simplistic) formulation, anti-Semitism served to ideologically mask the root cause of class conflict by positing the Jewish community as the source of class antagonism instead of the capitalist mode of production. Seen in this light, anti-Semitism represents "a mythical, bourgeois representation of the class struggle, and [as such] could not exist in a classless society." Following this logic, once the "social and economic causes" of anti-Semitism have been eliminated, the affirmation of Jewish difference will no longer be required; indeed, after the revolution has created a world stripped of the economic/social pluralism within which anti-Semitic racism flourishes, affirming Jewish difference would be at best redundant, or worse, it might serve to ideologically reproduce its own divisions and thus foreclose the possibility of a society free from conflict and social stratification.[28] Here the politics of difference is implicitly posited as an important *stage* in the struggle against anti-Semitic racism, but in no way should it be conceived as an end in itself.

Similar themes are further developed and elaborated by Sartre in "Black Orpheus," his well-known preface to Léopold Senghor's 1948 anthology of negritude poetry, *Anthologie de la nouvelle poésie nègre at malgache de langue française*.[29] However, unlike the situation sketched in *Anti-Semite and Jew* two years earlier, Sartre, now explicitly Marxist in orientation, begins "Black Orpheus" with an important distinction drawn between the situation faced by the Jew in his or her encounter with anti-Semitism, and that of the colonized black person in the context of anti-black racism. Like the condition of the Jew vis-à-vis anti-Semitic racism, and now the "white worker" vis-à-vis the capitalist mode of production, Sartre locates the oppression of colonized black people "in the capitalist structure of… society." However, unlike the situations of the Jew and the white worker, the black person finds him or herself a victim of capitalist exploitation and domination "*insofar as he is black* and by virtue of being a colonized native or deported African." In other words, for the colonized black worker, capitalist exploitation and domination is *mediated* through the lens of race and through the lived experience of racism. Now, as we saw previously, for Sartre, the victimization of Jews by capitalism is also mediated through anti-Semitism and their experience *as Jews*, but he then goes on to explain that, unlike the Jew, "there is no means of evasion" for the black person; "no 'passing' that he can consider: a Jew—a white man among white men—can deny that he is a Jew, can declare himself a man among men. The [N]egro cannot deny that he is a [N]egro, nor can he deny that he is part of some abstract colorless humanity: he is black."[30]

What does this mean for the black subject who chooses to act authentically in her or his situation? Here Sartre claims that the black person essentially has "his back up against the wall of authenticity."[31] As he explains: "Having been insulted and formally enslaved, [the black person] picks up the word 'nigger' which was thrown at him like a stone, he draws himself erect and proudly proclaims himself as black, in the face of the white man. The unity which will come eventually, bringing all oppressed peoples together in the same struggle, must be preceded in the colonies by what I shall call the moment of separation or negativity; this anti-racist racism is the only road that will lead to the abolition of racial differences."[32]

In positing negritude as an "anti-racist racism" that will eventually lead to the abolition of racial and class differentiation altogether, Sartre is situating the formation of black consciousness in relation to a distinction, often attributed to Marx, between a class that exists "in-itself" and one that exists "for-itself."[33] Without going into too much detail here, a class that exists in-itself represents the objective, structural positioning of a group in relation to the capitalist mode of production. Whereas a class that exists for-itself is one that has become *conscious* of itself *as a class* and then proceeds to struggle *for-itself* and thus in its own shared interests. And, of course, the primary agenda of a class that struggles for-itself is to root out the conditions (capitalist production) that determine its existence *as a class*. However, since the lived, subjective experience of race and racism occupies a mediating position in the exploitation and domination of black people by capitalism, "recognizing that socialism is the necessary answer to [the] immediate local claims" of black people first requires that they "learn to formulate these claims jointly; therefore they must [first] think of themselves *as blacks*." Hence, Sartre concludes that "becoming conscious" for black workers "is different from that which Marxism tries to awaken in the white worker." In the case of the European proletariat, "class consciousness" is "based on the objective characteristics of the *situation* of the proletariat. But since the selfish scorn that whites display for blacks . . . is aimed at the deepest recesses of the heart, [black people] must oppose it with a more exact view of black *subjectivity*.[34] For Sartre, developing this subjective opposition is the critical role played by negritude in anticapitalist and antiracist struggle.

So, then, for Sartre, becoming conscious of one's *objective* class position in the context of racialized capitalism requires that black people first work over the *subjective* dimension of race and racism. One cannot hope to uproot the social relations that give rise to both class exploitation and racial domination without first coming to grips with the corrosive effects that white supremacy has had on those subject to it. This is why Sartre attributes to negritude a revolutionary "function" in the struggle against capitalist imperialism.[35] In short, disalienation through the affirmative reconstruction of black subjectivity, which, as Aimé Césaire once noted, strikes at the core of what the negritude movement was all about,[36] serves as the precondition for establishing broader bonds of social solidarity and collective struggle. However, like the Marxist notion of a class that exists for-itself, the moment that black consciousness comes to fruition and affirms its worth as such, it must immediately seek to abolish itself as a form of individual/collective identification. In doing so, Sartre claims that the "subjective, existential, ethnic notion of *negritude* 'passes,' as Hegel says, into the objective, positive, and precise, notion of the *proletariat*."[37]

At this point we arrive at Sartre's infamous characterization of negritude as a transitional phase in a dialectical move from the particularity of identity

politics to the universality of class struggle.[38] "Negritude appears," writes
Sartre, "as a minor moment of a dialectical progression: the theoretical and
practical affirmation of white supremacy is the thesis; the position of negritude as the antithetical value is the moment of negativity. But this negative
moment is not sufficient in itself, and these blacks who use it know this per-
fectly well; they know that it aims at preparing the synthesis or realization of
the human in a raceless society." Sartre then goes on to conclude that "negritude is [thus] for destroying itself, it is a passage and not an outcome, *a means
and not an ultimate end*."[39] Once again, here Sartre appears to portray the politics of difference much like he did in *Anti-Semite and Jew*: as an important
(even necessary) *stage* in the struggle against capitalist exploitation and racial
domination, but ultimately insufficient as an end in itself.

Frantz Fanon on Negritude, Self-Recognition, and Decolonization

As discussed previously in chapter 1, one of the central concerns animating
Fanon's analysis in *Black Skin, White Masks* is the problem of recognition in
situations marked by colonial racism. In this sense, I argue that Fanon's early
work ought to be interpreted much like Sartre's *Anti-Semite and Jew* and "Black
Orpheus": as a practical reworking of Hegel's master/slave relation in contexts
where the possibility of achieving affirmative relations of mutual recognition
appears foreclosed. Like Sartre's portrayal of intersubjectivity discussed above,
Fanon's phenomenological account of "being-for-others" in *Black Skin, White
Masks* emphasizes the ultimately objectifying and alienating character of intersubjective recognition, especially when these relations are played out in contexts structured by racial or cultural inequality. Indeed, throughout his text,
Fanon describes the experience of colonial recognition in profoundly negative terms, like being "fixed" or "walled in" by the violating "gaze" of another.[40]
Far from being emancipatory and self-confirming, recognition is instead cast
as a "suffocating reification," a "hemorrhage" that causes the colonized to collapse into *self*-objectification.[41] However, unlike the situation of Sartre's Jew
in *Anti-Semite and Jew*, when fixated on the colonized black subject the gaze
takes on a new significance for Fanon: "I am not given a second chance. I am
overdetermined from the outside. I am a slave not to the 'idea' that others have of
me, but to my appearance."[42] This leads Fanon to declare that the "black man,"
unlike the Jew, "has no ontological resistance in the eyes of the white man."[43]

Here Fanon appears to be making a qualification in line with the distinction Sartre came to make in "Black Orpheus" regarding the difference between the situation of the Jew vis-à-vis anti-Semitic racism, and that of the colonized black person vis-à-vis anti-black racism.

How do colonized populations tend to respond to this situation? According to Fanon, like Sartre's Jew, the colonized black person's most common response is that of "flight."[44] As Fanon describes, colonial recognition will often provoke within the oppressed a desire to "escape" their particularity, to negate the differences that mark them as morally deficient and inferior in the eyes of the colonizer: "The Negro is an animal, the Negro is bad, the Negro is wicked, the Negro is ugly."[45] Once internalized, these derogatory images often produce a pathological yearning to "be recognized *not as Black, but as White*."[46] Fanon uses a number of terms to describe the result of this process: "inferiority complex," "psycho-existential complex," "neurosis," and "alienation" being the most common. All of these designations are used by Fanon to describe the subjectifying hold that colonial power can have on those within its reach. Seen in this light, there is nothing "inherent" about the perceived "inferiority" attributed to colonized subjects by the dominant society, nor is there anything "natural" about the so-called "complexes" they suffer as a result.[47] Both are the product of colonial social relations: "If there is a flaw, it lies not in the 'soul' of the [colonized] individual, but in his environment."[48]

This, then, is the problematic that Fanon sets out to address in the bulk of his work: namely, what forms of decolonial praxis must one individually and collectively undertake to subvert the interplay between structure and subjectivity that sustain colonial relations over time. Fanon's complex engagement with negritude is best understood when examined against this dual-structured conception of power. Fanon argued that insofar as the negritude movement sought to undercut the incapacitating effects of internalized racism by discursively reinscribing value and worth to those identity-related differences that colonial discourse had hitherto characterized as savage, dirty, and evil, it constituted a potentially powerful first move in the struggle for freedom.[49] The logic here is that one cannot hope to restructure the social relations of colonialism if the "inferiority complex" produced by these relations is left in place.[50] But Fanon's endorsement of negritude's approach to self-recognition was by no means absolute. Indeed, as his narrative continues it becomes apparent that the very attributes of negritude that he saw as potentially the most empowering in the subjective sphere—namely, the rehabilitation of the colonized subject based on a revaluation of black history and culture—are also the ones that threaten to undercut the movement's transformative potential in the structural sphere. What is important to keep in mind, then, is a distinction Fanon highlights between what Nigel Gibson has called, negritude's "objective" limitations, "and its subjective necessity."[51]

In *Black Skin, White Masks* negritude's subjective worth is expressed most in chapter 5, "The Lived Experience of the Black Man."[52] At this point in the text Fanon is faced with the realization that appealing "to the [white] Other" for recognition is a lost cause, and as a result he decides to instead "assert *himself* as a BLACK MAN."[53] "Since the Other was reluctant to recognize me, there was only one answer: *to make myself known*."[54] In doing so, Fanon found himself fervently excavating "black antiquity" and what he "discovered left [him] speechless": not only was the white man wrong, black people were not "primitive or subhuman" and belonged to a civilization in its own right—with its own history, values, traditions, and achievements.[55] This discovery, made possible by the path forged by the negritude poets, left Fanon feeling empowered, confident, and mobilized: it provided, if only momentarily, the sense of self-worth, dignity, and respect that recognition from the dominant society had not only failed to deliver, but undercut at every step of the way. Subsequently, Fanon was no longer willing to be recognized on terms imposed by the colonizer: "Accommodate me as I am; I'm not accommodating anyone."[56]

Later in the chapter negritude's subjective significance is again emphasized, this time in relation to Sartre's controversial portrayal of the movement as a mere "phase" in the unfolding trajectory of class struggle.[57] Fanon writes: "When I read this . . . I felt they had robbed me of my last chance. . . . We had appealed to a friend of the colored peoples, and this friend had found nothing better to do than demonstrate the relativity of [our] actions." After being denied affirmative recognition from the colonial society, Fanon now found himself having to defend his self-affirmative actions against the position of a self-professed ally. All approaches seemed to cash out in a loss: "I couldn't hope to win," writes Fanon; "I wanted to be typically black—that was out of the question. I wanted to be white—that was a joke. And when I tried to claim my negritude intellectually as a concept, they snatched it away from me."[58] Consequently, the foundation upon which Fanon had managed to carve out a constructive relation-to-self was again cut from under him: "I sensed my shoulders slipping from this world, and my feet no longer felt the caress of the ground. Without a black past, without a black future, it was impossible for me to live my blackness. Not yet white, no longer completely black, I was damned."[59] In characterizing negritude's reconstruction of black subjectivity as a temporary moment in the historical narrative of class struggle, Sartre effectively stripped Fanon of his newly won consciousness.

If it were not for the concluding chapter of *Black Skin, White Masks* it would be easy to see how Fanon's quite visceral response to Sartre's interpretation could be read as an unqualified endorsement of negritude's "plunge" into the "absolute" of black history, identity, and consciousness.[60] However, as his narrative continues, at least three problems or limitations with negritude are revealed. The first has to do with the power of negritude resting on a simple inversion of colonial discourse. Insofar as the negritude movement sought to undo colonial subjection by reversing the binary terms of domination—by reinscribing what was once denigrated and demeaned with worth and value—it remained, for Fanon, pathologically fixated around a value structure ultimately predetermined by colonial society. Thus, even though it might appear as though the empowerment derived from this process reflects an *authentic* instance of *self*-affirmation/determination, in reality this expression of resistance is still, for Fanon, "overdetermined from the outside."[61] Its is an expression of the colonized's *ressentiment* insofar as the colonizer remains the "actional" subject locked in their position of superiority as the creator of values, and the colonized remain the subject of "reaction" locked in their subordinated position whose values remain inversely bound by those of their masters.[62] As Fanon explains elsewhere, in this "initial phase," it is "the action, the plans of the occupier that determine the centres of resistance around which [the] peoples' will to survive becomes organized. . . . It is the white man who creates the Negro. But is the Negro who creates negritude."[63] Instead of disrupting the Manichean value structure of savage/civilized, colonizer/colonized itself, negritude's attempt to restore the Native subject as an agent of history through an inversion of colonial discourse remains comfortably within the very binary logic that has played such a crucial role in justifying the colonial relation in the first place.

The second contentious issue Fanon identifies involves what we might today call negritude's "essentialist" conception of black subjectivity. It is generally recognized among Fanon scholars that this angle of Fanon's analysis is directed largely at the "objectivist" strand within negritude, represented clear-est in the work of Léopold Senghor.[64] Fanon's anti-essentialist critique has two elements. The first is empirical: in Fanon's view the unified and undif-ferentiated "black" or "African" subject hailed by Senghor simply does not exist. "The black experience is ambiguous," writes Fanon, "for there is not *one* Negro—there are *many* black men."[65] Seen in this light, it is clearly nonsense to speak of negritude as the "totality of values" representing black "civilization" as such; "not only [the values] of the peoples of black Africa, but also of the black minorities of America, or even Asia or the South Sea Islands."[66] There are "Blacks of Belgium, French and British nationality, and there are Black republics," writes Fanon. "How can we claim to grasp *the essence* when such facts demand our attention?"[67] Fanon's second criticism has more to do with power. His concern here is that many of the specific characteristics and supposed cultural traits that Senghor targets for reinscription—irrationality, rhythm, animism, oneness with nature, sensuality—seem to be more the prod-uct of racist stereotyping disseminated through colonial discourse than em-pirically verifiable attributes of precontact African societies.[68] What negritude refers to as "the black soul" is in Fanon's view "a construction by white folk."[69] Fanon's point here is that if the structural foundation of colonial rule is at least in part justified through the ideological propagation of racially essentialized binaries, then, in the long run, the logic of negritude's own essentialist "revalu-ation of values" could undermine its emancipatory potential.

Fanon's third criticism is directed squarely at negritude's elitism and there-fore its questionable relevance to those struggling against colonial-capitalist domination and exploitation on the ground. According to Fanon, one of neg-ritude's main problems was that it tended to inadvertently displace or down-play contemporary questions of colonial political economy by focusing too narrowly on revaluing the historical achievements of colonized cultures and societies. Relating this issue back to the exploited blacks of Martinique's sugar-cane plantations, Fanon writes: "It would never occur to us to ask these men to rethink their concept of history." Indeed, the "few worker comrades that I have had the opportunity to meet in Paris have never thought to ask them-selves about discovering a black past. They knew they were black, but, they told me, that didn't change a thing. And damn right they were." For Fanon, the re-quired solution for this community is to "fight," to focus their struggle against the "ossified" structure of bourgeois colonial society directly. For Fanon, it is by taking a "stand against this living death" that we can hope to bring about decolonization in a truly substantive sense.[70]

Taken together, then, these three limitations inform Fanon's conclusion in *Black Skin, White Masks* that, although the process of self-affirmative recognition at the core of projects like negritude represents a potential source of empowerment for colonized populations suffering the effects of internalized racism, this potential hinges on its ability to motivate praxis that is attentive to the structural as well as the subjective features of colonial rule. Understood this way, I suggest that Fanon's position in *Black Skin, White Masks* is not entirely unlike that of Sartre's in "Black Orpheus," although they arrive at their respective views via markedly different paths. When Fanon reprimands Sartre for characterizing the self-affirmative reconstruction of black subjectivity as a phase in the unfolding dialectic of anticolonial class struggle, he is challenging Sartre's deterministic understanding of *the dialectic*, not his claim that this process represents "a stage" in a broader struggle for freedom and equality.[71] Indeed, by the time we reach Fanon's conclusion in *Black Skin, White Masks* it is clear that the cluster of practices associated with self-recognition are valuable only insofar as they reestablish the colonized as historical protagonists oriented toward a change in the colonial social structure.[72] The moment that this process takes hold, however, the emphasis placed on revaluing precolonial culture and history proceeds to either lose its critical purchase in the fight for freedom, or becomes *an impediment to freedom as such*. This leads Fanon to assert: "In no way do I have to dedicate myself to reviving a black civilization unjustly ignored. I will not make myself the man of any past. I do not want to sing my past to the detriment of my present and future."[73] Although Fanon concedes that articulating a positive vision of the future requires some prior effort to break the hold of colonial subjection, and that this step often involves revaluing those historical and cultural forms that colonialism sought to denigrate and destroy, in the end it is only by moving beyond these "historical and instrumental" givens that one can truly initiate the "cycle of freedom."[74] Like Sartre before him, Fanon portrays the identity politics of negritude as an important means to achieving anticolonial struggle, but not an end to the struggle itself.

In Fanon's later writings similar themes are developed and explored. For example, in his 1955 article "West Indians and Africans" Fanon begins by reiterating his earlier concern regarding negritude's essentialist portrayal of an undifferentiated black subject: "When one says 'Negro people,' one systematically assumes that all Negroes agree on certain things, that they share a principle of communion."[75] However, "the truth," writes Fanon, "is that there is nothing, *a priori*, to warrant the assumption that such a thing as a Negro people exists."[76] Again, here Fanon is not content with simply challenging the *empirical* validity of such a characterization; rather, the problem is fundamentally one of power: "The object of lumping Negroes together under the designation of 'Negro people' is to *deprive* them of any possibility of individual expression" and "to put them under the *obligation* of matching the idea one has of them."[77] Here it appears that where Fanon was initially concerned in *Black Skin, White Masks* with the ways in which self-essentialized constructions of black identity could inadvertently feed back into and justify hierarchical relations between the colonized and colonizer, now he seems to be equally attentive to how similar processes can work to constrain freedom *within* the colonized population itself. The problem with essentialism thus cuts in two directions for Fanon: it can serve to naturalize relations of dominance not only between but also within social groups.

Yet by grounding his analysis in the concrete operation of specific power relations Fanon is again able to maintain a critical stance toward negritude without denying its significance outright. This is made clear over the course of "West Indians and Africans" as Fanon begins to emphasize the social function played by negritude in mobilizing Antillean blacks against French racism in Martinique. Until this point, Fanon's endorsement of negritude rested largely on the transformative effects he saw the practice of self-affirmation having on the psychology of individuals, using his own experience in *Black Skin, White Masks* as an example. This stance undergoes a slight revision in "West Indians and Africans" as Fanon begins to historicize the movement's influence at the societal level. This is clearest in Fanon's discussion of Césaire, whose work he claims served to radicalize the local black population in ways that would have been unheard of before the popularization of his poetry and political activism. Indeed, it was Césaire's "scandalous" assertion that being black was a "good" thing, that it was not only "beautiful" but also a "source of truth" that provided the black community with a counterdiscourse to mobilize around and deploy in their efforts to collectively combat the heightened racism that came to plague Martinique as thousands of French sailors descended on the island during the Second World War.[78] "Without Césaire this would have been difficult," writes Fanon, for prior to this period "the West Indian identified himself with the white man, adopted a white man's attitude, was 'a white man.'"[79] This came to a grinding halt in 1939, however, for the colonized were now forced into a situation where they had to defend themselves against the derogatory images of blacks hurled at them by the stationed French troops. Césaire provided the discursive ammunition used in this defense, and as a result, "a new generation came into being."[80] Blackness was no longer considered an irrelevant category of identification (as blacks had convinced themselves it was before the influx of French sailors), nor was it seen as "a stain";[81] it was now a source of strength, an emergent consciousness, and a foundation for collective action.

Fanon also explores the social significance of negritude in "Racism and Culture."[82] Written with the Algerian context in mind, this groundbreaking essay traces the historical evolution of racism as a systematized form of oppression oriented around crude assumptions of biological inferiority to a more subtle form grounded on notions of cultural inferiority. What Fanon here calls the emergence of "cultural racism" anticipates what contemporary critical race scholars have termed the "culturalization of racism."[83] Under this new guise, the "object of racism" shifts from those genetically identifiable characteristics once thought to mark certain individuals or groups as inferior, to what Fanon calls entire "form[s] of existing" or "way[s] of life."[84] In colonial situations, this cultural variant of racism is what historically served to rationalize the host of repressive colonial practices associated with policies of forced assimilation. The underlying rationale here is that, if the perceived inferiority of non-European peoples does not appear to be attributable to innate characteristics, it then follows that these groups can, in theory, be elevated to the more "civilized" status of their European colonizers. In order to accomplish this, however, one has to first "destroy" the "primitive" "cultural values" thought to impede the so-called "development" of the colonized vis-à-vis the more "advanced" settler society. According to this scheme, colonial rule was (and for some, still is) thought to be justified insofar as it serves to facilitate the moral and cultural development of the colonized group.[85]

Witnessing firsthand the destructive effects of cultural racism in the Algerian context appears to have prompted a slight shift in the dismissive stance that Fanon adopts in his conclusion to Black Skin, White Masks toward strategies that seek to revalue precolonial history and culture as an ongoing feature of the decolonization process. This change is reflected in "Racism and Culture" and then again in the chapter "On National Culture" from *The Wretched of the Earth*. Fanon's argument in both texts can be stated like this: because colonialism tends to solidify its gains by normalizing the injustices it has perpetrated against the colonized population through a direct attack on the integrity of precontact history and culture, it follows that strategies that attempt to break the stranglehold of this subjection through practices of cultural self-affirmation can play an important role in anticolonial struggle as long as they remain grounded and oriented toward a change in the social structure of colonialism itself. What distinguishes Fanon's previous position in *Black Skin, White Masks* from the position articulated in "Racism and Culture" and *The Wretched of the Earth*, however, is that the arguments developed in the two latter texts were based on observations Fanon made while in Algeria, where expressions of cultural self-affirmation appeared to emerge organically among the colonized population as a whole, as opposed to being articulated solely among the elites of negritude. This is an important distinction to recognize because I think it alleviates to some degree Fanon's previous concern regarding the disassociation of cultural revitalization movements from questions of colonial political economy. This is why in "Racism and Culture" and *The Wretched of the Earth* we see Fanon's most biting criticisms directed more squarely at negritude as a specific practice of cultural self-affirmation, and less toward these types of practices as such.

However, even though Fanon is willing to assign a slightly more substantive value to practices of cultural self-recognition in his post–*Black Skin, White Masks* writings, he does so without abandoning his previous apprehensions entirely. Indeed, one of Fanon's lingering concerns is that the cultural forms and traditions exuberantly reclaimed and affirmed by the colonized no longer reflect the dynamic systems that existed prior to the colonial encounter: rather, "this culture, once living and open to the future, [has become] closed, fixed in the colonial status."[86] The problem here is that the cultural practices that the colonized passionately cling to as a source of pride and empowerment can easily become a cluster of antiquated attachments that divert attention away from the present and future needs of the Indigenous population.[87] In other words, what was initially empowering can quickly become a source of pacifying, *ressentiment*-infected nostalgia. This problem is compounded further in the activism of negritude elites like Senghor, whose work, Fanon claims, racializes and abstracts the past cultural achievements of the colonized to such a

degree that it bears little resemblance to the specificity of struggles occurring at the local, national level.[88] What ultimately needs to be realized in both
cases, then, whether it be in relation to the self-affirmative activities undertaken by the colonized intellectual or by the grassroots freedom-fighter, is
that the "native's hand-to-hand struggle with his culture" must be geared
toward "the total liberation of the national territory."[89] According to Fanon, it
is only under these radically transformed material conditions that a truly
national culture can emerge;[90] a "fighting culture" that "does not leave intact
either the *form or substance*" of previous cultural practices, but instead strives
toward the construction of a *totally new set of social, cultural and economic relations.*[91] Insofar as the "plunge into the chasm of the past" provides a possible
means of achieving this ultimate end,[92] then Fanon is more willing than he
was in his conclusion to *Black Skin, White Masks* to attribute a transformative
function to cultural self-affirmation in the fight for freedom against colonial
domination.

Conclusion

In her recent book on Anishinaabe political and cultural resurgence, *Dancing on Our Turtle's Back*, Leanne Simpson suggests that while non-Indigenous
critical theoretical frameworks still have much to offer our analyses of contemporary settler-colonialism, they are fundamentally limited in their ability
to provide insight into what a culturally grounded alternative to colonialism
might look like for Indigenous nations. "While theoretically, we have debated
whether Audre Lourde's 'the master's tools can dismantle the master's house,'"
writes Simpson, "I am interested in a different question." She continues: "I am
not so concerned with how we dismantle the master's house, that is, which
set of theories we use to critique colonialism; but I am very concerned with
how we (re)build our own house, or our own houses."[93] By now it should be
clear that although Fanon saw the revaluation of an Indigenous "past" as an
important means of temporarily breaking the colonized free from the interpellative stranglehold of colonial misrecognition, he was less willing to explore
the role that critically revitalized traditions might play in the (re)construction
of decolonized Indigenous nations. Subsequently, his work tends to treat "the
cultural" in a manner inappropriately similar to how Marxists treat the category of "class": as a transitional form of identification that subaltern groups

must struggle to overcome as soon as they become conscious of its existence as a distinct category of identification. In my concluding chapter I explore a different way of understanding the significance of Indigenous cultural politics in our struggles for national liberation—a *resurgent* approach to Indigenous decolonization that builds on the value and insights of our past in our efforts to secure a noncolonial present and future.

CONCLUSION

Lessons from Idle No More

The Future of Indigenous Activism

Personal and collective transformation is not instrumental to the surging against state power, it is the very means of our struggle.

—TAIAIAKE ALFRED, *Wasáse*

In writing this book I set out to problematize the increasingly commonplace assumption that the colonial relationship between Indigenous peoples and the Canadian state can be reconciled via a liberal "politics of recognition." I characterized the "politics of recognition" as a recognition-based approach to reconciling Indigenous peoples' assertions of nationhood with settler-state sovereignty via the accommodation of Indigenous identity-related claims through the negotiation of settlements over issues such as land, economic development, and self-government. I argued that this orientation to the reconciliation of Indigenous nationhood with state sovereignty is still *colonial* insofar as it remains structurally committed to the dispossession of Indigenous peoples of our lands and self-determining authority.

My conceptualization of settler-colonialism as a structure of domination predicated on the dispossession of Indigenous peoples' lands and political authority drew significantly from two theoretical resources: Karl Marx's writings on the "primitive accumulation" of capital and Frantz Fanon's anticolonial critique of Hegel's master/slave parable when applied to colonial situations. With respect to Marx, I argued that three issues must be addressed within his work to make his writings on colonialism relevant for analyzing the relationship between Indigenous peoples and liberal settler polities like Canada. First, I argued that Marx's thesis on primitive accumulation must be stripped of its rigidly *temporal* character; that is, rather than positing primitive accumulation as some historically situated, inaugural set of events that set the stage for the development of the capitalist mode of production through colonial expansion, we should see it as an ongoing practice of dispossession that never ceases to structure capitalist and colonial social relations in the present. *Settler-colonialism is territorially acquisitive in perpetuity*. Second, I argued that Marx's theory of primitive accumulation must be stripped of its early *normative developmentalist* character. While it is correct to view primitive accumulation as the condition of possibility for the development and ongoing reproduction of the capitalist mode of production, it is incorrect to view it as a *necessary* condition for developing the forms of critical consciousness and associated modes of life that ought to inform the construction of alternatives to capitalism in settler-colonial contexts. I also suggested that Marx himself came to acknowledge the problematic character of this early formulation of his thesis and worked to correct it in the last decade of his life. And finally, I argued that the forms of colonial power associated with primitive accumulation need not be understood as strictly coercive, repressive, or explicitly violent in nature; rather, the practices of dispossession central to the maintenance of settler-colonialism in liberal democratic contexts like Canada rely as much on the *productive* character of colonial power as it does on the coercive authority of the settler state. Seen from this angle, settler-colonialism should not be seen as deriving its reproductive force solely from its strictly repressive or violent features, but rather from its ability to produce *forms of life* that make settler-colonialism's constitutive hierarchies seem natural.

To tease out the productive character of settler-colonial power I turned to the theoretical contribution of Frantz Fanon. I used Fanon's work because it implicates the role played by *recognition* in the reproduction of settler-colonial forms of rule in a manner that still resonates today. More specifically, I used Fanon's critical engagement with the dialectic of recognition theorized in Hegel's master/slave narrative to identify the neocolonial function played by contemporary recognition politics in maintaining the settler-colonial relationship between Indigenous nations and the Canadian state. I drew three insights from Fanon in particular. First, I claimed that Fanon's critique of Hegel's theory of recognition convincingly unpacks the ways in which delegated exchanges of political recognition from the colonizer to the colonized usually ends up being structurally determined by and in the interests of the colonizer. Second, Fanon also identifies the subtle ways in which colonized populations often come to develop what he called "psycho-affective" attachments to these circumscribed, master-sanctioned forms of delegated recognition. For

Fanon, these psycho-affective or ideological attachments create an impression of "naturalness" to the colonial condition, which he referred to as "internalization" or "internalized" colonialism. Third, Fanon showed how colonized populations, despite the totalizing power of colonialism, are often able to turn these internalized forms of colonial recognition into expressions of Indigenous self-empowerment through the reclamation and revitalization of precolonial social relations and cultural traditions. In the end, however, Fanon viewed these practices of Indigenous cultural self-empowerment, or *self-recognition*, as insufficient for decolonization: they constitute a "means" but not an "end."

In this chapter I conclude my analysis by turning our attention to the contributions that Indigenous scholars and activists, particularly but not necessarily limited to those working within the emergent theory and practice of *Indigenous resurgence*, have added to our understanding of the entanglement of contemporary recognition politics with the operation of settler-colonial power.[1] I feel that it is important to conclude my study in this way because Indigenous contributions to anticolonial thought and practice have been generally underappreciated for their transformative value and insights. Indeed, as we saw in the previous chapter, even Fanon viewed the decolonial potential of Indigenous cultural politics as fundamentally undercut by its *ressentiment*-directed orientation toward the past. "We should not therefore be content to delve into the people's past to find *concrete examples* to counter colonialism's endeavour to distort or depreciate," writes Fanon in *The Wretched of the Earth*.[2] "Colonialism will never be put to shame by exhibiting unknown cultural treasures under its nose."[3] I suggest that it is on this point that we reach a limit to Fanon's anticolonial analysis, especially when applied to the settler-colonial dynamics that inform our current circumstances. Although Fanon eschews an evolutionary anthropological theory of historical development in which societies are viewed as developing along a linear path from primitive to civilized, he remains wedded to a *dialectical* conception of social transformation that privileges the "new" over the "old." When this dialectic is applied to colonial situations, the result, I claim, is a conceptualization of "culture" that mimics how Marxists understand "class": as a *transitional* category of identification that colonized peoples must struggle to *transcend* as soon as they become conscious of its existence as a form of identification. This view simply does not provide much insight into either what motivates Indigenous resistance to settler colonization or into the cultural foundations upon which Indigenous noncolonial alternatives might be constructed.

The concluding thoughts I offer in this chapter are organized into three sections. In the first one, I examine the work of two theorists of Indigenous resurgence, Taiaiake Alfred and Leanne Betasamosake Simpson, and parse out their significant contributions to our understanding of the dynamics that shape settler-colonialism and Indigenous decolonization in Canada. In the second section, I use the emergent Idle No More movement as a backdrop against which to explore what a resurgent decolonial politics might look like in practice. And finally, I conclude with "Five Theses on Indigenous Resurgence and Decolonization," in light of what we have learned throughout the preceding chapters.

INDIGENOUS RESURGENCE

To my mind, the most explicit theorization of the Indigenous resurgence paradigm can be found in the writings of two Indigenous scholar/activists working here in Canada: Mohawk political scientist Taiaiake Alfred and Anishinaabe feminist Leanne Simpson.[4] Like Fanon's quasi-Nietzschean invocation of self-affirmation in *Black Skin, White Masks*, both Alfred and Simpson start from a position that calls on Indigenous people and communities to "turn away" from the assimilative reformism of the liberal recognition approach and to instead build our national liberation efforts on the revitalization of "traditional" political values and practices.[5] "We [must] choose to *turn away* from the legacies of colonialism," writes Alfred in *Wasáse*, "and take on the challenge of creating a new reality for ourselves and for our people."[6] For Simpson, decolonization requires that Indigenous communities reorient our collective labor from attempts to transform "the colonial outside into a flourishment of the *Indigenous* inside." In other words, we need to decolonize "on our own terms, without the sanction, permission or engagement of the state, western theory or the opinions of Canadians."[7]

Unlike Fanon's notion of self-affirmation, however, the resurgence paradigm defended by Alfred and Simpson does not require us to dialectically transcend Indigenous practices of the past once the affirmation of these practices has served to reestablish us as historical protagonists in the present. For Alfred, the struggle to regenerate "traditional values" is assigned a far more substantive value: "We have a responsibility to recover, understand, and preserve these values, not only because they represent a unique contribution to the history of ideas, but because renewal of respect for traditional values is the only *lasting solution* to the political, economic, and social problems that beseech our people."[8] The same goes for Simpson's work: "Building diverse, nation-culture-based resurgences means significantly reinvesting in our own ways of being: regenerating our political and intellectual traditions; articulating and living our legal traditions; language learning; creating and using our artistic and performance based traditions. [Decolonization] requires us to reclaim the very best practices of our traditional cultures, knowledge systems and lifeways in the dynamic, fluid, compassionate, respectful context in which they were originally generated."[9] In *Peace, Power, Righteousness*, Alfred refers to these ethico-political practices of Indigenous resurgence as a form of "self-conscious traditionalism"—that is, a self-reflective program of culturally grounded de-subjectification that aims to undercut the interplay between subjectivity and structural domination that help maintain settler-colonial relationships in contexts absent pure force.[10]

For Alfred, colonial recognition politics serves the imperatives of capitalist accumulation by *appearing* to address its colonial history through symbolic acts of redress while in actuality "further entrenching in law and practice the real bases of its control."[11] As we have seen, over the last forty years Canada has recognized a host of rights specific to Aboriginal communities, including most importantly to land and self-government. Canada has always used this recognition, however, as evidence of its ultimately just relationship with Indigenous communities, even though this recognition continues to be structured with colonial power interests in mind. Simpson levels a similar charge against the more recent "turn to reconciliation" in Indigenous politics. "As reconciliation has become institutionalized," writes Simpson, "I worry our participation will benefit the state in an asymmetrical fashion."[12] In Simpson's view, the state's approach to reconciliation serves to neutralize the legitimacy of Indigenous justice claims by offering statements of regret and apology for harms narrowly conceived of as occurring in the past, thus off-loading Canada's responsibility to address structural injustices that continue to inform our settler-colonial present. In doing so the state can claim "that the historical 'wrong' has been 'righted' and further transformation is not needed."[13] In the end, the optics created by these grand gestures of recognition and reconciliation suggests to the dominant society that we no longer have a legitimate ground to stand on in expressing our grievances. Instead, Indigenous people appear unappreciative, angry, and resentful, as we saw in chapter 4.

The optics of recognition and reconciliation can also have a colonial impact on Indigenous subjects. For both Alfred and Simpson, settler-colonial rule is a form of *governmentality*: a relatively diffuse set of governing relations that operate through a circumscribed mode of recognition that structurally ensures continued access to Indigenous peoples' lands and resources by producing neocolonial subjectivities that coopt Indigenous people into becoming instruments of their own dispossession. According to this view, contemporary colonialism works *through* rather than entirely *against* freedom: In the "new relationship," writes Alfred, the "rusty cage [of colonialism] may be broken, but a new chain has been strung around the indigenous neck; *it offers more room to move, but it still ties our people to white men pulling on the strong end*."[14] Alfred's concern here is that many Indigenous people, particularly those leaders and community organizers heavily invested in the colonial politics of recognition, have come to associate this externally imposed field of maneuver with freedom or decolonization itself.

The biopolitics of settler-colonial recognition can also problematically inform our efforts at Indigenous resurgence. For both authors, recognizing this demands that we remain cognizant of the pitfalls associated with retreating into an uncritical essentialism in our practices of cultural revitalization. As Alfred states in *Peace, Power, Righteousness*: "Working within a traditional framework, we must acknowledge the fact that traditions change, and that any particular notion that constitutes 'tradition' will be contested."[15] A similar insistence on cultural dynamism informs Simpson's work. Resurgence does not "literally mean returning to the past," insists Simpson, "but rather re-creating the cultural and political flourishment of the past to support the well being of our contemporary citizens."[16] For Simpson this requires that we reclaim "the fluidity of our traditions, not the rigidity of colonialism."[17] Acknowledging culture's malleability, however, does not mean that we cannot still identify certain "beliefs, values and principles that form the persistent core of a community's culture," writes Alfred. It is this "traditional framework that we must use as the basis on which to build a better society." The resurgence Alfred and Simpson advocate is thus a *critical* one: an intellectual, social, political, and artistic movement geared toward the self-reflective revitalization of those "values, principles and other cultural elements that are best suited to the larger contemporary political and economic reality."[18] Resurgence, in this view, draws critically on the past with an eye to radically transform the colonial power relations that have come to dominate our present.

In *Wasáse* Alfred expands on the foundational critique he develops in *Peace, Power, Righteousness* in a way that provides more depth to our understanding of both the complexity of power relations that give shape to settler-colonialism and the types of practices we might engage in to transform these relations. To my mind, one of the more important layers of complexity Alfred adds in *Wasáse* has to do with the placement of gender in his theoretical framework, which was largely absent in previous work. I would suggest that there are two reasons that inform the inclusion of a gendered component to Alfred's more recent position. First, and most importantly, the crucial interventions of Indigenous feminist scholarship and activism over the years have made it *impossible* for any credible scholar working within the field to ignore the centrality of sexism to the colonial aims of land dispossession and sovereignty usurpation. This crucial area of work has also made it impossible to credibly ignore the impact that colonial patriarchy continues to have on our national liberation efforts. Second, I also think that gender figures its way into Alfred's more recent work because of the explicit collapse of any ends/means distinction in his notion of resurgence. One of the central "problems" with Indigenous politics, insists Alfred, "is that there is no consistency of means and ends in the way that we are struggling to empower ourselves."[19] For Alfred, we must remain cognizant of the subtle ways our methods can come to discursively shape the ends we seek to attain through our decolonization strategies.[20] This is why Alfred is quick to insist that the struggles of Indigenous peoples today cannot hold onto a concept of struggle "that is gendered in the way it once was and that is located in an obsolete view of men's and women's roles." Instead, Indigenous struggles must "be rethought and recast from the solely masculine view of the old traditional ways to a new concept of the warrior that is freed from colonial gender constructions."[21]

Critically, Simpson extends this gendered analysis to interrogate the subtle infiltration of heteropatriarchal norms in our practices of national liberation and resurgence. Drawing off the insights of recent scholars working at the intersection of queer theory and Indigenous studies, in particular the writings of Chris Finely and Andrea Smith,[22] Simpson challenges the perpetuation of heteropatriarchy within our movements on several fronts, including "[through the construction of] rigid (colonial) gender roles, pressuring women to wear certain articles of clothing to ceremonies, the exclusion of LGBQ2 individuals from communities and ceremonies, the dominance of male-centred narratives regarding Indigenous experience, the lack of recognition for women and LGBQ2's voices, experiences, contributions and leadership, and narrow interpretations of tradition used to control the contributions of women in ceremony, politics and leadership."[23] Although I am speculating here, I suspect that Simpson's important call to "queer resurgence" represents her own response to concerns raised by Métis feminist Emma LaRoque regarding the heteronormative conception of Indigenous womanhood that underwrites certain aspects of recent Indigenous feminist reclamation projects. Of particular concern to LaRoque is the manner in which Cree feminist Kim Anderson appears to foreground her particular view of Indigenous motherhood as "central to Aboriginal women's epistemology" in general. Although LaRoque recognizes that Anderson takes "great pains" to include as many nonmothers as possible in her analysis, including extended family members and other Indigenous women caregivers who do not have children, Anderson's normative privileging of "maternalization" nevertheless ends up being "totalizing and exclusionary." LaRoque's point here is not to dismiss the emancipatory potential of Anderson's invocation of a "maternal-based" ethical practice; rather, she is simply highlighting the way in which a specific practice of cultural empowerment can itself discursively rule out or constrain other equally legitimate and potentially empowering ways of being Indigenous in the present.[24] I think that Simpson's argument in "Queering Resurgence" is meant to clarify the decolonial role she attributes to her own experience of motherhood and childrearing in *Dancing on Our Turtle's Back*.[25] Perpetuating these heteronormative exclusions "cannot be part of our nation-building work," states Simpson unequivocally. "This is not resurgence."[26]

Alfred's call for a consistency between the means and ends of decolonization implicates more than oppressive gender constructions. It also has ramifications in the realm of political economy and governance. In relation to political economy, for example, Alfred's resurgent approach to decolonization demands that we challenge the commonsense idea that one can construct an equitable relationship with non-Indigenous peoples and a sustainable relationship with the land by participating more intensely in a capitalist economy that is environmentally unsustainable and founded, at its core, on racial, gender, and class exploitation and inequalities.[27] The same can be said regarding our attempts to negotiate a relation of nondomination with a structure of domination like the colonial nation-state. For Alfred, the best aspects of traditional Indigenous governing practices stand in "sharp contrast to the dominant understanding of 'the state': there is no absolute authority, no coercive enforcement of decisions, no hierarchy and no separate ruling entity."[28] In our thirty-year effort to achieve recognition of a right to self-government, we have come to accept the liberal democratic state as a legitimate, if not normative, mode of political organization. In doing so, Alfred claims that we have allowed "indigenous political goals to be framed and evaluated according to a 'statist' pattern."[29] In light of the productive capacity of the colonial state to call forth modes of life that mimic its constitutive power features, Alfred's concern is that our negotiations for self-government will end up replicating the worst manifestations of the state's power within the intensified context of our own communities and governance structures. We also saw in chapter 3 how a similar concern came to animate the late Mohawk legal theorist Patricia Monture's critique of the Canadian Charter of Rights and Freedoms as an appropriate tool in the gender justice struggles of Indigenous women. For Monture, when Native women seek legal protection from the patriarchal colonial state as a means of ameliorating the gendered violence that the state has disciplined into the minds and bodies of our citizens through the Indian Act, they risk reifying the subjective and structural relations required for their continued domination both as Indigenous women and as members of Indigenous nations.[30] To my mind, Monture's insight here adds a crucial gender dynamic to Alfred's claims that "structural change negotiated in a colonial cultural context will only achieve the further entrenchment of the social and political foundations of injustice, leading to reforms that are mere modifications to the pre-existing structures of domination."[31] By contrast, the resurgent approach to recognition advocated here explicitly eschews the instrumental rationality central to the liberal politics of recognition and instead demands that we *enact* or *practice* our political commitments to Indigenous national and women's liberation in the cultural form and content of our struggle itself. Indigenous resurgence is at its core a *prefigurative* politics—the methods of decolonization prefigure its aims.

Idle No More: A History

Below I want to turn our attention to the Idle No More movement that burst onto the Canadian political scene in the late fall/early winter of 2012/13. To my mind, Idle No More offers a productive case study against which to explore what a resurgent Indigenous politics might look like on the ground. Before I turn to this analysis, however, providing a bit of context to the movement is required.

On December 14, 2012, the Canadian senate passed the Conservative federal government's controversial omnibus Bill C-45. Bill C-45, also known as the Jobs and Growth Act, is a four-hundred-plus-page budget implementation bill that contains comprehensive changes to numerous pieces of federal legislation, including, but not limited to, the Indian Act, the Fisheries Act, the Canadian Environmental Assessment Act, and the Navigable Water Act.[32] From the perspective of many Indigenous people and communities, the changes contained in Bill C-45 threaten to erode Aboriginal land and treaty rights insofar as they reduce the amount of resource development projects that require environmental assessment; they change the regulations that govern on-reserve leasing in a way that will make it easier for special interests to access First Nation reserve lands for the purposes of economic development and settlement; and they radically curtail environmental protections for lakes and rivers.[33]

Indigenous opposition to Bill C-45 began in the fall of 2012 as a grassroots education campaign initiated by four women from the prairies—Jessica Gordon, Sylvia McAdam, Sheelah McLean and Nina Wilson—under the mantra "Idle No More." The campaign's original aim was to provide information to Canadians about the impending impacts of Bill C-45 on Aboriginal rights and environmental protections before the legislation was passed by the Canadian senate. Then, on December 4, Chief Theresa Spence of the Attawapiskat Cree Nation announced that she would begin a hunger strike on December 11 to bring attention to the deplorable housing conditions on her reserve in northern Ontario, to raise awareness about the impacts of Bill C-45, and to demonstrate her support for the emerging Idle No More movement. During her hunger strike Chief Spence consumed only liquids—a combination of lemon water, medicinal teas, and fish broth—which she claimed she would continue to do until she secured a meeting with Prime Minister Stephen Harper and Governor-General David Johnson to discuss treaty rights. Her hunger strike took place in a teepee on Victoria Island, near Parliament Hill in Ottawa, and lasted from December 11 until January 24, 2013.

By the second week in December the movement had exploded on social media under the Twitter hash tag #IdleNoMore (or #INM for short), with the first national "day of action" called for December 10. Protests erupted in cities across the country. At this point, the tactics favored by Idle No More participants involved a combination of "flash mob" round-dancing and drumming in public spaces like shopping malls, street intersections, and legislature grounds, coupled with an ongoing public education campaign organized through community-led conferences, teach-ins, and public panels. On December 21 an Idle No More protest involving thousands of Indigenous people and their supporters descended on Parliament Hill in Ottawa. During roughly the same time, Idle No More tactics began to diversify to include the use of blockades and temporary train and traffic stoppages, the most publicized of which involved a two-week railway blockade established in late December by the Aamjiwnaag First Nation near Sarnia, Ontario.[34]

By late December it was clear the something truly significant was underway with the Idle No More movement. Indeed, Canada had not seen such a sustained, united, and coordinated nationwide mobilization of Indigenous nations against a legislative assault on our rights since the proposed White Paper of 1969. What had begun in the fall of 2012 as an education campaign designed to inform Canadians about a particularly repugnant and undemocratic piece of legislation had erupted by mid-January 2013 into a full-blown defense of Indigenous land and sovereignty. By early January the momentum generated by Idle No More, in combination with the media attention paid to Chief Spence's hunger strike, had created such a national stir that the Prime Minister's Office was forced to respond by calling a January 11 meeting with the Assembly of First Nations, although the prime minister never explicitly stated that his decision to call the meeting was a result of pressure mounted by the escalating protests.[35]

At the height of the protest activities leading into the January 11 gathering, political analyses of the movement ranged from the entirely asinine to coverage that was both engaged and critically astute. Exemplifying the former, right-wing ideologue Christie Blatchford referred to Chief Spence's peaceful hunger strike as an act of "intimidation, if not terrorism: She is, after all, holding the state hostage to vaguely articulated demands."[36] The claim that Idle No More's "demands" were somehow abstruse was (and, at the time of writing this chapter in March 2013, continues to be) popular among mainstream media critics. In an especially laughable piece written for the *National Post* in January 2013, Kelly McParland speculated that Idle No More's lack of focus and clarity was a result of the movement having been "seized" by the forces of

Occupy Wall Street. "What are the aims of The Cause?" asks McParland condescendingly. "No one is really quite sure: just as with Occupy, the Idle forces are disparate and leaderless."[37] For others, however, it is precisely the diversity and bottom-up character of the movement that make decolonization movements like Idle No More so potentially transformative. Idle No More "is not led by any elected politician, national chief or paid executive director," explains Mi'kmaq legal scholar Pamela Palmater. "It is a movement originally led by indigenous women and has been joined by grassroots First Nations leaders, Canadians, and now the world."[38] Similarly, for Leanne Simpson, the strength of the movement lies in the fact that it is not led from above, but rather has "hundreds of eloquent spokespeople, seasoned organizers, writers, thinkers and artists acting on their own ideas in anyway and every way possible. This is the beauty of our movement."[39]

As with any grassroots political movement, the diversity at the heart of Idle No More resulted in debates and disagreements over what types of strategies and tactics to use in our efforts to forge meaningful change. These debates intensified in the days leading up to the January 11 meeting. On the one side, there was the perspective among many Native people working within mainstream Aboriginal organizations that saw the January 11 meeting as an important space to get Aboriginal issues and concerns on the federal government's political agenda. On the other side of the debate, however, were the voices emanating up from the communities (with some chiefs following suit), that saw the turn to high-level political negotiations as yet another attempt by the state and Aboriginal organizations, in particular the Assembly of First Nations, to coopt the transformative potential of the movement by redirecting it in a more moderate and reformist direction.[40] Longtime Secwepemc activist and leader Arthur Manuel gets to the core of the debate when he writes that "one thing is clear: that certain Indigenous leaders only know how to meet with government and not fight with government. In situations like Friday [January 11] they say that it is important to 'engage' with government when they open the door to discussion. The real problem is that you get sucked into basically supporting the government's position unless you walk out. In this case it is just another 'process' and not 'change in policy' that the AFN left the room with."[41] There is much historical evidence to support Manuel's concern. If we take a step back and look at the history that led to our present juncture, especially since the late 1960s, the state has always responded to increased levels of

Indigenous political assertiveness and militancy by attempting to contain these outbursts through largely symbolic gestures of political inclusion and recognition. Indeed, as we saw in chapter 4, this was precisely the manner in which the federal government attempted to address the fallout of the decade-long escalation of First Nations' militancy that culminated in the Meech Lake Accord and the conflict at Kanesatake in 1990. And if we push our view back a bit further yet, we see a similar strategy used by the federal government to quell the upsurge of struggle that eventually defeated the White Paper of 1969. It was at this time that the entire policy orientation of Canada's approach to solving the "Indian problem" began to shift from willfully ignoring Aboriginal peoples' rights to recognizing them in the manageable form of land claims and eventually self-government agreements. I suggest that Idle No More is an indication of the ultimate failure of this approach to reconciliation. After forty years the subtle lure of Canada's vacuous gestures of accommodation have begun to lose their political sway.

All of this is to say that the January 11 meeting did not transpire without major controversy. One of the most significant points of contention involved the refusal of Prime Minister Harper to include the participation of Governor-General David Johnson in the meeting, thwarting the demand of Chief Spence and a growing number of First Nations leaders and Idle No More supporters. As the Crown's official representative in Canada, the governor-general's roles and responsibilities are today largely symbolic in nature. However, from the perspective of treaty First Nations, securing a meeting with the governor-general would have emphasized the nation-to-nation character of the relationship between First Nations and the Crown. This is especially important given the manner in which Canada has failed to live up to the spirit and intent of these historic agreements. Prime Minister Harper's refusal to concede to Chief Spence's demand on this point signified a refusal by Canada to take the treaty relationship seriously more generally, which was the central point of demanding a meeting with the governor-general's participation to begin with. Combined with the previously mentioned concern of cooptation, the failure to invite the governor-general resulted in a boycott of the meeting by a number of prominent leaders within the Assembly of First Nations, including the Assembly of Manitoba Chiefs, which represents sixty-four First Nations in the province of Manitoba.[42] Chief Spence also declined to attend the meeting as well as break with her hunger strike.

Native anger and frustration in the immediate lead-up to the January 11 gathering resulted in a call among some Idle No More supporters for an escalation in land-based direct action, including by Grand Chief Derek Nepinak of the Assembly of Manitoba Chiefs: "The Idle No More movement has the people," warned Nepinak at a January 10 press conference, "it has the people and the numbers that can bring the Canadian economy to its knees. . . . We have the warriors that are standing up now that are willing to go that far."[43] Apparently many activists shared Chief Nepinak's sentiment, and on January 16 another national day of action was called, this time focusing on more assertive forms of Indigenous protest. Actions including rallies, railway blockades, and traffic stoppages swept across the country, including railway barricades erected in Manitoba, Ontario, and British Columbia; highway and bridge stoppages in British Columbia, Ontario, New Brunswick, and Alberta; as well as the now regular display of marches, flash-mob round-dances, drumming, and prayer circles.[44]

By the last week in January media speculation was beginning to circulate about the possibility of Chief Spence ending her hunger strike after securing a "Declaration of Commitment" by the executive committee of the Assembly of First Nations, the Native Women's Association of Canada, and the caucuses of two of Canada's federal opposition parties, the New Democrats and the Liberals. On January 23 it was confirmed that Chief Spence (along with Raymond Robinson of Cross Lake, Manitoba, who was also on a hunger strike) would be ending her strike the following day. The "Declaration of Commitment" that ended the two hunger strikes was the culmination of a week's worth of negotiations led by Native leader Alvin Fiddler and interim Liberal Party leader Bob Rae. Among the thirteen points of the declaration is a call for a "national inquiry" into the hundreds of cases of murdered and missing Aboriginal women that have gone unsolved in Canada; improving Aboriginal education and housing; fully implementing the United Nations Declaration on the Rights of Indigenous Peoples; reform of the federal government's comprehensive lands claims policy; the establishment of an implementation framework for First Nations' treaty rights; and, of course, a comprehensive review of Bill C-45, undertaken with meaningful consultation with Aboriginal peoples.[45]

As I was a close observer of the movement in general and a regular participant in the Idle No More events and teach-ins in the Vancouver area in particular, by late January it had become clear to me that a relative decline in Idle

No More's more overt and thus publically conspicuous forms of protest was underway. Somewhat predictably, this was interpreted by many outlets of Canada's corporate media as a decline in the movement itself. In newspeak, Idle No More had "lost its legs." At that time, I sensed that a moment of pause and critical reflection was underway, yes, but this should not be interpreted as a deterioration of the movement's spirit and resolve. Prime Minister Stephen Harper has stated that, despite the outcry of informed concerns emanating from Indigenous communities and their allies through spring 2013, Bill C-45 is not up for negotiation. Business, in other words, will proceed as usual. As long as the land remains in jeopardy, supporters of movements like Idle No More will continue the struggle. "We're in this for the long haul," explains Pamela Palmater. "It was never meant to be a flashy one month, then go away. This is something that's years in the making. . . . You'll see it take different forms at different times, but it's not going away anytime soon."[46] Indeed, the recent escalation and increased public visibility of Indigenous anti-fracking protests in places like Elsipogtog, New Brunswick, along with the ongoing anti–oil sands activism led by Native communities in northern Alberta, and the unrelenting antipipeline campaigns mounted by First Nations communities across British Columbia, are a clear demonstration of Indigenous peoples' continued resolve to defend their land and sovereignty from further encroachments by state and capital.

FIVE THESES ON INDIGENOUS RESURGENCE AND DECOLONIZATION

As a conclusion to this study I want to critically reflect on the Idle No More movement in light of what we have discussed up to this point. With this as my aim, I will organize my thoughts around five theses on Indigenous resurgence. These theses are not meant to be overly prescriptive or conclusive. Instead I propose them with the aim of both consolidating and contributing to the constructive debates and critical conversations that have already animated the movement to date. They also indicate areas where future research is required.

Thesis 1: On the Necessity of Direct Action

I am going to structure my comments on direct action around a discursive restraint that has increasingly been placed on movements like Idle No More (both from within and from without) since the debates that emerged leading into the January 11 meeting with Prime Minister Harper and the January 16 national day of action. This constraint involves the type of tactics that are being represented as morally legitimate in our efforts to defend our land and rights as Indigenous peoples, on the one hand, and those that are increasingly being presented as either morally illegitimate or at least politically self-defeating because of their disruptive, extralegal, and therefore potentially alienating character, on the other hand.

With respect to those approaches deemed "legitimate" in defending our rights, emphasis is usually placed on formal "negotiations"—usually carried out between "official" Aboriginal leadership and representatives of the state—and if need be coupled with largely symbolic acts of peaceful, nondisruptive protest that abide by Canada's "rule of law." Those approaches that are increasingly deemed "illegitimate" include, but are not limited to, forms of "direct action" that seek to influence power through less mediated and sometimes more disruptive and confrontational measures. In the context of Indigenous peoples' struggles, the forms of "direct action" often taken to be problematic include activities like temporarily blocking access to Indigenous territories with the aim of impeding the exploitation of Indigenous peoples' land and resources, or in rarer cases still, the more-or-less permanent reoccupation of a portion of Native land through the establishment of a reclamation site which also serves to disrupt, if not entirely block, access to Indigenous peoples' territories by state and capital for sustained periods of time. Even though these actions may be oriented toward gaining some solid commitment by the state to curtail its colonial activities, I think that they still ought to be considered "direct action" for three reasons: first, the practices are directly undertaken by the subjects of colonial oppression themselves and seek to produce an immediate power effect; second, they are undertaken in a way that indicates a loosening of internalized colonialism, which is itself a precondition for any meaningful change; and third, they are prefigurative in the sense that they build the skills and social relationships (including those with the land) that are required within and among Indigenous communities to construct alternatives to the colonial relationship in the long run. Regardless of their diversity and specificity, however, most of these actions tend to get branded in the media as the typical Native "blockade." Militant, threatening, disruptive, and violent.

The following positions are typical of those that emerged in the wake of the January 11 meeting regarding use of these direct action tactics to defend

Indigenous peoples' land and interests. The first position is drawn from a statement made by the former national chief of the Assembly of First Nations, Ovide Mercredi, at an Aboriginal leadership gathering in the spring of 2013. In his speech Mercredi boldly stated that it is "only through talk, not through blockades that [real] progress will be made."[47] The assumption here, of course, is that the most productive means to forge lasting change in the lives of Indigenous people and communities is through the formal channels of negotiation. The second example is slightly more predictable. It is drawn from a statement made by Prime Minister Stephen Harper: "People have the right in our country to demonstrate and express their points of view peacefully as long as they obey the law, but I think the Canadian population expects everyone will obey the law in holding such protests."[48]

There are three arguments that typically get used when critics rail against the use of more assertive forms of Indigenous protest actions. The first is the one clearly articulated by Mecredi in the statement I just quoted: negotiations are, objectively speaking, simply more effective in securing the rights and advancing the interests of Indigenous communities. This is simply false. Historically, I would venture to suggest that all negotiations over the scope and content of Aboriginal peoples' rights in the last forty years have piggybacked off the assertive direct actions—including the escalated use of blockades—spearheaded by Indigenous women and other grassroots elements of our communities. For example, there would likely have been *no* negotiations over Aboriginal rights and title in British Columbia through the current land claims process (as problematic as it is) if it were not for the ongoing commitment of Indigenous activists willing to put their bodies on the line in defense of their lands and communities. There would have likely been *no* Royal Commission on Aboriginal Peoples without the land-based direct actions of the Innu in Labrador, the Lubicon Cree in Alberta, the Algonquin of Barrier Lake, the Mohawks of Kanesatake and Kahnawake, the Haida of Haida Gwaii, the Anishanaabe of Temagami, and the countless other Indigenous communities across Canada that have put themselves directly in harm's way in the defense of their lands and distinct ways of life. Likewise, there would have likely been *no* provincial inquiry (there has yet to be a national one) into the shameful number of murdered and missing Indigenous women in Vancouver and across the province if it were not for the thousands of Native women and their allies who have formed lasting networks of mutual care and support and taken to the streets every year on February 14 for more than two decades to ensure that state-sanctioned sexual violence against Indigenous women ends here and now. All of this is to say that if there has been any progress in securing our rights to land and life—including through the largely male-dominated world of formal negotiations—this progress is owed to the courageous activists practicing their obligations to the land and to each other in these diverse networks and communities of struggle.

The second argument that gets used to denounce or criticize more "disruptive" forms of Indigenous direct action involve these actions' supposedly "self-defeating" or "alienating" character.[49] The idea this time is that insofar as these tactics disrupt the lives of perhaps well-intentioned but equally uninformed non-Indigenous people, First Nations will increasingly find themselves alienated and our causes unsupported by average, working-class Canadians. I have two brief points to make here.

First, I think that getting this reaction from the dominant society is unavoidable. Indigenous people have within their sights, now more than ever, a restructuring of the fundamental relationship between Indigenous nations and Canada. For more than two centuries the manifestations of this relationship have run roughshod over the rights of Indigenous peoples, which has resulted in a massive stockpiling of power and privilege by and for the dominant society. Land has been stolen, and significant amounts of it must be returned. Power and authority have been unjustly appropriated, and much of it will have to be reinstated. This will inevitably be very upsetting to some; it will be incredibly inconvenient to others. But it is what needs to happen if we are to create a more just and sustainable life in this country for the bulk of Indigenous communities, and for the majority of non-Indigenous people as well. To my mind, the apparent fact that many non-Indigenous people are "upset" or feel "alienated" by the aims of decolonization movements like Idle No More simply means that we are collectively doing something right.

My second point is that this criticism or concern smells of a double standard. I suspect that equally "disruptive" actions undertaken by various sectors of, for example, the mainstream labor movement, including job actions ranging from the withdrawal of teaching, transit, and healthcare services to full-blown strike activity, does not often undergo the same criticism and scrutiny by progressive non-Natives that Indigenous peoples' movements are subjected to.

When these sectors of society courageously defend their rights outside of the increasingly hostile confines of imposed labor legislation—actions that also tend to disproportionately "disrupt" the lives of ordinary Canadians—it is crucial that we educate ourselves about the causes that inform these efforts. All Indigenous people ask is that the same courtesy and respect be offered our communities in our struggles.

The third critique involves what we might characterize as a neo-Nietzschean concern over the largely *reactive* stance that such acts of resistance take in practice. On the surface, blockades in particular appear to be the epitome of *reaction* insofar as they clearly embody a resounding "no" but fail to offer a more *affirmative* gesture or alternative built into the practice itself. The risk here is that, in doing so, these *ressentiment*-laden modalities of Indigenous resistance reify the very structures or social relationships we find so abhorrent. In Nietzsche's terms, insofar as this "No" becomes our "creative deed" we end up dependent on the "hostile world" we have come to define ourselves *against*.[50] We become dependent on "external stimuli to act at all—[our] action is fundamentally *reaction*."[51]

This concern, I claim, is premised on a fundamental misunderstanding of what these forms of direct action are all about. In his own creative engagement with Nietzsche at the end of *Black Skin, White Masks*, Frantz Fanon exclaims that, yes, "man is an *affirmation*. . . and that we shall not stop repeating it. Yes to life. Yes to love. Yes to generosity." "But man," he continues on to insist, "is also a *negation*. No to man's contempt. No to the indignity of man. To the exploitation of man. To the massacre of what is most human in man: freedom."[52] Forms of Indigenous resistance, such as blockading and other explicitly disruptive oppositional practices, are indeed *reactive* in the ways that some have critiqued, but they are also very important. Through these actions we physically say "no" to the degradation of our communities and to exploitation of the lands upon which we depend. But they also have ingrained within in them a resounding "yes": they are the affirmative *enactment* of another modality of being, a different way of relating to and with the world. In the case of blockades like the one erected by the Anishinaabe people of Grassy Narrows in northwest Ontario, which has been in existence since 2002, they become a *way of life*, another form of *community*. They embody through praxis our ancestral obligations to protect the lands that are core to who we are as Indigenous peoples.

Thesis 2: Capitalism, No More!

What the recent direct actions of First Nation communities like Elsipogtog in New Brunswick demonstrate is that Indigenous forms of economic disruption through the use of blockades are both a negation and an *affirmation*.[53] They are a crucial act of negation insofar as they seek to impede or block the flow of resources currently being transported to international markets from oil and gas fields, refineries, lumber mills, mining operations, and hydroelectric facilities located on the dispossessed lands of Indigenous nations. These modes of direct action, in other words, seek to have a negative impact on the economic infrastructure that is core to the colonial accumulation of capital in settler-political economies like Canada's.[54] Blocking access to this critical infrastructure has historically been quite effective in forging short-term gains for Indigenous communities. Over the last couple of decades, however, state and corporate powers have also become quite skilled at recuperating the losses incurred as a result of Indigenous peoples' resistance by drawing our leaders off the land and into negotiations where the terms are always set by and in the interests of settler capital.

What tends to get ignored by many self-styled pundits is that these actions are also an affirmative gesture of Indigenous resurgence insofar as they embody an enactment of Indigenous law and the obligations such laws place on Indigenous peoples to uphold the relations of reciprocity that shape our engagements with the human and nonhuman world—the land. The question I want to explore here, albeit very briefly, is this: how might we begin to scale up these often localized, resurgent land-based direct actions to produce a more general transformation in the colonial economy? Said slightly differently, how might we move beyond a resurgent Indigenous politics that seeks to inhibit the destructive effects of capital to one that strives to create *Indigenous alternatives* to it?

In her recent interview with Naomi Klein, Leanne Simpson hints at what such an alternative or alternatives might entail for Indigenous nations: "People within the Idle No More movement who are talking about Indigenous nationhood are talking about a massive transformation, a massive decolonization"; they are calling for a "resurgence of Indigenous political thought" that is "land-based and very much tied to that intimate and close relationship to the land, which to me means a revitalization of sustainable local Indigenous economies."[55]

Without such a massive transformation in the political economy of contemporary settler-colonialism, any efforts to rebuild our nations will remain parasitic on capitalism, and thus on the perpetual exploitation of our lands and labor. Consider, for example, an approach to resurgence that would see Indigenous people begin to reconnect with their lands and land-based practices on either an individual or small-scale collective basis. This could take the form of "walking the land" in an effort to refamiliarize ourselves with the landscapes and places that give our histories, languages, and cultures shape and content; to revitalizing and engaging in land-based harvesting practices like hunting, fishing, and gathering, and/or cultural production activities like hide-tanning and carving, all of which also serve to assert our sovereign presence on our territories in ways that can be profoundly educational and empowering; to the reoccupation of sacred places for the purposes of relearning and practicing our ceremonial activities.

A similar problem informs self-determination efforts that seek to ameliorate our poverty and economic dependency through resource revenue sharing, more comprehensive impact benefit agreements, and affirmative action employment strategies negotiated through the state and with industries currently tearing up Indigenous territories. Even though the capital generated by such an approach could, in theory, be spent subsidizing the revitalization of certain cultural traditions and practices, in the end they would still remain dependent on a predatory economy that is entirely at odds with the deep reciprocity that forms the cultural core of many Indigenous peoples' relationships with land.

What forms might an Indigenous political-economic alternative to the intensification of capitalism on and within our territories take? For some communities, reinvigorating a mix of subsistence-based activities with more contemporary economic ventures is one alternative.[56] As discussed in chapter 2, in the 1970s the Dene Nation sought to curtail the negative environmental and cultural impacts of capitalist extractivism by proposing to establish an economy that would apply traditional concepts of Dene governance—decentralized, regional political structures based on participatory, consensus decision-making—to the realm of the economy. At the time, this would have seen a revitalization of a bush mode of production, with emphasis placed on the harvesting and manufacturing of local renewable resources through traditional activities like hunting, fishing, and trapping, potentially combined with and partially subsidized by other economic activities on lands communally held and managed by the Dene Nation. Economic models discussed during the time thus included the democratic organization of production and distribution through Indigenous cooperatives and possibly worker-managed enterprises.[57]

Revisiting Indigenous political-economic alternatives such as these could pose a real threat to the accumulation of capital on Indigenous lands in three ways. First, through mentorship and education these economies reconnect Indigenous people to land-based practices and forms of knowledge that emphasize radical sustainability. This form of grounded normativity is antithetical to capitalist accumulation. Second, these economic practices offer a means of subsistence that over time can help break our dependence on the capitalist market by cultivating self-sufficiency through the localized and sustainable production of core foods and life materials that we distribute and consume within our own communities on a regular basis. Third, through the application of Indigenous governance principles to nontraditional economic activities we open up a way of engaging in contemporary economic ventures in an Indigenous way that is better suited to foster sustainable economic decision-making, an equitable distribution of resources within and between Indigenous communities, Native women's political and economic emancipation, and empowerment for Indigenous citizens and workers who may or must pursue livelihoods in sectors of the economy outside of the bush. Why not critically apply the most egalitarian and participatory features of our traditional governance practices to all of our economic activities, regardless of whether they are undertaken in land-based or urban contexts?

The capacity of resurgent Indigenous economies to challenge the hegemony of settler-colonial capitalism in the long term can only happen if certain conditions are met, however. First, all of the colonial, racist, and patriarchal legal and political obstacles that have been used to block our access to land need to be confronted and removed.[58] Of course, capitalism continues to play a core role in dispossessing us of our lands and self-determining authority, but it only does so with the aid of other forms of exploitation and domination configured along racial, gender, and state lines. Dismantling all of these oppressive structures will not be easy. It will require that we continue to assert our presence on all of our territories, coupled with an escalation of confrontations with the forces of colonization through the forms of direct action that are currently being undertaken by communities like Elsipogtog.

Second, we also have to acknowledge that the significant political leverage required to simultaneously block the economic exploitation of our people and homelands while constructing alternatives to capitalism will not be generated through our direct actions and resurgent economies alone. Settler colonization has rendered our populations too small to affect this magnitude of change. This reality demands that we continue to remain open to, if not actively seek out and establish, relations of solidarity and networks of trade and mutual aid with national and transnational communities and organizations that are also struggling against the imposed effects of globalized capital, including other Indigenous nations and national confederacies; urban Indigenous people and organizations; the labor, women's, GBLTQ2S (gay, bisexual, lesbian, trans, queer, and two-spirit), and environmental movements; and, of course, those racial and ethnic communities that find themselves subject to their own distinct forms of economic, social, and cultural marginalization. The initially rapid and relatively widespread support expressed both nationally and internationally for the Idle No More movement in spring 2013, and the solidarity generated around the Elsipogtog antifracking resistance in the fall and winter of 2013, gives me hope that establishing such relations are indeed possible.

It is time for our communities to seize the unique political opportunities of the day. In the delicate balancing act of having to ensure that his social conservative contempt for First Nations does not overwhelm his neoconservative love of the market, Prime Minister Harper has erred by letting the racism and sexism of the former outstrip his belligerent commitment to the latter. This is a novice mistake that Liberals like Jean Chrétien and Paul Martin learned how to manage decades ago. As a result, the federal government has invigorated a struggle for Indigenous self-determination that must challenge the relationship between settler colonization and free-market fundamentalism in ways that refuse to be coopted by scraps of recognition, opportunistic apologies, and the cheap gift of political and economic inclusion. For Indigenous nations to live, capitalism must die. And for capitalism to die, we must actively participate in the construction of Indigenous alternatives to it.

Thesis 3: Dispossession and Indigenous Sovereignty in the City

In Canada, more than half of the Aboriginal population now lives in urban centers.[59] The relationship between Indigenous people and the city, however, has always been one fraught with tension. Historically, Canadian cities were originally conceived of in the colonial imagination as explicitly non-Native spaces—as *civilized* spaces—and urban planners and Indian policy makers went through great efforts to expunge urban centers of Native presence.[60] In 1911, for example, Prime Minister Wilfrid Laurier announced in Parliament that "where a reserve is in the vicinity of a growing town, as is the case in several places, it becomes a source of nuisance and an impediment to progress."[61] This developmentalist rationale, which at the time conceived of Native space, particularly reserves, as uncultivated "waste" lands, justified an amendment to the Indian Act a month later, which stipulated that the residents of any "Indian reserve which adjoins or is situated wholly or partly within an incorporated town having a population of not less than eight thousand" could be legally removed from their present location without their consent if it was deemed in the "interest of the public and of the Indians of the band for whose use the reserve is held."[62] This situated Indian policy in a precarious position, as by the turn of the nineteenth century the reserve system, originally implemented to isolate and marginalize Native people for the purpose of social engineering (assimilation), was increasingly being seen as a failure because of the geographical distance of reserves from the civilizational influence of urban centers.[63] Here you have the economic imperatives of capitalist accumulation through the dispossession of Indigenous peoples' land come into sharp conflict with the white supremacist impulses of Canada's assimilation policy and the desire of settler society to claim "the city for themselves—and only themselves."[64]

The civilizational discourse that rationalized both the theft of Indigenous peoples' land base and their subsequent confinement onto reserves facilitated a significant geographical separation of the colonizer and the colonized that lasted until the mid-twentieth century.[65] As Sherene Razack notes, the segregation of urban from Native space that marked the colonial era began to break down with the increase in urbanization that took hold in the 1950s and 1960s, which resulted in a new racial configuration of space. Within this new colonial spatial imaginary,

> The city belongs to the settlers and the sullying of civilized society through the presence of the racialized Other in white spaces gives rise to a careful management of boundaries within urban space. Planning authorities require larger plots in the suburbs, thereby ensuring that larger homes and wealthier families live there. Projects and Chinatowns are created, cordoning off the racial poor.

Such spatial practices, often achieved through law (nuisance laws, zoning laws, and so on), mark off the spaces of the settler and the native both conceptually and materially. The inner city is racialized space, the zone in which all that is not respectable is contained. Canada's colonial geographies exhibit this same pattern of violent expulsions and the spatial containment of Aboriginal peoples to marginalized areas of the city, processes consolidated over three hundred years of colonization.[66]

The dispossession that originally displaced Indigenous peoples from their traditional territories either onto reserves or disproportionally into the inner cities of Canada's major urban centers is now serving to displace Indigenous populations from the urban spaces they have increasingly come to call home. To this end, I suggest that the analytical frame of *settler-colonialism* developed throughout the previous chapters offers an important lens through which to interrogate the power relations that shape Indigenous people's experiences in the city, especially those disproportionately inhabiting low-income areas. As we learned in previous chapters, defenders of settler-colonial power have tended to rationalize these practices by treating the lands in question as *terra nullius*—the racist legal fiction that declared Indigenous peoples too "primitive" to bear rights to land and sovereignty when they first encountered European powers on the continent, thus rendering their territories legally "empty" and therefore open for colonial settlement and development.

In the inner cities of Vancouver, Winnipeg, Regina, Toronto, and so forth, we are seeing a similar logic govern the gentrification and subsequent displacement of Indigenous peoples from Native spaces within the city. Commonly defined as the transformation of working-class areas of the city into middle-class residential or commercial spaces, gentrification is usually accompanied by the displacement of low-income, racialized, Indigenous, and other marginalized segments of the urban population.[67] Regardless of these violent effects, however, gentrifiers often defend their development projects as a form of "improvement," where previously "wasted" land or property (rooming houses, social housing, shelters, small businesses that cater to the community, etc.) and lives (sex-trade workers, homeless people, the working poor, mentally ill people, those suffering from addictions, etc.) are made more socially and economically productive. This Lockean rationale has led scholars like Neil Smith, Nicholas Blomley, and Amber Dean to view the gentrification of urban space through a colonial lens, as yet another "frontier" of dispossession central to the accumulation of capital.[68] Through gentrification, Native spaces in the city are now being treated as *urbs nullius*—urban space void of Indigenous sovereign presence.

All of this is to say that the efficacy of Indigenous resurgence hinges on its ability to address the interrelated systems of dispossession that shape Indigenous peoples' experiences in *both* urban and land-based settings. Mi'kmaq scholar Bonita Lawrence suggests that this will require a concerted effort on the part of both reserve- and urban-based Indigenous communities to reconceptualize Indigenous identity and nationhood in a way that refuses to replicate the "colonial divisions" that contributed to the urban/reserve divide through racist and sexist policies like enfranchisement.[69] Although Lawrence's work has shown how Native individuals, families, and communities are able to creatively retain and reproduce Indigenous traditions in urban settings, she also recognizes the importance for urban Native people to have "some form of mutually agreed upon, structured access to land-based communities."[70] Access to land is essential.

Similar struggles are seen in land-based communities, which would no doubt benefit from the numbers and human capital offered through the forging of political relations and alliances with the over 50 percent of Indigenous people now living in cities.[71] For Lawrence, all of this suggests that urban Native people and First Nations need ways of forging national alliances strategically in a manner that does not demand that First Nation governments endlessly open their membership to those who grew up disconnected from the life and culture of their original communities, or urban Indigenous people having to engage in the arduous struggle of maintaining an Indigenous identity cut off from the communities and homelands that ground such identities.[72] In other words, we need to find ways of bringing together through relations of solidarity and mutual aid "the strengths that urban and reserve-based Native people have developed in their different circumstances, in the interests of our mutual empowerment."[73]

Thesis 4: Gender Justice and Decolonization

According to Anishinaabe feminist Dory Nason, if Idle No More showed us anything, it is the "boundless love that Indigenous women have for their families, their lands, their nations, and themselves as Indigenous people."

This love has encouraged Indigenous women everywhere "to resist and protest, to teach and inspire, and to hold accountable both Indigenous and non-Indigenous allies to their responsibilities to protect the values and traditions that serve as the foundation for the survival of the land and Indigenous peoples." Nason is also quick to point out, however, that the same inspirational power of Indigenous women's love to mobilize others to resist "settler-colonial misogyny's" inherently destructive tendencies has also rendered them subjects of "epidemic levels of violence, sexual assault, imprisonment and cultural and political disempowerment."[74]

The violence that Indigenous women face is both systemic and symbolic. It is systemic in the sense that it has been structured, indeed institutionalized, into a relatively secure and resistant set of oppressive material relations that render Indigenous women more likely than their non-Indigenous counterparts to suffer severe economic and social privation, including disproportionately high rates of poverty and unemployment, incarceration, addiction, homelessness, chronic and/or life-threatening health problems, overcrowded and substandard housing, and lack of access to clean water, as well as face discrimination and sexual violence in their homes, communities, and workplaces.[75] Just as importantly, however, the violence that Indigenous women face is also "symbolic" in the sense that Pierre Bourdieu used the term: "gentle, invisible violence, unrecognized as such, chosen as much as undergone."[76] Symbolic violence, in other words, is the subjectifying form of violence that renders the crushing materiality of systemic violence invisible, appear natural, acceptable.

As we saw in chapter 3, the symbolic violence of settler-colonial misogyny, institutionalized through residential schools and successive Indian Acts, has become so diffuse that it now saturates all of our relationships. The misogyny of settler-colonial misrecognition through state legislation, writes Bonita Lawrence, "has functioned so completely—and yet so invisibly—along gendered lines" that it now informs many of our struggles for recognition and liberation.[77] In such contexts, what does it mean to be "held accountable" to our "responsibilities to protect the values and traditions that serve as the foundation for the survival of the land and Indigenous peoples"? To start, it demands that Indigenous people, in particular Native men, commit ourselves *in practice* to uprooting the symbolic violence that structures Indigenous women's lives as much as we demand *in words* that the material violence against Indigenous women come to an end. This is what I take Nason to mean when she asks that all of us "think about what it means for men, on the one hand, to publicly profess an obligation to 'protect our women' and, on the other, take leadership positions that uphold patriarchal forms of governance or otherwise ignore the contributions and sovereignty of the women, Indigenous or not."[78] Here, the paternalistic and patriarchal insistence that we "protect *our* women" from the material violence they disproportionately face serves to reinforce the symbolic violence of assuming that Indigenous women are "ours" to protect. Although many Native male supporters of Idle No More have done a fairly decent job symbolically recognizing the centrality of Indigenous women to the movement, this is not the recognition that I hear being demanded by Indigenous feminists. The demand, rather, is that society, including Indigenous society and particularly Indigenous men, stop collectively *conducting ourselves* in a manner that denigrates, degrades, and devalues the lives and worth of Indigenous women in such a way that epidemic levels of violence are the norm in too many of their lives. Of course, this violence must be stopped in its overt forms, but we must also stop practicing it in its more subtle expressions—in our daily relationships and practices in the home, workplaces, band offices, governance institutions, and, crucially, in our practices of *cultural resurgence*. Until this happens we have reconciled ourselves with defeat.

Thesis 5: Beyond the Nation-State

We are now in a position to revisit the concern I raised at the end of chapter 1 regarding a problematic claim made by Dale Turner in *This Is Not a Peace Pipe*. Turner's claim is that if Indigenous peoples want the political and legal relationship between ourselves and the Canadian state to be informed by and reflect our distinct worldviews, then we "will have to engage the state's legal and political discourses in more effective ways."[79] This form of engagement, I claimed, assumes that the structure of domination that frames Indigenous–state relations in Canada derives its legitimacy and sustenance by excluding Indigenous people and voices from the legal and political institutional/discursive settings within which our rights are determined. Seen from this light, it would indeed appear that "critically undermining colonialism" requires that Indigenous peoples find more effective ways of "participating in the Canadian legal and political practices that determine the meaning of Aboriginal rights."[80]

Yet, I would venture to suggest that over the last forty years Indigenous peoples have become incredibly skilled at participating in the Canadian legal and political practices that Turner suggests. In the wake of the 1969 White Paper, these practices emerged as the *hegemonic* approach to forging change in our political relationship with the Canadian state. We have also seen, however, that our efforts to engage these discursive and institutional spaces to secure recognition of our rights have not only failed, but have instead served to subtly reproduce the forms of racist, sexist, economic, and political configurations of power that we initially sought, through our engagements and negotiations with the state, to challenge. Why has this been the case? Part of the reason has to do with the sheer magnitude of discursive and nondiscursive power we find ourselves up against in our struggles. Subsequently, in our efforts to *interpolate* the legal and political discourses of the state to secure recognition of our rights to land and self-determination we have too often found ourselves *interpellated* as subjects of settler-colonial rule.

What are the implications of this profound power disparity in our struggles for land and freedom? Does it require that we vacate the field of state negotiations and participation entirely? Of course not. Settler-colonialism has rendered us a radical minority in our own homelands, and this necessitates that we continue to engage with the state's legal and political system. What our present condition does demand, however, is that we begin to approach our engagements with the settler-state legal apparatus with a degree of critical self-reflection, skepticism, and caution that has to date been largely absent in our efforts. It also demands that we begin to shift our attention away from the largely rights-based/recognition orientation that has emerged as hegemonic over the last four decades, to a resurgent politics of recognition that seeks to practice decolonial, gender-emancipatory, and economically nonexploitative alternative structures of law and sovereign authority grounded on a critical refashioning of the best of Indigenous legal and political traditions. It is only by privileging and grounding ourselves in these normative lifeways and resurgent practices that we have a hope of surviving our strategic engagements with the colonial state with integrity and as Indigenous peoples.

NOTES

INTRODUCTION

1. When deployed in the Canadian context, I use the terms "Indigenous," "Aboriginal," and "Native" interchangeably to refer to the descendants of those who traditionally occupied the territory now known as Canada before the arrival of European settlers and state powers. At a more general level I also use these terms in an international context to refer to the non-Western societies that have suffered under the weight of European colonialism. I use the specific terms "Indian" and "First Nation" to refer to those legally recognized as Indians under the Canadian federal government's Indian Act of 1876 (unless indicated otherwise).

2. Dene Nation, "Dene Declaration," in *Dene Nation: The Colony Within*, ed. Mel Watkins (Toronto: University of Toronto Press, 1977), 3–4 (emphasis added).

3. Assembly of First Nations (AFN), *Our Nations, Our Governments: Choosing our Own Paths* (Ottawa: Assembly of First Nations, 2005), 18.

4. Ibid., 18–19. The Royal Commission on Aboriginal Peoples (RCAP) was established by the federal government in 1991 to investigate the social, cultural, political, and economic impact of the colonial relationship between Aboriginal peoples and the state in Canada. The commission culminated in a five-volume *Final Report*, which was published in 1996. The RCAP report will be examined in detail in chapter 4.

5. For discussion, see Michael Murphy, "Culture and the Courts: A New Direct in Canadian Aboriginal Rights Jurisprudence?," *Canadian Journal of Political Science* 34, no. 1 (2001): 109–29; Murphy, "The Limits of Culture in the Politics of Self-Determination," *Ethnicities* 1, no. 3 (2001): 367–88.

6. Department of Indian Affairs and Northern Development (DIAND), *The Government of Canada's Approach to Implementation of the Inherent Right and the Negotiation of Aboriginal Self-Government* (Ottawa: Published by the Department of Indian Affairs and Northern Development, 1995).

7. Will Kymlicka, *Multicultural Odysseys: Navigating the New International Politics of Diversity* (Don Mills, Ont.: Oxford University Press, 2007); Sheryl Lightfoot, "Indigenous Rights in International Politics: The Case of 'Overcompliant' Liberal States,"

Alternatives: Global Local Political 33, no. 1 (2008): 83–104; Ronald Niezen, *The Origins of Indigenism: Human Rights and the Politics of Identity* (Berkeley: University of California Press, 2003); James (Sa'ke'j) Henderson, *Indigenous Diplomacy and the Rights of Indigenous Peoples: Achieving UN Recognition* (Saskatoon: Purich Publishing, 2008).

8. Alan Cairns makes the argument that recognition politics have required the state to reconceptualize the relationship with Indigenous peoples; see his *Citizens Plus: Aboriginal Peoples and the Canadian State* (Vancouver: University of British Columbia Press, 2000); and *First Nations and the Canadian State: In Search of Coexistence* (Kingston, Ont.: Institute of Intergovernmental Relations, 2005). The language of "mutual recognition" is used explicitly in RCAP, *Report of the Royal Commission on Aboriginal Peoples*, 5 vols. (Ottawa: Minister of Supply and Services, 1996); Department of Indian Affairs and Northern Development, *Gathering Strength: Canada's Aboriginal Action Plan* (Ottawa: Published under the authority of the Minister of Indian Affairs and Northern Development, 1997); *A First Nations–Federal Crown Political Accord on the Recognition and Implementation of First Nation Governments* (Ottawa: Published under the authority of the Minister of Indian Affairs and Northern Development, 2005). For a more substantive, postcolonial articulation, see James Tully, *Strange Multiplicity: Constitutionalism in the Age of Diversity* (New York: Cambridge University Press, 1995).

9. Richard J. F. Day, *Multiculturalism and the History of Canadian Diversity* (Toronto: University of Toronto Press, 2000). Also see Richard Day and Tonio Sadik, "The BC Land Question, Liberal Multiculturalism, and the Spectre of Aboriginal Nationhood," *BC Studies* 134 (Summer 2002): 5–34. The following writings provide a sample of the more influential works in the diverse field of recognition-based approaches to liberal pluralism: Charles Taylor, "The Politics of Recognition," in *Re-Examining the Politics of Recognition*, ed. Amy Gutmann, 27–73 (Princeton: Princeton University Press, 1994); Will Kymlicka, *Multicultural Citizenship: A Liberal Theory of Minority Rights* (Don Mills, Ont.: Oxford University Press, 1995); Kymlicka, *Finding Our Way: Rethinking Ethnocultural Relations in Canada* (Don Mills, Ont.: Oxford University Press, 1998); Kymlicka, *Politics in the Vernacular: Nationalism, Multiculturalism, and Citizenship* (Don Mills, Ont.: Oxford University Press, 2001); Kymlicka, *Multicultural Odyssey*; Tully, *Strange Multiplicity*; Patrick Macklem, *Indigenous Difference and the Constitution of Canada* (Toronto: University of Toronto Press, 2001); RCAP, *Report of the Royal Commission on Aboriginal Peoples*; Keith Banting, Thomas Courchene, and F. Leslie Seidle, eds., *The Art of the State*, vol. 3, *Belonging? Diversity, Recognition and Shared Citizenship in Canada* (Kingston, Ont.: Institute for Research on Public Policy, 2007); Siobhán Harty and Michael Murphy, *In Defence of Multinational Citizenship* (Vancouver: University of British Columbia Press, 2005).

10. Department of Indian Affairs and Northern Development, *Statement of the Government of Canada on Indian Policy* (Ottawa: Department of Indian Affairs and Northern Development, 1969). For an authoritative analysis of the philosophical underpinnings of the 1969 White Paper, see Dale Turner, *This Is Not a Peace Pipe: Towards a Critical Indigenous Philosophy* (Toronto: University of Toronto Press, 2007).

11. For a history of this period, see John Tobias, "Protection, Assimilation, Civilization," in *Sweet Promises: A History of Indian-White Relations in Canada*, ed. J. R. Miller, 127–44 (Toronto: University of Toronto Press, 1991); RCAP, *Report of the Royal Commission on Aboriginal Peoples*, vol. 1.

12. J. R. Miller, *Shingwauk's Vision: A History of Indian Residential Schools* (Toronto: University of Toronto Press, 1996). This book provides an authoritative history of residential schools in Canada.

13. Sarah Carter, *Lost Harvests: Prairie Indian Reserve Farmers and Government Policy* (Montreal: McGill-Queen's University Press, 1993); Helen Buckley, *From Wooden Ploughs to Welfare: Why Indian Policy Failed the Prairie Provinces* (Montreal: McGill-Queen's University Press, 1992).

14. Bonita Lawrence, "Gender, Race and the Regulation of Native Identity in Canada and the United States," *Hypatia* 18, no. 2 (2003): 3–31; Lawrence, *"Real" Indians and Others: Mixed-Blood Urban Native Peoples and Indigenous Nationhood* (Vancouver: University of British Columbia Press, 2005).

15. Christopher Walmsley, *Protecting Aboriginal Children* (Vancouver: University of British Columbia Press, 2005).

16. On settler-colonialism and the "logic of elimination," see Patrick Wolfe, "Settler Colonialism and the Elimination of the Native," *Journal of Genocide Studies* 8, no. 4 (2006): 387–409.

17. "Statement of the National Indian Brotherhood," in *Recent Statements by the Indians of Canada*, Anglican Church of Canada General Synod Action 1969, Bulletin 201, 1970, 28, quoted in Olive Patricia Dickason, *Canada's First Nations: A History of Founding Peoples from Earliest Times* (Toronto: McClelland and Stewart, 1992), 386.

18. Sally Weaver, cited in Leonard Rotman, *Parallel Paths: Fiduciary Doctrine and the Crown-Native Relationship in Canada* (Toronto: University of Toronto Press, 1996), 7.

19. Dickason, *Canada's First Nations*, 388.

20. *Calder et al. v. Attorney-General of British Columbia* (1973).

21. *St Catherine's Milling and Lumber Company v. The Queen* (1888).

22. For an excellent discussion of the *Calder* case and its influence, see Michael Asch, "From 'Calder' to 'Van der Peet': Aboriginal Rights and Canadian Law, 1973–96", in *Indigenous Peoples' Rights in Australia, Canada and New Zealand*, ed. Paul Havemann, 428–46 (New York: Oxford University Press, 1999).

23. Ibid., 430–32.

24. Department of Indian Affairs and Northern Development, *Statement on Claims of Indian and Inuit People: A Federal Native Claims Policy* (Ottawa: Department of Indian Affairs and Northern Development), 1973.

25. Francis Abele, Katherine Graham, and Allan Maslove, "Negotiating Canada: Changes in Aboriginal Policy over the Last Thirty Years," in *How Ottawa Spends, 1999–2000*, ed. Leslie Pal (Don Mills, Ont.: Oxford University Press, 2000), 259.

26. Jean Chrétien in *Montreal Gazette*, June 16, 1972, 1, quoted in Robert Davis and Mark Zanis, *The Genocide Machine in Canada* (Montreal: Black Rose Books, 1973), 42.

27. Mel Watkins, ed., *Dene Nation: The Colony Within* (Toronto: University of Toronto Press, 1977); Thomas Berger, *Northern Frontier, Northern Homeland: The Report of The Mackenzie Valley Pipeline Inquiry* (Vancouver: Douglas and McIntyre, 1977). These texts summarize the struggle of the Métis and Dene during this period. On the efforts of the James Bay Cree, see Boyce Richardson, *Strangers Devour the Land* (Vancouver: Douglas and McIntyre, 1991).

28. Wolfe, "Settler-Colonialism and the Elimination of the Native," 388. Throughout the following chapters I will often use the terms "settler-colonialism," "colonialism," and (on occasion) "imperialism" interchangeably to avoid repetitiveness. I do so, however, acknowledging the distinction that Wolfe, Lorenzo Veracini (*Settler Colonialism: A Theoretical Overview* [London: Palgrave Macmillan, 2010]), Robert Young (*Postcolonialism: A Historical Introduction* [Oxford: Wiley-Blackwell, 2001]), and James Tully (*Public Philosophy in a New Key*, vol 1. [Cambridge: Cambridge University Press, 2004]) have drawn between these interrelated concepts. In the work of all of these scholars, settler-colonial and colonial relationships are conceptualized as more *direct* forms or practices of maintaining an imperial system of dominance. Settler-colonialism, in particular, refers to contexts where the territorial infrastructure of the colonizing society is built on and overwhelms the formerly self-governing but now dispossessed Indigenous nations; indeed, settler-colonial polities are predicated on maintaining this dispossession. Imperialism is a much broader concept, which may include colonial and settler-colonial formations, but could also be carried out indirectly through noncolonial means.

29. Karl Marx, *Capital*, vol 1. (New York: Penguin, 1990).

30. Ibid., 874.

31. Ward Churchill, ed., *Marxism and Native Americans* (Boston: South End Press, 1983). The character of the debate is well represented in this text.

32. Charles Menzies, "Indigenous Nations and Marxism: Notes on an Ambivalent Relationship," *New Proposals: Journal of Marxism and Interdisciplinary Inquiry* 3, no. 3 (2010): 5.

33. Peter Kropotkin, *Conquest of Bread and Other Writings* (Cambridge: Cambridge University Press, 1995), 221.

34. Jim Glassman, "Primitive Accumulation, Accumulation by Dispossession, Accumulation by 'Extra-Economic' Means," *Progress in Human Geography* 30, no. 5 (2005): 611.

35. Marx, *Capital*, 1:899. The degree to which Marx is susceptible to this general line of criticism is itself the subject of debate. For instance, an interesting argument developed by Massimo De Angelis suggests that if we conceive of primitive accumulation as a set of strategies that seeks to permanently maintain a *separation* of workers from the means of production then it would follow that this process must be ongoing insofar as this separation is constitutive of the capital relation as such. The specific character of primitive accumulation strategies might change at any given historical juncture, but as a general process of ongoing separation it must remain in effect indefinitely. See Massimo De Angelis, "Marx and Primitive Accumulation: The Continuous

Character of Capital's 'Enclosures,'" *The Commoner*, no. 2 (September 2001): 1–22. However, the question this position raises is why then utilize the historical marker "primitive" to refer to the process at all, instead of simply referencing the "accumulation of capital" proper? This latter question is explored in Paul Zarembka, "Primitive Accumulation in Marxism, Historical or Trans-Historical Separation from Means of Production?," *The Commoner* (March 2002), 1–9, as a qualification to Angelis's earlier contribution to the same journal.

36. David Harvey, *The New Imperialism* (New York: Oxford University Press, 2003); Silvia Federici, *Caliban and the Witch: Women, the Body, and Primitive Accumulation* (New York: Autonomedia, 2004); Taiaiake Alfred, *Wasáse: Indigenous Pathways of Actions and Freedom* (Peterborough, Ont.: Broadview Press, 2005); Rauna Kuokkanen, "Globalization as Racialized, Sexual Violence: The Case of Indigenous Women," *International Feminist Journal of Politics* 10, no. 2 (2008): 216–33; Andrea Smith, *Conquest: Sexual Violence and American Indian Genocide* (Boston: South End Press, 2005). Also see Retort Collective, *Afflicted Powers: Capital and Spectacle in a New Age of War* (New York: Verso, 2005); Michael Pearlman, *The Invention of Capitalism: Classical Political Economy and the Secret History of Primitive Accumulation* (Durham: Duke University Press, 2000); Todd Gordon, "Canada, Empire, and Indigenous Peoples in the Americas, *Socialist Studies* 2, no. 1 (2006): 47–75; Robin Blackburn, *The Making of New World Slavery* (London: Verso, 1997). Also see De Angelis, "Marx and Primitive Accumulation"; De Angelis's article is one of many contributions in the issue devoted to examining the continual relevance of Marx's dispossession thesis in the contemporary period.

37. Robert Nichols, "Indigeneity and the Settler Contract Today," *Philosophy and Social Criticism* 39, no. 2 (2013): 166.

38. Michael Hardt and Antonio Negri, *Commonwealth* (Cambridge, Mass.: Harvard University Press, 2009), 84.

39. Karl Marx, "The British Rule in India," in Karl Marx and Fredrick Engels, *On Colonialism* (Honolulu: University Press of the Pacific, 2001), 41–42. This is also the underlying thrust of Marx and Engels's famous assertion in *The Communist Manifesto*: "The bourgeoisie, by the rapid improvement of all instruments of production, by the immensely facilitated means of communication, draws all, even the most barbarian, nations into civilization. The cheap prices of its commodities are the heavy artillery with which it batters down all Chinese walls, with which it forces the barbarians' intensely obstinate hatred of foreigners to capitulate. It compels all nations, on pain of extinction, to adopt the bourgeois mode of production; it compels them to introduce what it calls civilization into their midst, i.e., to become bourgeois themselves. In one word it creates the world after its own image" (*Karl Marx: Selected Writings*, ed. David McClelland [Oxford: Oxford University Press, 1987], 225). For a useful discussion of this aspect of Marx's argument, see Aijaz Ahmad, *In Theory: Classes, Nations, Literatures* (New York: Verso, 1994); Epifanio San Juan Jr., *Beyond Postcolonial Theory* (New York: Saint Martin's Press, 1999); Arif Dirlik, *The Postcolonial Aura: Third World Criticism in the Age of Global Capitalism* (Boulder, Colo.: Westview Press, 1998); Crystal

Bartolovich and Neil Lazarus, eds., *Marxism, Modernity, and Postcolonial Studies* (Cambridge: Cambridge University Press, 2002).

40. Georg Wilhelm Friedrich Hegel, *The Philosophy of History* (New York: Dover, 1956), 99; Karl Marx, "The Future Results of the British Rule in India," in *On Colonialism*, by Karl Marx and Frederick Engels (Honolulu: University Press of the Pacific, 2001), 81.

41. This rigidly unilinear understanding of historical development began to shift significantly in Marx's work after the collapse of the European labor movement following the defeat of the Paris Commune in 1871. It was at this point that Marx began to again turn his attention to the study of non-Western societies. Marx scholars have tended to identify three areas of Marx's late writings (1872–83) that reflect this shift in perspective: (1) editorial changes introduced by Marx to the 1872–75 French edition of *Capital*, vol. 1, that strip the primitive accumulation thesis of any prior suggestion of unilinearism; (2) a cluster of late writings on Russia that identify the Russian communal village as a potential launching point for socialist development; and (3) the extensive (but largely ignored) ethnological notebooks produced by Marx between 1879 and 1882. See, in particular, Kevin Anderson, "Marx's Late Writings on Non-Western and Pre-Capitalist Societies and Gender," *Rethinking Marxism* 14, no. 4 (2002): 84–96; and Gareth Stedman Jones, "Radicalism and the Extra-European World: The Case of Karl Marx," in *Victorian Visions of Global Order: Empire and International Relations in Nineteenth-Century Political Thought*, ed. Duncan Bell, 186–214 (Cambridge: Cambridge University Press, 2007). Although each of these three strands in Marx's late scholarship are instructive in their own right, his 1872–75 French revisions to *Capital* are of particular interest for us here because of the specific focus paid to the primitive accumulation thesis. Marx referred to these revisions in a well-known 1877 letter he wrote to Russian radical N. K. Mikailovsky, in which he states that the "chapter on primitive accumulation" *should not* be read as a "historico-philosophical theory of the general course imposed *on all peoples*"; but rather as a historical examination of the "path by which, *in Western Europe*, the capitalist economic order emerged from the womb of the feudal economic order" (Karl Marx, "A Letter to N. K. Mikailovsky," transcribed and reprinted in *The New International* 1, no. 4 [November 1934]: 1). Marx makes the virtually analogous point in his well-known letter to Russian populist Vera Zasulich (Karl Marx, "A Letter to Vera Zasulich," in McClelland, *Karl Marx: Selected Writings*, 576–80).

42. Marx, *Capital*, 1:932.

43. Ibid., 1:940. For a discussion of this feature of Marx's project, see R. Young, *Postcolonialism*, 101–3.

44. Marx, *Capital*, 1:932.

45. As David McNally succinctly puts it: at its "heart" primitive accumulation is ultimately about "the commodification of human labour power" (*Another World Is Possible: Globalization and Anti-Capitalism* [Winnipeg: Arbeiter Ring Press, 2006], 107).

46. Federici, *Caliban and the Witch*, 12.

47. For an example of this line of argument drawn from the neoliberal right, see Thomas Flanagan, *First Nations, Second Thoughts* (Montreal: McGill-Queen's University Press, 2000). For an example claiming to speak from the left, see Frances Widdowson and Albert Howard, *Disrobing the Aboriginal Industry: The Deception behind Indigenous Cultural Preservation* (Montreal: McGill-Queen's University Press, 2008).

48. Aidan Foster-Carter, "The Modes of Production Controversy," *New Left Review* 107 (1978): 47–77. This text provides an excellent introduction to the "articulation of modes of production" debate.

49. For an autonomous Marxist critique of socialist primitive accumulation that also draws off the insights of Kropotkin, see Harry Cleaver, "Kropotkin, Self-Valorization, and the Crisis of Marxism," *Anarchist Studies* 2, no. 2 (2003): 119–36.

50. Frances Abele and Daiva Stasiulis, "Canada as a 'White Settler Colony': What about Natives and Immigrants," in *The New Canadian Political Economy*, ed. Wallace Clement and Glen Williams (Montreal: McGill-Queen's University Press, 1989), 252–53. Also see Terry Wotherspoon and Vic Satzewich, *First Nations: Race, Class, and Gender Relations* (Regina: Canadian Plains Research Centre, 2000); David Bedford and Danielle Irving, *The Tragedy of Progress: Marxism, Modernity and the Aboriginal Question* (Halifax: Fernwood Publishing, 2001). On the importance of Native labor to Canadian political economic development, see John Lutz, *Makuk: A New History of Aboriginal–White Relations* (Vancouver: University of British Columbia Press, 2008).

51. Cole Harris, "How Did Colonialism Dispossess? Comments from an Edge of Empire," *Annals of the Association of American Geographers* 94, no. 1 (2004): 167.

52. Canada, "Annual Report Department of Indian Affairs," *Sessional Papers*, 1890, no. 12, 165.

53. Taiaiake Alfred articulates this point well in the context of Canada's land claims and self-government policies when he writes: "The framework of current reformist or reconciling negotiations are about handing us the scraps of history: self-government and jurisdictional authorities for state-created Indian governments within the larger colonial system and subjection of Onkwehonwe [Indigenous peoples] to the blunt force of capitalism by integrating them as wage slaves into the mainstream resource-exploitation economy" (*Wasáse*, 37).

54. Marx, *Capital*, 1:876.

55. Joel Kovel, *The Enemy of Nature: The End of Capitalism of the End of the World?* (Halifax: Fernwood Publishing, 2007); John Bellamy Foster, *Marx's Ecology: Materialism and Nature* (New York: Monthly Review Press, 2000). These authors provide a constructive conversation regarding both the limits and potential of Marx's ecological insights.

56. On intersectionality as a methodological approach to studying questions of race, class, gender and state power, I am indebted to a number of critical works, including the following: Rita Dhamoon, *Identity/Difference Politics: How Difference Is Produced, and Why It Matters* (Vancouver: University of British Columbia Press, 2009); Yasmin Jiwani, *Discourses of Denial: Mediations of Race, Gender and Violence*

(Vancouver: University of British Columbia Press, 2006); Smith, *Conquest*; Chandra Talpade Mohanty, *Feminism without Borders* (Durham: Duke University Press, 2003); Razak Sherene, *Looking White People in the Eye: Gender, Race and Culture in Courtrooms and Classrooms* (Toronto: University of Toronto Press, 1998).

57. Marx, *Capital*, 1:874.

58. Ibid., 1:926.

59. In framing this question, I do not intend to suggest that the day-to-day effects of colonial dispossession within our communities have not been incredibly violent in character. All evidence points to the contrary. Nor am I suggesting that the era of overtly coercive colonial rule has come to an end. The frequency of what have at times been spectacular displays of state power deployed against relatively small numbers of Indigenous community activists has shown this not to be the case either. The violent state interventions that transpired at Kanesatake in 1990 and Gustafsen Lake in 1995 demonstrate this all too well. I am merely suggesting that strategically deployed state violence no longer constitutes the *first response* in maintaining settler-colonial hegemony vis-à-vis Indigenous nations. On the military and paramilitary attacks at Kanesatake and Gustafsen Lake, see Geoffrey York and Loreen Pindera, *People of the Pines: The Warriors and the Legacy of Oka* (Toronto: Little, Brown and Company, 1991); and Sandra Lambertus, *Wartime Images, Peacetime Wounds: The Media and the Gustafsen Lake Standoff* (Toronto: University of Toronto Press, 2004).

60. See in particular, Frantz Fanon, *Black Skin, White Masks*, trans. Charles Lam Markmann (1967; repr., Boston: Grove Press, 1991); Fanon, *A Dying Colonialism* (Boston: Grove Press, 1965); Fanon, *Toward the African Revolution* (Boston: Grove Press, 1967); Fanon, *The Wretched of the Earth* (Boston: Grove Press, 2005). For a theory of colonial governmentality that draws more centrally from Michel Foucault's contributions, see David Scott, "Colonial Governmentality," *Social Text* 43 (Autumn 1995): 191–220. Also see, Michel Foucault, "Governmentality" and "The Subject of Power," in *Power: The Essential Works of Michel Foucault*, vol. 3, ed. James Faubian (New York: The New Press, 1994), 201–22, 326–48.

61. Fanon, *The Wretched of the Earth*, 4.

62. Georg Wilhelm Friedrich Hegel, *Phenomenology of Spirit* (Oxford: Oxford University Press, 1977).

63. Fanon, *Black Skin, White Masks* (1991), 45.

64. Taylor, "The Politics of Recognition," 32–33.

65. James Clifford, "Taking Identity Politics Seriously: The Contradictory Stony Ground . . . ," in *Without Guarantees: Essays in Honour of Stuart Hall*, ed. Paul Gilroy, Lawrence Grossberg, and Angela McRobbie, 94–112 (London: Verso, 2000).

66. Brian Barry, *Culture and Equality: An Egalitarian Critique of Multiculturalism* (Cambridge: Polity Press, 2001), 325.

67. Nancy Fraser, "Rethinking Recognition: Overcoming Displacement and Reification in Cultural Politics," in *Recognition Struggles and Social Movements: Identities, Agency and Power*, ed. Barbara Hobson (Cambridge: Cambridge University Press, 2003), 22.

68. I would argue that this claim applies to other identity-related struggles as well. As James Tully suggests, when "struggles over recognition" are conceived of in "broad" or "ontological" terms, it is clear that any effort to alter "the norms under which citizens are led to recognize themselves [and each other] will have effects in the distribution or redistribution of the relations of power among them." This is as true in cases where workers collectively struggle to challenge the prevailing norms of exploitative nonrecognition that have hitherto excluded them from participating in the democratic governance of a site of production, as it is in contexts where a group of Indigenous women challenge a patriarchal norm of misrecognition which has functioned to exclude, assimilate, or dominate them. When seen in this light, many, if not most, of today's prominent social movements clearly "exhibit both recognition and distribution aspects" (*Public Philosophy in a New Key* [Cambridge: Cambridge University Press, 2008], 1:293–300).

69. Nancy Fraser and Axel Honneth, *Redistribution or Recognition? A Political Philosophical Exchange* (New York: Verso, 2003), 72–78.

70. Cressida Heyes, *Line Drawings: Defining Women through Feminist Practice* (Ithaca: Cornel University Press, 2000), 35.

71. Anne Philips, *Multiculturalism without Culture* (Princeton: Princeton University Press, 2007), 14.

72. Richard J. F. Day, *Gramsci Is Dead: Anarchist Currents in the Newest Social Movements* (Ann Arbor, Mich.: Pluto Press, 2005), 15.

1. The Politics of Recognition in Colonial Contexts

1. Hegel, *The Phenomenology of Spirit*.

2. Fanon, *Black Skin, White Masks* (1991), 148.

3. R. Young, *Postcolonialism*, 275.

4. Fraser and Honneth, *Redistribution or Recognition?*, 1.

5. Hegel, *Phenomenology of Spirit*, 11–119.

6. See in particular, Alexander Kojève, *Introduction to the Reading of Hegel: Lectures on the Phenomenology of Spirit* (New York: Basic Books, 1969). Also see Jean-Paul Sartre, *Being and Nothingness* (New York: Washington Square Press, 1956); Sartre, *Anti-Semite and Jew: An Exploration of the Etiology of Hate* (New York: Schocken Books, 1974); Sartre, "Black Orpheus," in *Race*, ed. Robert Bernasconi, 115–42 (Malden, Mass.: Blackwell Publishing, 2001). The relationship between Fanon and Sartre on the question of recognition will be taken up in more detail in chapter 5.

7. Nigel Gibson, "Dialectical Impasses: Turning the Table on Hegel and the Black," *Parallax* 8, no. 2 (2002): 31.

8. Fraser and Honneth, *Redistribution or Recognition?* 11.

9. Hegel, *Phenomenology of Spirit*, 178.

10. Robert Pippin, "What Is the Question for Which Hegel's Theory of Recognition Is the Answer?," *European Journal of Philosophy* 8, no. 2 (2000): 156.

11. Hegel, *Phenomenology of Spirit*, 191–92.

12. Ibid., 191, 192.

13. Ibid., 195.

14. Robert Williams, "Hegel and Nietzsche: Recognition and Master/Slave," *Philosophy Today* 45, no. 5 (2001): 16.

15. Patchen Markell, *Bound by Recognition* (Princeton: Princeton University Press, 2003), 25–32. One could argue that this is not necessarily the case with respect to Hegel's later works, particularly *The Philosophy of Right* (Oxford: Oxford University Press, 1952), where the state is understood to play a key role in mediating relations of recognition.

16. Markell, *Bound by Recognition*, 25.

17. Taylor, "The Politics of Recognition," 61, 40.

18. Ibid., 61.

19. Ibid., 32–34; and Charles Taylor, *Sources of the Self: The Making of the Modern Identity* (Cambridge, Mass.: Harvard University Press, 1989), 27.

20. Charles Taylor, *The Malaise of Modernity* (Toronto: Anansi Press, 1991), 45–46.

21. Taylor, "The Politics of Recognition," 25

22. Ibid., 26, 36.

23. Ibid., 36, 64.

24. Ibid., 26.

25. Ibid., 40; also see Charles Taylor, *Reconciling the Solitudes: Essays on Canadian Federalism and Nationalism* (Montreal: McGill-Queen's University Press, 1993), 148, 180.

26. Taylor, *Reconciling the Solitudes*, 180. Also see Charles Taylor, "On the Draft Nisga'a Treaty," *BC Studies* 120 (Winter 1998/1999): 37–40.

27. Taylor, "The Politics of Recognition," 40.

28. Richard Day and Tonio Sadik, "The BC Land Question, Liberal Multiculturalism, and the Spectre of Aboriginal Nationhood," *BC Studies* 134 (2002): 6. Taylor, *Reconciling the Solitudes*, 148. Taylor, "Politics of Recognition," 41.

29. Taylor, "The Politics of Recognition," 65–66.

30. Fanon, *Black Skin, White Masks* (1991), 12; Taylor, "Politics of Recognition," 65–66. Also see Charles Taylor, *Philosophical Papers*, vol. 2, *Philosophy and the Human Sciences* (Cambridge: Cambridge University Press, 1985), 235.

31. A number of studies have mapped the similarities and differences between the dialectic of recognition as conceived by Fanon and Hegel, but relatively few have applied Fanon's insights to critique the groundswell appropriation of Hegel's theory of recognition to address contemporary questions surrounding the recognition of cultural diversity. Even fewer have used Fanon's writings to problematize the utility of a politics of recognition for restructuring hierarchical relations among disparate identities in colonial contexts. For a survey of the available literature, see Irene Gendzier, *Fanon: A Critical Study* (New York: Grove Press, 1974); Hussien Bulhan, *Frantz Fanon and the Psychology of Oppression* (New York: Plenum Press, 1985); Lou Turner, "On the Difference between the Hegelian and Fanonian Dialectic of Lordship and Bondage," in *Fanon: A Critical Reader*, ed. Lewis Gordon, Denean Sharpley-Whiting, and Renee White, 134–51 (Oxford: Blackwell Publishers, 1996); Beatrice Hanssen, "Ethics of the Other," in *A Turn to Ethics*, ed. Marjorie Garber, Beatrice Hanssen, and Rebecca Walkowitz, 127–80 (New York: Routledge, 2000); Sonia Kruks, *Retrieving Experience:*

Subjectivity and Recognition in Feminist Politics (Ithaca: Cornell University Press, 2001); Kelly Oliver, *Witnessing: Beyond Recognition* (Minneapolis: University of Minnesota Press, 2001); Nigel Gibson, "Dialectical Impasse: Turning the Table on Hegel and the Black," *Parallax* 23 (2002): 30–45; Gibson, *Fanon: The Postcolonial Imagination* (Cambridge: Polity Press, 2003); Anita Chari, "Exceeding Recognition," *Sartre Studies International* 10, no. 2 (2004): 110–22; Andrew Schaap, "Political Reconciliation through a Struggle for Recognition?," *Social and Legal Studies* 13, no. 4 (2004): 523–40.

32. Louis Althusser, "Ideology and Ideological State Apparatuses," in *Mapping Ideology*, ed. Slavoj Žižek (London: Verso, 1994), 100–140.

33. Fanon, *Black Skin, White Masks* (1991), 84 (emphasis added).

34. Fanon's contemporary Albert Memmi drew a similar conclusion five years later, in 1957: "Constantly confronted with this image of himself, set forth and imposed on all institutions and in every human contact, how could the colonized help reacting to this portrait? It cannot leave him indifferent and remain a veneer which, like an insult, blows with the wind. He ends up *recognizing it* as one would a detested nickname which has become a familiar description.... Wilfully created and spread by the colonizer, this mythical and degrading portrait ends up being *accepted* and *lived* to a certain extent by the colonized. It thus acquires a certain amount of reality and contributes to the true portrait of the colonized" (*The Colonizer and the Colonized* [Boston: Beacon Press, 1991], 87–88 [emphasis added]).

35. Fanon, *Black Skin, White Masks* (1991), 111–12.

36. Ibid., 109.

37. Ibid., 111.

38. Ibid., 112.

39. Ibid., 109.

40. Taylor, "The Politics of Recognition," 26.

41. Fanon, *Black Skin, White Masks* (1991), 11–12.

42. Ibid.

43. Ibid., 11.

44. Ibid., 202.

45. Ibid., 11.

46. Fanon, *Wretched of the Earth*, 5.

47. Georg Lukacs, *History and Class Consciousness: Studies in Marxist Dialectics* (Cambridge: Cambridge University Press, 1994), 83.

48. For example, see Himani Bannerji, *Dark Side of the Nation* (Toronto: Canadian Scholars Press, 2001); Richard Rorty, *Achieving Our Country: Leftist Thought in Twentieth-Century America* (Cambridge, Mass.: Harvard University Press, 1998); Rorty, "Is 'Cultural Recognition' a Useful Notion for Leftist Politics?," *Critical Horizons* 1, no. 1 (2000): 7–20; Richard Day, "Who Is This We That Gives the Gift? Native American Political Theory and *The Western Tradition*," *Critical Horizons* 2, no. 2 (2001): 173–201; Day and Sadik, "The BC Land Question," 5–34; Brian Barry, *Culture and Equality: An Egalitarian Critique of Multiculturalism* (Cambridge Mass.: Harvard University Press, 2002); Fraser and Honneth, *Redistribution or Recognition?*

49. Fraser and Honneth, *Redistribution or Recognition?*, 12–13.

50. Day, "Who Is This We That Gives the Gift?," 189.

51. In particular, see Howard Adams, *Prison of Grass: Canada from a Native Point of View* (Saskatoon: Fifth House Publishers, 1975); Adams, *A Tortured People: The Politics of Colonization* (Penticton, Ont.: Theytus Books, 1999). Also see Marie Small-face Marule, "Traditional Indian Government: Of the People, By the People and For the People," in *Pathways to Self-Determination: Canadian Indians and the Canadian State*, ed. Menno Boldt, J. Anthony Long, and Leroy Little Bear, 36–53 (Toronto: University of Toronto Press, 1984); Watkins, *Dene Nation*.

52. For example, see: Lee Maracle, *I Am Woman: A Native Perspective on Sociology and Feminism* (Vancouver: Press Gang Publishers, 1988); Taiaiake Alfred, *Peace Power Righteousness: An Indigenous Manifesto* (Don Mills, Ont.: Oxford University Press, 1999); Alfred, *Wasáse*; Smith, *Conquest*; Gord Hill, "Indigenous Anti-Colonialism," *Upping the Anti* 5 (2007), 4–15.

53. Alfred, *Peace Power Righteousness*, 60.

54. Alfred, *Wasáse*, 133.

55. A more thorough treatment of Indigenous anticapitalism in Canada will be examined in chapters 2 and my concluding chapter.

56. Fraser and Honneth, *Redistribution or Recognition?*, 29.

57. Day, "Who Is This We That Gives the Gift?," 176. Also see Nancy Fraser, "Against Anarchism," *Public Seminar Blog*, October 9, 2013, http://www.publicseminar.org/2013/10/against-anarchism/#.UzR7nTKcXok.

58. Fraser and Honneth, *Redistribution or Recognition?*, 100.

59. Ibid., 31.

60. Fanon, *Black Skin, White Masks* (1991), 11.

61. For a comprehensive evaluation of Fraser's critique of "psychologization" in the work of Charles Taylor and Axel Honneth, see Simon Thompson, *The Political Theory of Recognition* (Cambridge: Polity Press, 2006), 31–41.

62. Fanon, *Black Skin, White Masks* (1991), 217 (emphasis added).

63. Ibid.

64. Hegel, *Phenomenology of Spirit*, 113–14.

65. Fanon, *Black Skin, White Masks* (1991), 220 (emphasis added).

66. Ibid., 18.

67. Ibid., 12.

68. Turner, "On the Difference," 146.

69. Fanon, *Black Skin, White Masks* (1991), 221.

70. Oliver, *Witnessing*.

71. Fanon, *Wretched of the Earth*, 9.

72. Fanon, *Black Skin, White Masks* (1991), 220–22.

73. Taylor, "Politics of Recognition," 50 (emphasis added).

74. Fanon, *Black Skin, White Masks* (1991), 220 (emphasis added).

75. Will Kymlicka frames the problem of colonialism as a matter of unjust incorporation into dominant state structures; see his *Multicultural Citizenship: A Liberal Theory of Minority Rights* (Don Mills, Ont.: Oxford University Press, 1995); *Finding*

Our Way: Rethinking Ethnocultural Relations in Canada (Don Mills, Ont.: Oxford University Press, 1998); *Politics in the Vernacular: Nationalism, Multiculturalism, and Citizenship* (Don Mills, Ont.: Oxford University Press, 2001).

76. Todd Gordon, "Canada, Empire and Indigenous Peoples in the Americas," *Socialist Studies* 2, no. 1 (2006): 47–75.

77. Isabelle Schulte-Tenckhoff, "Reassessing the Paradigm of Domestication: The Problematic of Indigenous Treaties," *Review of Constitutional Studies* 4, no. 2 (1998): 239–89.

78. Michael Asch, "From 'Calder' to 'Van der Peet': Aboriginal Rights and Canadian Law," in *Indigenous Peoples' Rights in Australia, Canada, and New Zealand*, ed. Paul Havemann, 428–46 (Auckland: Oxford University Press, 1999); Patrick Macklem, *Indigenous Difference and the Constitution of Canada* (Toronto: University of Toronto Press, 2001); James Tully, "The Struggles of Indigenous Peoples for and of Freedom," in *Political Theory and the Rights of Indigenous Peoples*, ed. Duncan Ivison, Paul Patton, and Will Saunders, 36–59 (Cambridge: Cambridge University Press, 2001).

79. Supreme Court of Canada, *Delgamuukw v. British Columbia* (1997), 3 SCR 1010, in *Delgamuukw: The Supreme Court of Canada Decision on Aboriginal Title* (Vancouver: David Suzuki Foundation, 1998), 35, quoted in James Tully, "Aboriginal Peoples: Negotiating Reconciliation," in *Canadian Politics*, ed. James Bickerton and Alain-G. Gagnon, 3rd ed. (Peterborough, Ont.: Broadview Press, 2000), 413.

80. Elizabeth Povinelli, *The Cunning of Recognition: Indigenous Alterities and the Making of Australian Multiculturalism* (Durham: Duke University Press, 2002).

81. Eduardo Duran and Bonnie Duran, *Native American Postcolonial Psychology* (Albany: State University of New York Press, 1995).

82. Alfred, *Wasáse*.

83. Bill Ashcroft, *Post-Colonial Transformations* (New York: Routledge, 2001), 35.

84. Ashcroft, *Post-Colonial Transformations*; David Scott, *Refashioning Futures: Criticism after Postcoloniality* (Princeton: Princeton University Press, 1999); Scott, *Conscripts of Modernity: The Tragedy of Colonial Enlightenment* (Durham: Duke University Press, 2004).

85. I think Taylor's own account of recognition demands an answer to this question also. For instance, in relying on Hegel's master/slave dialectic to make his point about the constitutive relation between recognition and freedom, Taylor seems to downplay the fact that the agency and self-understanding fought for and won by the slave occurs in a condition marked by inequality and misrecognition, not reciprocity. As Nikolas Kompridis points out, here the slave is "able, at least partially, to resolve the 'epistemological crisis' set in motion by his unsatisfied . . . desire for recognition without receiving the kinds of recognition [theorist's such as Taylor regard] as necessary and sufficient conditions of successful agency and personal identity." This same point can be made with respect to the background political context animating Taylor's essay: namely, since confederation the respective relationships of Quebec and Indigenous peoples to the Canadian state have been marked by domination, yet both Quebec and Indigenous peoples routinely resist this dominance through creative displays of political agency and collective empowerment; the Quiet Revolution and Red Power

movements provide two particularly salient examples of this. In light of this, the question that needs to be asked again is where are these manifestations of collective empowerment coming from if not from recognition provided by the Canadian state? See Nikolas Kompridis, "Struggling over the Meaning of Recognition: A Matter of Identity, Justice or Freedom?," *European Journal of Political Theory* 6 (2007): 283.

86. Fanon, *Black Skin, White Masks* (1991), 222.

87. Fanon, *The Wretched of the Earth*, 148.

88. Fanon, *Black Skin, White Masks* (1991), 221.

89. Kruks, *Retrieving Experience*, 101. Fanon's position on the emancipatory potential of negritude will be explored further in chapter 5.

90. Fanon, *Black Skin, White Masks* (1991), 222.

91. R. Young, *Postcolonialism*, 275. For an authoritative treatment of the historical successes and failures of the Third World's postcolonial political projects, see Vijay Prashad, *The Darker Nations: A People's History of the Third World* (New York: The New Press, 2007).

92. Jorge Larrain, "Stuart Hall and the Marxist Concept of Ideology," in *Stuart Hall: Critical Dialogues in Cultural Studies*, ed. David Morley and Kuan-Hsing Chen (New York: Routledge, 1996), 48; John Scott, *Power* (Cambridge: Polity Press, 2001), 10. Also see Stuart Hall, "The Problem of Ideology: Marxism without Guarantees," in *Stuart Hall: Critical Dialogues in Cultural Studies*, ed. David Morley and Kuan-Hsing Chen, 25–46 (New York: Routledge, 1996).

93. Larrain makes a similar point but without reference to Fanon in "Stuart Hall and the Marxist Concept of Ideology," 49.

94. Fanon, *Black Skin, White Masks* (1991), 183.

95. Fanon, *Wretched of the Earth*, 8.

96. R. Young, *Postcolonialism*, 295.

97. Dale Turner, *This Is Not a Peace Pipe: Towards a Critical Indigenous Philosophy* (Toronto: University of Toronto Press, 2006), 5.

98. Ibid., 31.

99. Ibid., 111.

100. Ibid., 114.

101. Fanon, *Wretched of the Earth*, 51.

102. Ibid., 54.

103. Ibid., 44.

104. Alfred, *Wasáse*, 58, 30.

105. bell hooks, *Yearning: Race, Gender and Cultural Politics* (Boston: South End Press, 1990), 22.

2. FOR THE LAND

1. Lois McNay, *Against Recognition* (London: Polity, 2008), 3.

2. Frances Widdowson and Albert Howard, *Disrobing the Aboriginal Industry: The Deception behind Indigenous Cultural Preservation* (Montreal: McGill-Queen's Press, 2007), 264.

3. Frances Widdowson, March 15, 2010, comment on Peter Kulchyski, "With friends like this, aboriginal people don't need enemies," *Canadian Dimension*, http://canadiandimension.com (emphasis added).

4. Widdowson and Howard, *Disrobing the Aboriginal Industry*, 264.

5. Ian Angus, *A Border Within: National Identity, Cultural Plurality, and Wilderness* (Montreal: McGill-Queen's Press, 1997), 3.

6. Fraser and Honneth, *Redistribution or Recognition?*, 72–78.

7. Day, *Gramsci Is Dead*, 4.

8. See Kerry Abel, *Drum Songs: Glimpses of History* (Montreal: McGill-Queen's Press, 1993), 3–16.

9. Department of Indian Affairs and Northern Development, *Gwich'in Comprehensive Land Claims Agreement*, 2 vols. (Ottawa: Minister of Public Works and Government Services Canada, 1992). For background information on the Inuvialuit comprehensive claim, see Department of Indian Affairs and Northern Development, *NWT Plain Facts: On Land and Self-Government, The Inuvialuit Final Agreement* (Ottawa: Minister of Public Works and Government Services Canada, 2007).

10. Department of Indian Affairs and Northern Development, *Sahtu Dene and Metis Comprehensive Land Claim Agreement*, 2 vols. (Ottawa: Minister of Public Works and Government Services Canada, 1993).

11. For background information on the Tlicho Agreement, see Department of Indian Affairs and Northern Development, Tlicho Agreement—Highlights, http://www.aadnc-aandc.gc.ca.

12. Under federal policy, specific claims differ from comprehensive claims insofar as the latter do not involve an Aboriginal title claim but rather seek to implement the specific rights and provisions outlined in a historical treaty (which the Crown has failed to live up to), or those that flow from the state's fiduciary obligation to protect the interests of Aboriginal peoples in its management of band money, lands or other assets. See Department of Indian Affairs and Northern Development, *Specific Claims: Justice at Last* (Ottawa: Minister of Public Works and Government Services, 2007).

13. Martha Johnson and Robert A. Ruttan, *Traditional Dene Environmental Knowledge* (Hay River, N.W.T.: Published by the Dene Cultural Institute, 1993), 98–99; Michael Asch, "The Economics of Dene Self-Determination," in *Challenging Anthropology*, ed. David H. Turner and Gavin A. Smith (Toronto: McGraw-Hill, 1980), 345–47; Asch, "The Dene Economy," in Watkins, *Dene Nation*, 56–57; Peter Usher, "The North: One Land, Two Ways of Life," in *Heartland and Hinterland: A Geography of Canada*, ed. L. D. McCann (Scarborough, Ont.: Prentice-Hall, 1982), 483–529.

14. Asch, "The Dene Economy," 56–58.

15. Abel, *Drum Songs*, 244.

16. Mark Dickerson, *Whose North? Political Change, Political Development, and Self-Government in the Northwest Territories* (Vancouver: University of British Columbia Press, 1992), 89–90.

17. Ibid., 90.

18. Statistics Canada, *2001 Census Analysis Series—A Profile of the Canadian Population: Where We Live* (Ottawa: Government of Canada, 2001), 1.

19. Dene Nation, *Denendeh: A Dene Celebration* (Yellowknife, N.W.T.: Dene Nation, 1984), 19.

20. Dickerson, *Whose North?*, 83–84.

21. Garth M. Evans, "The Carrothers Commission Revisited," in *Northern Transitions*, vol. 2, *Second National Workshop on People, Resources and the Environment North of 60°*, ed. Robert Keith and Janet Wright (Ottawa: Canadian Arctic Resources Committee, 1978), 299.

22. Dickerson, *Whose North?*, 86.

23. Institute for Psycho-Political Research and Education, "Political Development in the Northwest Territories," in Keith and Wright, *Northern Transitions*, 2:318.

24. Gerald Sutton, "Aboriginal Rights," in Watkins, *Dene Nation*, 149.

25. Department of Indian Affairs and Northern Development, *Oil and Gas North of 60: A Report of Activities in 1969* (Ottawa: Queen's Printer, 1970), 4, quoted in Bruce Alden Cox, "Changing Perceptions of Industrial Development in the North," in *Native Peoples, Native Lands*, ed. Bruce Alden Cox (Ottawa: Carleton University Press, 1991), 223.

26. Berger, *Northern Frontier, Northern Homeland*, 1:ix.

27. Ibid.

28. Edgar Dosman, *The National Interest: The Politics of Northern Development, 1968–75* (Toronto: McClelland and Stuart, 1975), xiii.

29. Ibid., 25.

30. Peter Kulchyski, *Like the Sound of a Drum: Aboriginal Cultural Politics in Denendeh and Nunavut* (Winnipeg: University of Manitoba Press, 2005), 61–62. On the differing ideological perspectives of each organization vis-à-vis northern development, see Peter Usher, "Northern Development, Impact Assessment, and Social Change," in *Anthropology, Public Policy and Native Peoples in Canada*, ed. Noel Dick and James Waldram (Montreal: McGill-Queen's University Press, 1993), 110–11.

31. *Re: Paulette and Registrar of Land Titles, (1973)*. For a discussion of the caveat, also see Abel, *Drum Songs*, 250.

32. Abel, *Drum Songs*, 250.

33. Quoted in Miggs Wynne Morris, *Return to the Drum: Teaching among the Dene in Canada's North* (Edmonton: NeWest Press, 2000), 138.

34. On the history of Treaties 8 and 11 see Rene Fumoleau, *As Long as This Land Shall Last: A History of Treaty 8 and Treaty 11, 1870–1939* (Calgary: University of Calgary Press, 2004).

35. Department of Indian Affairs and Northern Development, *Statement on Claims of Indian and Inuit People*.

36. Department of Indian Affairs and Northern Development, "Comprehensive Claims Policy and Status of Claims," March 2002, 1.

37. Berger, *Northern Frontier, Northern Homeland*, xxvi–xxvii.

38. Frances Abele, "The Berger Inquiry and the Politics of Transformation in the Mackenzie Valley" (PhD diss., York University, 1983), 1.

39. Usher, "Northern Development, Impact Assessment and Social Change," 111.

40. Vine Deloria Jr., *God Is Red: A Native View of Religion* (Golden, Colo.: Fulcrum Publishing, 1992), esp. 61–76.

41. Ibid., 62 (emphasis added).

42. Ibid.

43. Ibid., 63.

44. Vine Deloria Jr., "Power and Place Equal Personality," in *Power and Place: Indian Education in America*, by Vine Deloria Jr. and Daniel Wildcat (Golden, Colo.: Fulcrum Publishing, 2001), 23.

45. Tim Cresswell, *Place: A Short Introduction* (New York: Blackwell, 2004), 11.

46. For further elaboration, see Allice Legat, *Walking the Land, Feeding the Fire: Knowledge and Stewardship among the Tlicho Dene* (Tucson: University of Arizona Press, 2012).

47. Bill Erasmus, foreword to *Finding Dahshaa: Self-Government, Social Suffering, and Aboriginal Policy in Canada*, by Stephanie Irlbacher-Fox (Vancouver: University of British Columbia Press, 2009), x–xv; Sally Anne Zoe, Madelaine Chocolat, and Allice Legat, "Tlicho Nde: The Importance of Knowing," unpublished research paper prepared for the Dene Cultural Institute, Dogrib Treaty 11 Council and BHP Diamonds Inc. (1995), 5. These references discuss land-as-relationship in the Dene context. For similar accounts in other Indigenous contexts, see, Paul Nadasdy, "The Gift in the Animal: The Ontology of Hunting and Human–Animal Sociality," *American Ethnologist* 34, no. 1 (2007): 25–43; Keith Basso, *Wisdom Sits in Places: Language and Landscape among the Western Apache* (Albuquerque: University of New Mexico Press, 1996); Thomas F. Thornton, *Being and Place among the Tlingit* (Seattle: University of Washington Press, 2008).

48. George Blondin, *When the World Was New: Stories of the Sahtu Dene* (Yellowknife, N.W.T.: Outcrop Publishers, 1990), 155–56.

49. Kulchyski, *Like the Sound of a Drum*, 88.

50. Philip Blake, "Statement to the Mackenzie Valley Pipeline Inquiry," in Watkins, *Dene Nation*, 7–8 (emphasis added).

51. See, for example, Lesley Malloch, *Dene Government: Past and Future* (Yellowknife, N.W.T.: Western Constitutional Forum, 1984). Also see Berger, *Northern Frontier, Northern Homeland*, 93–100; George Barnaby, George Kurszewski, and Gerry Cheezie, "The Political System and the Dene," in Watkins, *Dene Nation*, 120–29.

52. Dene Nation, "Dene Declaration," in Watkins, *Dene Nation*, 3.

53. Gerald (Taiaiake) Alfred, *Heeding the Voices of Our Ancestors: Kahnawake and the Rise of Native Nationalism* (Don Mills, Ont.: Oxford University Press, 1995), 14.

54. Ibid., 178. On the nationalism as "invented tradition" thesis see Eric Hobsbawm and Terence Ranger, eds., *The Invention of Tradition* (Cambridge: Cambridge University Press, 1983); Benedict Anderson, *Imagined Communities* (London: Verso, 1983).

55. Alfred, *Heeding the Voices of Our Ancestors*, 14.

56. Abel, *Drum Songs*, 231.

57. Usher, "Northern Development, Impact Assessment and Social Change," 99.

58. On the application of the "mode of production" concept to Dene self-determination, I am indebted to the work of Peter Kulchyski and Michael Asch in particular. See Kulchyski, *Like the Sound of a Drum*, 34–42, 103–4; Michael Asch, "Dene Self-Determination and the Study of Hunter-Gatherers in the Modern World," in *Politics and History in Band Societies*, ed. Eleanor Leacock and Richard Lee, 347–71 (Cambridge: Cambridge University Press, 1982). Also see: Hugh Brody, *The Living Arctic: Hunters of the Canadian North* (Vancouver: Douglas and McIntyre, 1987); Brody, *Maps and Dreams* (Vancouver: Douglas and McIntyre, 1988); Brody, *The Other Side of Eden: Hunters, Farmers and the Shaping of the Modern World* (Vancouver: Douglas and McIntyre, 2000). Also see these writings on the subject: Peter J. Usher, "The Class System, Metropolitan Dominance, and Northern Development in Canada," *Antipode* 8, no. 3 (1976): 28–32; Usher, "Staple Production and Ideology in Northern Canada," in *Culture, Communications and Dependency*, ed. W. H. Melody, L. Salter, and P. Heyer, 177–86 (Norwood, N.J.: Ablex Publishing, 1982); Usher, "The North: One Land, Two Ways of Life," in *Heartland and Hinterland: A Geography of Canada*, ed. L. D. McCann, 483–529 (Scarborough, Ont.: Prentice-Hall, 1982); Usher, "Environment, Race and Nation Reconsidered: Reflections on Aboriginal Land Claims in Canada," *Canadian Geographer* 47, no. 4 (2003): 365–82.

59. Kulchyski, *Like the Sound of a Drum*, 38.

60. Marx, "The German Ideology" in *Karl Marx: Selected Writings*, ed. David McLelland (New York: Oxford University Press, 1987), 161 (emphasis added). The full quote reads: "[A] mode of production must not be considered simply as being the production of the physical existence of the individuals. Rather it is a definite form of activity of these individuals, a definite form of *expressing their life*, a definite *mode of life* on their part. As individuals express their life, so they are. What they are, therefore, coincides with their production, both with what they produce and with how they produce [it]" (emphasis added).

61. Kulchyski, *Like the Sound of a Drum*, 38.

62. See Asch, "The Dene Economy."

63. Joan Ryan, *Doing Things the Right Way: Dene Traditional Justice in Lac La Martre, NWT* (Calgary: University of Calgary Press, 1995), 1.

64. Barnaby, Kurszewski, and Cheezie, "The Political System and the Dene," 120.

65. For a comprehensive elaboration on this point in the context of land claims in British Columbia, see Andrew Woolford, *Between Justice and Certainty: Treaty-Making in British Columbia* (Vancouver: University of British Columbia Press, 2005); Taiaiake Alfred, "Deconstructing the British Columbia Treaty Process," *Balayi: Culture, Law and Colonialism* 3 (2001): 37–66. Also see, Gabrielle Slowey, *Navigating Neoliberalism: Self-Determination and the Mikisew Cree First Nation* (Vancouver: University of British Columbia Press, 2008).

66. Joyce Green, "Decolonization and Recolonization," in *Changing Canada: Political Economy as Transformation*, ed. Wallace Clement and Leah Vosko (Montreal: McGill-Queen's University Press, 2003), 52.

67. United Nations Commission on Human Rights, *Study on Treaties, Agreements and Other Constructive Arrangements between States and Indigenous Populations*, final

report by Miguel Alfonso Martinez, Special Rapporteur, Sub-Commission on Prevention of Discrimination and Protection of Minorities, 51st Session, June 22, 1999, 30.

68. Indian Brotherhood of the Northwest Territories, "A Proposal to the Government and People of Canada," in Watkins, *Dene Nation*, 185–87.

69. June Helm, *The People of Denendeh: An Ethnohistory of the Indians of Canada's Northwest Territories* (Montreal: McGill-Queen's Press, 2000), 265.

70. On the importance of "political form" to Indigenous politics in the North, see Kulchyski, *Like the Sound of the Drum*. More generally, see Day, "Who Is This We That Gives the Gift?," 173–201; Taiaiake Alfred, "Sovereignty," in *Sovereignty Matters: Locations of Contestation and Possibility in Indigenous Struggles for Self-Determination*, ed. Joanne Barker (Lincoln: University of Nebraska Press, 2005), 33–50; Andrea Smith, "Native American Feminism, Sovereignty, and Social Change," *Feminist Studies* 31, no. 1 (2005): 116–32; and Rauna Kuokkanen, "The Politics of Form and Alternative Autonomies: Indigenous Women, Subsistence Economies, and the Gift Paradigm," paper published by the Institute on Globalization and the Human Condition, McMaster University, 2007, 1–31.

71. On the IB-NWT boycott of the 8th Legislative Assembly of the NWT, see Gurston Dacks, *A Choice of Futures: Politics in the Canadian North* (Toronto: Methuen, 1981), 99–100; Dickerson, *Whose North*, 102; Abel, *Drum Songs*, 259; Barnaby, Kurszewski, and Cheezie, "The Political System and the Dene," 120–29.

72. George Barnaby, *Native Press*, October 22, 1975, 12, quoted in June Helm, *The People of Denendeh*, 267.

73. IB-NWT, "Agreement in Principle," 184.

74. On the relevance of cooperative and workplace democracy models of economic development to Indigenous societies, see Gurston Dacks, "Worker-Controlled Native Enterprises: A Vehicle for Community Development in Northern Canada," *Canadian Journal of Native Studies* 3, no. 2 (1983): 289–310; Lou Ketilson and Ian MacPherson, *Aboriginal Co-operatives in Canada: Current Situation and Potential for Growth* (Saskatoon: Centre for the Study of Co-operatives, 2001). Also see Robert Ruttan and John T'Seleie, "Renewable Resource Potentials for Alternative Development in the Mackenzie River Region," report prepared for the Indian Brotherhood of the NWT and Metis Association of the NWT, 1976.

75. Indian Brotherhood of the Northwest Territories, "Annual Report, 1975" (Yellowknife, N.W.T.: Indian Brotherhood of the Northwest Territories, 1975), 24–25.

76. The conversation occurred via mail between a representative for the Kahnawake Sub-Office and then Vice President of the IB-NWT, Richard Nerysoo. The letter was included as part of an information package compiled in 1977 by the NWT Legislative Assembly to generate public concern over the "radical" nature of the Dene self-determination movement. Also included in the package was a list of reading materials that the then IB-NWT community development program director, Georges Erasmus, suggested might be useful in constructing a "development philosophy" for the Dene Nation. The list of readings included, among others, Frantz Fanon's *Wretched of the Earth*, Paulo Freire's *Pedagogy of the Oppressed*, Albert Memmi's *The Colonizer and*

the Colonized, and Regis Debray's *Revolution in the Revolution*. According to Erasmus, these "alternative" sources on development were to supplement research and perspectives drawn from the communities: "Many alternatives must be looked at," wrote Erasmus in a memo addressed to Dene fieldworkers, "especially the example of our culture, the approach to development and distribution of material and ownership that our forefathers took. We may wish to keep some aspects of the old way in this industrial era." Georges Erasmus became president of the IB-NWT the following year (in 1976) and served in this capacity until 1983. Information package on file with author and can be found in the Price of Wales Northern Heritage Centre, Yellowknife NWT.

77. Indian Brotherhood of the Northwest Territories, "Annual Report, 1975," 25.

78. Indian Brotherhood of the Northwest Territories, "A Proposal to the Government and People of Canada," 184.

79. Ibid., 187.

80. Abel, *Drum Songs*, 254.

81. Judd Buchanan, quoted in Martin O'Malley, *Past and Future Land: An Account of the Berger Inquiry into the Mackenzie Valley Pipeline* (Toronto: Peter Martin Associates Limited, 1976), 98.

82. Harold Cardinal, *The Rebirth of Canada's Indians* (Edmonton: Hurtig, 1977), 15.

83. Ted Byfield, "Wah-Shee and the Left: A Tale of the Territories," *Saint John's Edmonton Report* 4, no. 24, May 23, 1977, quoted in Peter Puxley, "A Model of Engagement: Reflections of the 25th Anniversary of the Berger Report" (Ottawa: Canadian Policy Research Network, 2002), 9.

84. Stuart Demelt, quoted in O'Malley, *Past and Future Land*, 29–30.

85. Government of the Northwest Territories, *You've Heard from the Radical Few about Canada's North* (pamphlet), quoted in Kenneth Coates and Judith Powell, *The Modern North: People, Politics and the Rejection of Colonialism* (Toronto: James Lorimer and Company, 1989), 112.

86. IB-NWT, "The FBI War Game and the NWT," *Native Press*, November 12, 1976, 1, 8. This information was obtained by the IB-NWT from a report made by the United States' Federal Bureau of Investigation's Counterintelligence Program (COINTELPRO).

87. Dene Nation, *Denendeh*, 29.

88. Coates and Powell, *The Modern North*, 113.

89. Government of the Northwest Territories, "Priorities for the North: A Submission to the Honourable Warren Allmand, Minister of Indian Affairs and Northern Development," in Keith and Wright, *Northern Transitions*, 2:259–64.

90. Ibid., 260, 262. The legislative assembly even went as far as to irresponsibly suggest that Thomas Berger's recommendations would amount to the establishment of an "apartheid" regime in northern Canada: "These same people (i.e., the Dene and their supporters) think that much of the territories should be converted into racial states along native lines. Like Mr. Thomas Berger. If you're for what he seems to believe, then you've got to support something that has always been abhorrent to Canadians and violates our history—separating people according to race. Frankly, support Mr.

Berger and you have to support South Africa and its policy of apartheid—the separate development for each of its founding races." Quoted in Free South Africa Committee, "Dene Nation: Apartheid?" (Edmonton: Pamphlet published by the Free South Africa Committee, University of Alberta, 1977).

91. Indian Brotherhood of the Northwest Territories, "Metro Proposal," in Keith and Wright, *Northern Transitions*, 2:265–66.

92. Ibid., 265.

93. Ibid., 266.

94. Government of the Northwest Territories, "Priorities for the North," 259–62.

95. Office of the Prime Minister, "Political Development in the Northwest Territories," in Keith and Wright, *Northern Transitions*, 2:211–83.

96. Office of the Prime Minister, "Special Government Representative for Constitutional Development in the Northwest Territories," in Keith and Wright, *Northern Transitions*, 2:275.

97. Office of the Prime Minister, "Political Development," 280.

98. Ibid., 279.

99. Somewhat tellingly, the federal government would immediately go on to qualify this assertion by stating that it would not sanction racially determined "political structures" *unless* this meant "the establishment of reserves under the Indian Act" (ibid., 280).

100. Office of the Prime Minister, "Special Government Representative," 275.

101. Peter Russell, "An Analysis of Prime Minister Trudeau's Paper on Political Development in the Northwest Territories," in Keith and Wright, *Northern Transitions*, 2:297.

102. Government of the Northwest Territories, "Priorities for the North," 262.

103. Ibid., 263.

104. Office of the Prime Minister, "Political Development," 278.

105. Dene Nation and Metis Association of the Northwest Territories, *Public Government for the People of the North* (Yellowknife, N.W.T.: Dene Nation and Metis Association of the Northwest Territories, 1981), 3.

106. Ibid., 7.

107. Ibid., 13.

108. Ibid., 13, 21–23.

109. Ibid., 17.

110. Ibid., 9–10.

111. Ibid., 9.

112. Ibid., 11.

113. Dene Nation, *Denendeh*, 42.

114. Aboriginal Rights and Constitutional Development Secretariat, "Discussion Paper on the Denendeh Government Proposal," working paper prepared for the Special Committee of the Legislative Assembly on Constitutional Development, September 1982, 30.

115. Dene Nation, *Denendeh*, 42.

116. Abel, *Drum Songs*, 256–57.

117. Dene/Metis Claims Secretariat, "The Dene/Metis Land Claim: Information Package," (Yellowknife, N.W.T.: Produced by the Dene/Metis Negotiations Secretariat, 1986), 8.

118. Ibid. Following the leadership change in 1983 from Georges Erasmus to Stephen Kakfwi, the Dene Nation made a strategic decision to pursue the recognition of political rights though the territorial government and land issues through the negotiation of the land claim. See Kulchyski, *Like the Sound of a Drum*, 87.

119. Marina Devine, "The Dene Nation: Coming Full Circle," *Arctic Circle*, March/April 1992, 15.

120. Ibid.; Kulchyski, *Like the Sound of a Drum*, 94–97. These authors discuss the fragmentation of the Dene Nation and unified nationalist movement.

121. For critical discussions of the newly proposed MPG, see: Petr Cizek, "Northern Pipe Dreams and Nightmares: Return of the Mackenzie Valley Pipeline," *Canadian Dimension* (May/June 2005): http://canadiandimension.com/articles/1930; Erin Freeland and Jessica Simpson, "Petro-Capitalism and the Fight for Indigenous Culture in Denendeh," *New Socialist* 62 (Fall 2007): 9–11.

122. Frank T'Seleie quoted in Ed Struzik, "Things Change in 25 Years Says Anti-Pipeline Activist: Frank T'Seleie Is Now in Favor of a Pipeline along the Mackenzie," *Edmonton Journal*, July 7, 2001.

123. Stuart Kirsch, "Indigenous Movements and the Risks of Counter Globalization," *American Ethnologist* 34, no. 2 (2007): 304.

124. Todd Gordon, "Canada, Empire and Indigenous Peoples in the Americas," *Socialist Studies* 2, no. 1 (2006): 47–75.

125. Paul Nadasdy, "'Property' and Aboriginal Land Claims in the Canadian Subarctic: Some Theoretical Considerations," *American Anthropologist* 104, no. 1 (2002): 248.

3. Essentialism and the Gendered Politics
of Aboriginal Self-Government

1. Seyla Benhabib, *The Claims of Culture: Equality and Diversity in the Global Era* (Princeton: Princeton University Press, 2002).

2. See, in particular, James Clifford, "Taking Identity Politics Seriously," in *Without Guarantees: In Honor of Stuart Hall*, ed. Paul Gilroy, Lawrence Grossberg, and Angel McRobbie, 94–112 (London: Verso, 2000); Arif Dirlik, *Postmodernity's Histories: The Past as Legacy and Project* (New York: Rowman and Littlefield, 2000); Michael Hardt and Antonio Negri, *Empire* (Cambridge, Mass.: Harvard University Press, 2000); Nikolas Kompridis, "Normativizing Hybridity/Neutralizing Culture," *Political Theory* 33, no. 3 (2005): 318–43; Bonita Lawrence, *"Real" Indians and Others: Mixed-Blood Urban Native Peoples and Indigenous Nationalism* (Vancouver: University of British Columbia Press, 2004); David Scott, "The Social Construction of Postcolonial Studies," in *Postcolonial Studies and Beyond*, ed. Ania Loomba, Suvir Kaul, Matti Bunzl, Antoinette Burton, and Jed Esty, 385–400 (Durham: Duke University Press, 2005);

Peter Kulchyski, *Like the Sound of a Drum: Aboriginal Cultural Politics in Denendeh and Nunavut* (Winnipeg: University of Manitoba Press, 2006).

3. Benhabib, *The Claims of Culture*, 8 (emphasis added).

4. Ibid.

5. Ibid., ix.

6. Ibid., 7–8, 4.

7. Terence Turner, "Anthropology and Multiculturalism: What Is Anthropology That Multiculturalists Should Be Mindful of It?," *Cultural Anthropology* 8, no. 4 (1993): 412, quoted in Benhabib, *The Claims of Culture*, 4.

8. Benhabib, *The Claims of Culture*, 68.

9. Ibid., 184.

10. Ibid., 184, ix.

11. Ibid., 7.

12. Ibid., ix.

13. Ibid., 19.

14. Ibid., 20.

15. Ibid. 184.

16. Ibid., 54. For a comprehensive discussion of the gendered character of Canadian Indian policy, to which I am much indebted, see Lawrence, *"Real" Indians and Others*; Joanne Barker, "Gender, Sovereignty, and the Discourse of Rights in Native Women's Activism," *Meridians: Feminism, Race, Transnationalism* 7, no. 1 (2006): 127–61. Also see Kathleen Jamieson, *Indian Women and the Law in Canada: Citizens Minus* (Ottawa: Advisory Council on the Status of Women and Indian Rights for Indian Women, 1978).

17. Megan Furi and Jill Wherrett, *Indian Status and Band Membership Issues* (Ottawa: Parliamentary Research Branch, 2003), 2.

18. Lawrence, *"Real" Indians and Others*, 50.

19. Ibid., 54–55.

20. Barker, "Gender, Sovereignty and the Discourse of Rights in Native Women's Activism," 135–36.

21. *Re: Lavell and Attorney-General of Canada (1971), 22 DLR (3d) 182.*

22. Lawrence, *"Real" Indians and Others*, 56.

23. Barker, "Gender, Sovereignty, and the Discourse of Rights in Native Women's Activism," 137.

24. Ibid.

25. Kathleen Jamieson, "Sex Discrimination and the Indian Act," in *Arduous Journey: Canadian Indians and Decolonization*, ed. J. R. Ponting (Toronto: McClelland and Stewart, 1986), 126–27.

26. *Attorney-General of Canada v. Lavell; Isaac v. Bedard (1973), 38 DLR (3d), 481* (emphasis added).

27. Ibid.

28. For an authoritative account of this struggle, see Janet Silman, ed., *Enough Is Enough: Aboriginal Women Speak Out* (Toronto: The Women's Press, 1987).

29. Lawrence, *"Real" Indians and Others*, 57.

30. Barker, "Gender, Sovereignty, and the Discourse of Rights in Native Women's Activism," 138–39.

31. Ibid., 139.

32. UN Office of the High Commissioner for Human Rights, *International Covenant on Civil and Political Rights*, adopted and opened for signature, ratification and accession by General Assembly resolution 2200A (XXI) of December 16, 1966. Available online at http://www.ohchr.org.

33. Janet Silman, *Enough Is Enough: Aboriginal Women Speak Out*, 149–72.

34. *Sandra Lovelace v. Canada, Communication No. R. 6/34 (29 December 1977), UN Doc. Supp. No. 40 (A/36/40) at 166 (1981).*

35. Joyce Green, "Balancing Strategies: Aboriginal Women and Constitutional Rights in Canada," in *Women Making Constitutions: New Perspectives and Comparative Perspectives*, ed. Alexandra Dobrowolsky and Vivian Hart (New York: Palgrave Macmillan, 2004), 47.

36. Joyce Green, "Canaries in the Mines of Citizenship: Indian Women in Canada," *Canadian Journal of Political Science* 34, no. 4 (2001): 728.

37. Barker, "Gender, Sovereignty, and the Discourse of Rights in Native Women's Activism," 141.

38. Bryan Schwartz, *First Principles, Second Thoughts: Aboriginal Peoples, Constitutional Reform and Canadian Statecraft* (Montreal: Institute for Research on Public Policy, 1986), 337.

39. For a discussion of Aboriginal participation in the Charlottetown negotiations, see Peter H. Russell, *Constitutional Odyssey: Can Canada Become a Sovereign People?*, 3rd ed. (Toronto: University of Toronto Press, 2004), 154–227.

40. Native Women's Association of Canada, *Aboriginal Women, Self-Government and the Canadian Charter of Rights and Freedoms* (Ottawa: Published by the Native Women's Association of Canada, 1991), 17–18.

41. Lawrence, *"Real" Indians and Others*, 69.

42. The Assembly of First Nations, quoted in Menno Boldt and J. Anthony Long, "Tribal Philosophies and the Charter of Rights and Freedoms," in *The Quest for Justice: Aboriginal Peoples and Aboriginal Rights* (Toronto: University of Toronto Press, 1985), 171.

43. Benhabib, *The Claims of Culture*, 19.

44. The following interpretation of Benhabib's critique of essentialism is indebted to Michael Hardt and Antonio Negri's analysis of Homi Bhabha's postcolonial criticism (Hardt and Negri, *Empire*, 143–46). See also Homi K. Bhabha, *The Location of Culture* (New York: Routledge, 1994).

45. Benhabib, *The Claims of Culture*, 106; also see Monique Deveau, "A Deliberative Approach to Conflicts of Culture," *Political Theory* 31, no. 6 (2003): 780–807.

46. Or, stated the other way around: when cultural obligations are conferred on individuals without these deliberative mechanisms in place, then "the obligations that ensue can only be regarded as an imposition. In such cases, any defense of cultural

traditions will be regarded as a [potential] source of coercive power applied against an unwilling membership" (Tim Schouls, *Shifting Boundaries: Aboriginal Identity, Pluralist Theory, and the Politics of Self-Government* [Vancouver: University of British Columbia Press, 2003], 106).

47. Hardt and Negri, *Empire*, 137–50.

48. Ibid., 139.

49. Lawrence, *"Real" Indians and Others*, 2.

50. Rodolfo Stavenhagen, *Human Rights and Indigenous Issues: Report of the Special Rapporteur on the Situation of Human Rights and Fundamental Freedoms of Indigenous Peoples: Mission to Canada*, UN Commission of Human Rights report, 2004, 2.

51. Patricia Monture-Angus, *Thunder in My Soul: A Mohawk Woman Speaks* (Halifax: Fernwood, 1995), 184; Lawrence, *"Real" Indians and Others*, 64–84.

52. Peter Kulchyski, "Human Rights or Aboriginal Rights?" *Briarpatch Magazine*, July 1, 2011, 3.

53. The Assembly of First Nations, quoted in Menno Boldt and J. Anthony Long, "Tribal Philosophies and the Charter of Rights and Freedoms," in *The Quest for Justice*, 171.

54. Take, for instance, Homi Bhabha's suggestion that by highlighting the fractured and in-between spaces of social identities we "open up" the very "possibility of a cultural hybridity that entertains difference without an assumed or imposed hierarchy." See Bhabha, *The Location of Culture*, 4. For a discussion of both the transformative possibilities and limits of Bhabha's project, see, Hardt and Negri, *Empire*, 137–59.

55. Judith Butler, Ernesto Laclau, and Slavoj Žižek, *Contingency, Hegemony, Universality: Contemporary Dialogues on the Left* (London: Verso, 2000), 14–15.

56. Benhabib, *The Claims of Culture*, 8.

57. Ibid., x, 19–20, 184.

58. Butler, Laclau and Žižek, *Contingency, Hegemony, Universality*, 15.

59. Duncan Ivison, "Deliberative Democracy and the Politics of Reconciliation," in *Deliberative Democracy in Practice*, ed. David Kahane, Daniel Weinstock, Dominque Leydet, and Melissa Williams, 115–37 (Vancouver: University of British Columbia Press, 2010).

60. Dirlik, *Postmodernity's Histories*, 207.

61. Arif Dirlik and Roxann Prazniak, "Introduction: Cultural Identity and the Politics of Place," in *Places and Politics in an Age of Globalization*, ed. Arif Dirlik and Roxann Prazniak (Lanham, Md.: Rowman and Littlefield, 2000), 9.

62. Ibid.

63. Benhabib, *The Claims of Culture*, 185.

64. Ibid.

65. James Tully, "Aboriginal Peoples: Negotiating Reconciliation," in *Canadian Politics*, ed. James Bickerton and Alain-G. Gagnon, 3rd ed. (Peterborough, Ont.: Broadview Press, 2000), 419. Also see Royal Commission on Aboriginal Peoples, *Report of the Royal Commission on Aboriginal Peoples*, vol. 1: ch. 6.

66. For a survey of literature in the Canadian context, see Alfred, *Peace, Power, Righteousness*; Tully, "Aboriginal Peoples: Negotiating Reconciliation"; Michael Asch, "From 'Calder' to 'Van der Peet': Aboriginal Peoples and Canadian Law," in *Indigenous Peoples' Rights in Australia, Canada, and New Zealand*, ed. Paul Havemann (Auckland: Oxford University Press, 1997), 428–46; Patrick Macklem, *Indigenous Difference and the Constitution of Canada* (Toronto: University of Toronto Press, 2001). In the American context, see Robert A. Williams, *The American Indian in Western Legal Thought: The Discourses of Conquest* (New York: Oxford University Press, 1990). In the Australian context, see Henry Reynolds, *Aboriginal Sovereignty: Three Nations, One Australia?* (Sydney: Allan and Unwin Publishers, 1996).

67. Michael Asch, "Self-Government in the New Millennium," in *Nation-to-Nation: Aboriginal Sovereignty and the Future of Canada*, ed. John Bird, Lorraine Land, and Murray MacAdam, 65–73 (Toronto: Irwin Publishing, 2002); and Asch, "From 'Calder' to 'Van der Peet.'"

68. Patricia Monture, *Thunder in My Soul: A Mohawk Woman Speaks* (Halifax: Fernwood Press, 1995).

69. Ibid., 175.

70. Wendy Brown, *States of Injury: Power and Freedom in Late Modernity* (Princeton: Princeton University Press, 1995), 173.

71. Sarah Hunt, "More Than a Poster Campaign: Redefining Colonial Violence," *Decolonization: Indigeneity, Education and Society Blog*, February 14, 2013, http://decol onization.wordpress.com/2013/02/14/more-than-a-poster-campaign-redefining -colonial-violence/.

72. Ibid.

73. Dory Nason, "We Hold Our Hands Up: On Indigenous Women's Love and Resistance," *Decolonization: Indigeneity, Education and Society Blog*, February 12, 2013, http://decolonization.wordpress.com/2013/02/12/we-hold-our-hands-up-on-indig enous-womens-love-and-resistance/.

74. Day, *Multiculturalism and the History of Canadian Diversity*, 222.

75. Dirlik, *Postmodernity's Histories*, 205.

76. Stuart Hall, "The Work of Representation," in *Representation: Cultural Representations and Signifying Practices*, ed. Stuart Hall (London: Sage Publications, 1997), 44.

77. Jeffrey Tobin, "Cultural Construction and Native Nationalism," *Boundary 2* 22, no. 2 (1994): 131.

4. Seeing Red

1. Prime Minister of Canada, "Statement and Apology" (Ottawa: Indian Affairs and Northern Development, 2008). Online as "Prime Minister Harper Offers Full Apology on Behalf of Canadians for the Indian Residential Schools System," Prime Minister of Canada website, June 11, 2008, http://www.pm.gc.ca/eng/news/2008/06/ 11/pm-offers-full-apology-behalf-canadians-indian-residential-schools-system.

2. Courtney Young, "Canada and the Legacy of Indian Residential Schools: Transitional Justice for Indigenous People in a Non-Transitional Society," in *Identities in*

Transition: Challenges for Transitional Justice in Divided Societies, ed. Paige Arthur (Cambridge: Cambridge University Press, 2011), 217–50; "Native Groups Shut out of Residential School Apology," *Canadian Press*, June 5, 2008; "Aboriginal Leaders Hail Historic Apology," *Ottawa Citizen*, June 11, 2008.

3. David Ljunggren, "Every G20 Nation Wants to Be Canada, Insists PM," *Reuters*, September 25, 2009.

4. Stephen Hui, "Sean Atleo Criticizes Stephen Harper over 'No History of Colonialism' Remark," *Georgia Straight*, October 2, 2009.

5. Jeff Corntassel and Cindy Holder, "Who's Sorry Now? Government Apologies, Truth Commissions and Indigenous Self-Determination in Australia, Canada, Guatemala, and Peru," *Human Rights Review* 9, no. 4 (2008): 465–89.

6. For a genealogy of the emergence of "the field of transitional justice," see Paige Arthur, "How 'Transitions' Reshaped Human Rights: A Conceptual History of Transitional Justice," *Human Rights Quarterly* 31 (2009): 321–67. For a discussion of the application of transitional justice concepts and mechanisms to the context of Indigenous–state relations, see C. Young, "Canada and the Legacy of Indian Residential Schools"; Will Kymlicka and Bashir Bashir, eds., *The Politics of Reconciliation in Multicultural Societies* (Oxford: Oxford University Press, 2008); Damian Short, *Reconciliation and Colonial Power: Indigenous Rights in Australia* (Burlington, Vt.: Ashgate Publishers, 2008).

7. Andrew Schaap, "Political Reconciliation through a Struggle for Recognition?," *Social and Legal Studies* 13, no. 4 (2004): 523 (emphasis added).

8. For example, see Axel Honneth, "Integrity and Disrespect: Principles of the Concept of Morality Based on the Theory of Recognition," *Political Theory* 20, no. 2 (1992): 187–201. For a discussion of Honneth's approach, see Fraser and Honneth, *Redistribution or Recognition?* Indigenous people often equate this form of reconciliation with individual and collective "healing."

9. Trudy Govier, *Forgiveness and Revenge* (New York: Routledge, 2002), viii.

10. Will Kymlicka and Bashir Bashir, "Introduction: Struggles for Inclusion and Reconciliation in Modern Democracies," in Kymlicka and Bashir, *The Politics of Reconciliation in Multicultural Societies*, 1–24.

11. Trudy Govier, *Forgiveness and Revenge*; Govier, "Acknowledgement and Truth Commissions: The Case of Canada," in *Philosophy and Aboriginal Rights: Critical Dialogues*, ed. Sandra Tomsons and Lorraine Mayer (Don Mills, Ont.: Oxford University Press, 2013). Also see Thomas Brudholm, *Resentment's Virtue: Jean Améry and the Refusal to Forgive* (Philadelphia: Temple University Press, 2008).

12. Oxford English Dictionary quoted in Dale Turner, "Aboriginal Relations in Canada: The Importance of Political Reconciliation," Federation for the Humanities and Social Sciences Blog, *Equity Matters*, May 3, 2011, http://www.idees-ideas.ca/blog/aboriginal-relations-canada-importance-political-reconciliationx.

13. Brudholm, *Resentment's Virtue*, 3.

14. Jean Améry, *At the Mind's Limit: Contemplations by a Survivor on Auschwitz and its Realities*, trans. Sidney and Stella Rosenfeld (Bloomington: Indiana University

Press, 1980). Also see, Friedrich Nietzsche, *On the Genealogy of Morals and Ecce Homo*, ed. Walter Kaufmann (New York: Vintage, 1989).

15. Brudholm, *Resentment's Virtue*, 4.

16. Ibid., 4–5.

17. I say "explicitly" here because achieving reconciliation in the three senses noted above always implicitly informed the turn to recognition politics that began in the early 1970s. Also, I borrow the term "nontransitional" from Courtney Young, "Transitional Justice for Indigenous People in a Non-Transitional Society," Research Brief for Identities in Transition, *International Center for Transitional Justice*, October 2009.

18. Jean Améry, "The Birth of Man from the Spirit of Violence: Frantz Fanon the Revolutionary," *Wasafiri* 44 (2005): 14.

19. Thomas Brudholm, "Revisiting Resentments: Jean Améry and the Dark Side of Forgiveness," *Journal of Human Rights* 5, no. 1 (2006): 7–26; Robert Solomon, *Living with Nietzsche: What the Great "Immoralist" Has to Teach Us* (Oxford: Oxford University Press, 2003); Alice MacLachlan, "Unreasonable Resentments," *Journal of Social Philosophy* 41, no. 4 (2010): 422–41.

20. See under "resentment," http://oxforddictionaries.com (emphasis added).

21. On the political significance of anger in the face of gendered and racial oppression, I have learned much from the foundational analysis in Audre Lorde, "The Uses of Anger," *Women Studies Quarterly* 25, nos. 1/2 (1997): 278–85. Also see the fierce poem by queer Menominee poet Chrystos, "They're Always Telling Me I'm Too Angry," *Fugitive Colors* (Cleveland: Cleveland State University Poetry Center, 1995), 44.

22. Adam Smith, *The Theory of Moral Sentiments* (New York: Penguin Modern Classics, 2010); John Rawls, *A Theory of Justice* (Cambridge, Mass.: Harvard University Press, 2005); Solomon, *Living with Nietzsche*; Jeffrie Murphy, *Getting Even: Forgiveness and Its Limits* (New York: Oxford University Press, 2003); MacLachlan, "Unreasonable Resentments"; Brudholm, *Resentment's Virtue*.

23. John Rawls, *A Theory of Justice* (Cambridge, Mass.: Harvard University Press, 1971), 533.

24. Murphy, *Getting Even*.

25. MacLachlan, "Unreasonable Resentments," 422–23.

26. Brudholm, *Resentment's Virtue*, 9–10.

27. For example, in the context of post-Holocaust demands for reconciliation, Jean Améry wrote: there "seems to be general agreement that the final say on resentment is that of Friedrich Nietzsche" (Améry, *At the Mind's Limit*, 67).

28. Ibid., 68.

29. Friedrich Nietzsche, *Thus Spoke Zarathustra*, ed. Adrian Del Caro and Robert Pipin (Cambridge: Cambridge University Press, 2006), 111.

30. Ibid. (emphasis added).

31. Nietzsche, *On the Genealogy of Morals and Ecce Homo*, 230.

32. Ibid, 38–39, 57–58.

33. Richard Wagamese, "Returning to Harmony," in *Response, Responsibility and Renewal*, ed. Aboriginal Healing Foundation (Ottawa: Aboriginal Healing Foundation Research Series, 2009), 144.

34. Fanon, *The Wretched of the Earth*, 89.

35. Jean-Paul Sartre, preface to Fanon, *The Wretched of the Earth*, liv.

36. See Antonio Gramsci, *Selections from the Prison Notebooks* (New York: International Publishers, 1999).

37. Fanon, *The Wretched of the Earth*, 27.

38. Frantz Fanon, *Black Skin, White Masks*, trans. Richard Philcox (Boston: Grove Press, 2008), 18.

39. Fanon, *The Wretched of the Earth*, 15 (emphasis added).

40. Fanon, *Black Skin, White Masks* (2008), xiii–xiv.

41. The arguments of both Hegel and early Marx are paradigmatic of the former view.

42. Fanon, *The Wretched of the Earth*, 15–16, 94.

43. Ibid., 4, 5, 16, 89.

44. Ibid., 5. On "envy" and its close relationship to "resentment," see Marguerite La Caze, "Envy and Resentment," *Philosophical Explorations: An International Journal for the Philosophy of Mind and Action* 4, no. 1 (2007): 141–47.

45. Fanon, *Wretched of the Earth*, 89.

46. Ibid., 31.

47. Améry, "The Birth of Man from the Spirit of Violence," 15.

48. Fanon, *Wretched of the Earth*, 31.

49. Ibid., 8.

50. Ibid., 89.

51. In the following chapter I explore the limitations of Fanon's views on the instrumentality of Indigenous cultural politics in more detail.

52. Georges Erasmus, "Twenty Years of Disappointed Hopes," in *Drum Beat: Anger and Renewal in Indian Country*, ed. Boyce Richardson (Ottawa: Summerhill Press with the Assembly of First Nations, 1990), 24–28.

53. Newfoundland also failed to ratify the deal.

54. Kiera Ladner and Leanne Simpson, eds., *This Is an Honour Song: Twenty Years since the Barricades* (Winnipeg: Arbeiter Ring Press, 2010), 1–2.

55. Linda Pertusati, *In Defence of Mohawk Land: Ethno Political Conflict in Native North America* (New York: State University of New York Press, 1997), 101–2.

56. "Oka Costs Natives Canada's Sympathy," *Toronto Star*, November 27, 1990, A9.

57. For examples of such representations, see Mark Kennedy, "PM Brands Warriors 'Terrorists,' Calls for Surrender," *Ottawa Citizen*, August 29, 1990, A2; "Army Moving In on Mohawks; 'No One above the Law' PM Says of Warriors," *Edmonton Journal*, August 29, 1990, A1; William Johnson, "Oka Symbolizes Meech Aftermath," *Edmonton Journal*, July 24, 1990, A7; "Judge Recognizes Native 'Rage' as Oka Standoff Leaders Jailed," *Toronto Star*, February 20, 1992, A13; "Thousands of Okas Loom," *The*

Gazette, September 28, 1990, A4. For critical analyses of such representations, see James Winter, *Common Cents: The Media's Portrayal of the Gulf War and Other Issues* (Montreal: Black Roade Press, 1992); Gail Valaskakis, "Rights and Warriors," *Ariel: A Review of International English Literature* 25, no. 1 (1994): 60–72.

58. Boyce Richardson, ed., *Drumbeat: Anger and Renewal in Indian Country* (Ottawa: Summerhill Press and the Assembly of First Nations, 1989).

59. Daniel Ashini, "David Confronts Goliath: The Innu of Ungava versus the NATO Alliance," in Richardson, *Drumbeat*, 43–72; Marie Wadden, *Nitassinan: The Innu Struggle to Reclaim Their Homeland* (Vancouver: Douglas and McIntyre, 1991).

60. Ward Churchill, "Last Stand at Lubicon Lake," *Struggle for the Land: Native North American Resistance to Genocide, Ecocide and Colonization* (Winnipeg: Arbeiter Ring Press, 1999), 190–238; Dawn Martin-Hill, *The Lubicon Lake Nation: Indigenous Knowledge and Power* (Toronto: University of Toronto Press, 2008).

61. See Nicholas Blomley, "'Shut the Province Down': First Nations' Blockades in British Columbia, 1884–1995," *BC Studies* 111 (1996): 5–35.

62. Jean-Maurice Matchewan, "Mitchikanibikonginik Algonquins of Barrier Lake: Our Long Battle to Create a Sustainable Future," in Richardson, *Drumbeat*, 139–68.

63. Bruce W. Hodgins, Ute Lischke, and David McNab, eds., *Blockades and Resistance: Studies in Action and Peace at the Temegami Blockades of 1989–90* (Waterloo, Ont.: Wilfrid Laurier University Press, 2003).

64. Fanon, *The Wretched of the Earth*, 15.

65. "Act or Face Threat of Violence, Native Leader Warns Ottawa," *Toronto Star*, June 1, 1988, A1.

66. In Commonwealth countries a "royal commission" is a major commission of inquiry into an issue of perceived national public importance.

67. Royal Commission on Aboriginal Peoples, *Report of the Royal Commission on Aboriginal Peoples*, 5 vols. (Ottawa: Minister of Supply and Services, 1996); available online at http://www.collectionscanada.gc.ca and http://www.aadnc-aandc.gc.ca.

68. Mary Hurley and Jill Wherrett, *The Report of the Royal Commission on Aboriginal Peoples* (Ottawa: Parliamentary Information and Research Service, 2000), 2.

69. See in particular, Kiera Ladner, "Negotiated Inferiority: The Royal Commission on Aboriginal Peoples' Vision of a Renewed Relationship," *American Review of Canadian Studies* 31, nos. 1/2 (2001): 241–64.

70. Trudy Grovier, "Acknowledgement and Truth Commissions: The Case of Canada," in Tomsons and Mayer, *Philosophy and Aboriginal Rights*, 44.

71. Alfred, *Wasáse*, 53.

72. Taiaiake Alfred, "Restitution is the Real Pathway for Justice of Indigenous Peoples," in Aboriginal Healing Foundation, *Response, Responsibility, and Renewal*, 179–87; Stephanie Irlbacher-Fox, *Finding Dahshaa: Self-Government, Social Suffering, and Aboriginal Policy in Canada* (Vancouver: University of British Columbia Press, 2009). These two texts embody both of these criticisms.

73. Irlbacher-Fox, *Finding Dahshaa*, 33.

74. Fanon, *The Wretched of the Earth*, 89.

75. Department of Indian Affairs and Northern Development, *Gathering Strength: Canada's Aboriginal Action Plan* (Ottawa: Minister of Public Works and Government Services Canada, 1998).

76. Ibid., 1.

77. Irlbacher-Fox, *Finding Dahshaa*, 106–8.

78. Sam McKegney, "From Trickster Poetics to Transgressive Politics: Substantiating Survivance in Tomson Highway's *Kiss of the Fur Queen*," *Studies in American Indian Literatures* 17, no. 4 (2005): 85.

79. Department of Indian Affairs and Northern Development website, "Notes for an Address by the Honourable Jane Stewart, Minister of Indian Affairs and Northern Development, on the Occasion of the Unveiling of *Gathering Strength—Canada's Aboriginal Action Plan*," Ottawa, January 7, 1998, http://www.aadnc-aandc.gc.ca/eng/1100100015725/1100100015726.

80. Aboriginal Healing Foundation, *FAQs*, http://www.ahf.ca/faqs.

81. Alfred, *Wasáse*, 152.

82. Department of Indian Affairs and Northern Development, *Gathering Strength*, 11.

83. Bonita Lawrence, *Fractured Homeland: Federal Recognition and Algonquin Identity in Ontario* (Vancouver: University of British Columbia Press, 2012), 71. Lawrence offers a discussion of "alternative" comprehensive claim options.

84. Kulchyski, *Like the Sound of a Drum*, 100.

85. Department of Indian Affairs and Northern Development website, *The Government of Canada's Approach to Implementation of the Inherent Right and Negotiation of Self-Government* (Ottawa: Department of Indian Affairs and Northern Development, 1995), http://www.aadnc-aandc.gc.ca/eng/1100100031843/1100100031844 (emphasis added).

86. Michael Asch, "Self-Government in the New Millennium," in *Nation to Nation: Aboriginal Sovereignty and the Future of Canada*, ed. John Bird, Lorraine Land, and Murray MacAdam (Toronto: Irwin Publishing, 2002), 70.

87. *R. v. Van der Peet*, (1996), Supreme Court Ruling, 507, 539.

88. Lisa Dufraimont, "From Regulation to Recolonization: Justifiable Infringement of Aboriginal Rights at the Supreme Court of Canada," *University of Toronto Faculty of Law Review*, 58, no. 1 (2000): 1–30.

89. Prime Minister of Canada, "Statement and Apology."

90. Wolfe, "Settler Colonialism and the Elimination of the Native," 388.

91. Ibid.

92. Jefferie Murphy, "Moral Epistemology, the Retributive Emotions, and the 'Clumsy Moral Philosophy' of Jesus Christ," in *The Passions of Law*, ed. S. Bandes, 152, quoted in Brudholm, "Revisiting Resentments," 13.

93. Paulette Regan, *Unsettling the Settler Within: Indian Residential Schools, Truth Telling, and Reconciliation in Canada* (Vancouver: University of British Columbia Press, 2010), 7.

94. Alfred, "Restitution Is the Real Pathway to Justice for Indigenous Peoples," 182–84.

5. The Plunge into the Chasm of the Past

1. Sonia Kruks, *Retrieving Experience: Subjectivity and Recognition in Feminist Politics* (Ithaca: Cornell University Press, 2001), 88; Azzedine Haddour, "Sartre and Fanon on Negritude and Political Empowerment," *Sartre Studies International* 2, no. 1 (2005): 286–301.

2. David Caute, *Fanon* (New York: Fontana, 1970), 21–31; Irene Grendzier, *Frantz Fanon: A Critical Study* (New York: Vintage, 1974), 44; David Macey, *Frantz Fanon: A Life* (London: Granta, 2000), 186.

3. Jock McCullock, *Black Soul, White Artifact: Fanon's Clinical Psychology and Social Theory* (Cambridge: Cambridge University Press, 2003), 36.

4. I attribute this third interpretation to Nigel Gibson, *Fanon: The Postcolonial Imagination* (Cambridge: Polity, 2003); Robert Benasconi, "The Assumption of Negritude: Aimé Césaire, Frantz Fanon, and the Vicious Circle of Racial Politics," *Parallax* 8, no. 2 (2002): 69–83; Lou Turner, "Marginal Note on Minority Questions in the Thought of Frantz Fanon," *Philosophia Africana* 4, no. 2 (2001): 37–46 ; and to a slightly lesser extent, Anita Parry, "Resistance Theory/Theorizing Resistance or Two Cheers for Nativism," in *Rethinking Fanon: The Continuing Dialogue*, ed. Nigel Gibson, 215–50 (Amherst, Mass.: Humanity Books, 1999). Within this third approach authors tend to situate Fanon more in line with the "subjectivist" conception of negritude advanced by Césaire—which conceptualizes black subjectivity as a "construction" representing "the colonized condition and its refusal"—as opposed to the "objectivist" notion promulgated by Senghor, where negritude is aligned with a "biologically determined notion of blackness as a distinctive mode of being and collective identity" (Parry, "Resistance Theory/Theorizing Resistance," 230).

5. Katherine Gines, "Fanon and Sartre 50 Years Later: To Retain or Reject the Concept of Race," *Sartre Studies International* 9, no. 2 (2003): 55–70.

6. Kruks, *Retrieving Experience*, 98. Also see Azzedine Haddour, "Sartre and Fanon on Negritude and Political Empowerment," *Sartre Studies International* 2, no. 1 (2005): 286–301.

7. Jean-Paul Sartre, *Anti-Semite and Jew: An Exploration of the Etiology of Hate* (New York: Schocken Books, 1974).

8. Ibid., 69, 143.

9. Jean Paul Sartre, *Being and Nothingness* (New York: Washington Square Press, 1956), 324–29.

10. Ibid., 362.

11. Ibid., 340–400, 471–74.

12. Sonia Kruks, "Sartre, Fanon and Identity Politics," in *Fanon: A Critical Reader*, ed. Lewis Gordon, T. Denean Sharpley-Whiting, and Renee T. White (Malden, Mass.: Blackwell, 1996), 124.

13. Sartre, *Being and Nothingness*, 473. For a helpful discussion of Sartre's "pessimistic" reading of Hegel, see Majid Yar, "Recognition and the Politics of Human(e) Desire," *Theory, Culture and Society* 18, nos. 2–3 (2001): 58–62. Also see Axel Honneth, *The Struggle for Recognition: The Moral Grammar of Social Conflicts* (Cambridge: MIT

Press, 1995), 145–59; Robert Williams, *Hegel's Ethics of Recognition* (Berkeley: University of California Press, 1997), 371–79.

14. Yar, "Recognition and the Politics of Human(e) Desire," 60–61.

15. Sartre, *Being and Nothingness,* 475. For a less pessimistic account of Sartre's theory of recognition, see T. Storm Heter, "Authenticity and Others: Sartre's Ethics of Recognition," *Sartre Studies International* 12, no. 2 (2006): 17–43. Sartre scholars generally agree that Sartre eventually sought to establish the foundation for an existential ethics that recognizes, within the frame of authenticity, the freedom of others. To act authentically would under this formulation require that one respect the freedom of others. The beginnings of Sartre's existential ethics are sketched in *Notebooks for an Ethics* (Chicago: University of Chicago Press, 1992).

16. Ibid. Sartre, *Anti-Semite and Jew,* 79.

17. Ibid., 59–60.

18. Ibid., 92.

19. Ibid., 94.

20. Ibid., 90–135.

21. Ibid., 93.

22. Ibid., 94–95.

23. Ibid., 137.

24. Ibid.

25. Ibid., 138 (emphasis added).

26. Ibid., 141.

27. Ibid., 148.

28. Ibid., 149.

29. Jean-Paul Sartre, "Black Orpheus," in *Race,* ed. Robert Bernasconi (New York: Blackwell, 2001), 115–42.

30. Ibid., 118.

31. Ibid.

32. Ibid.

33. This distinction in Marx shapes Sartre's views on the role played by negritude in the struggle against capitalist imperialism. The following is the most commonly cited passage by Marx that makes this distinction: "The economic conditions have in the first place transformed the mass of the people of the country into wage-workers. The domination of capital has created for this mass of people a common situation with common interests. This mass is already a class, as opposed to capital, but not yet for itself. In the struggle . . . this mass unites, and constitutes itself as a class for itself. The interests which it defends are the interests of its class. But the struggle of class against class is a political struggle" (Karl Marx, *The Poverty of Philosophy* [New York: Prometheus Books, 1995], 188–89). Whether or not it is correct to read this distinction into Marx is a matter of debate. Edward Andrew, "Class in Itself and Class against Capital: Karl Marx and His Classifiers," *Canadian Journal of Political Science* 16, no. 3 (1983): 577–84.

34. Sartre, "Black Orpheus," 119.

35. Ibid.

36. Aimé Césaire and René Depestre , "An Interview with Aimé Césaire," in *Aimé Césaire: Discourse on Colonialism* (New York: Monthly Review Press, 2000), 89–90.

37. Sartre, "Black Orpheus," 137.

38. Ibid.

39. Ibid. (emphasis added).

40. Ibid., 89, 95, 97.

41. Ibid., 89, 92.

42. Ibid., 95 (emphasis added).

43. Ibid., 90.

44. Sartre, *Anti-Semite and Jew*, 93. For a discussion of the similarities between Sartre and Fanon on this matter, see Kruks, "Sartre, Fanon and Identity Politics," 128–29.

45. Fanon, *Black Skin, White Masks* (2008), 42, 157, 93.

46. Ibid., 45.

47. This is the main argument that Fanon develops in the chapter "The So-Called Dependency Complex of the Colonized," in *Black Skin, White Masks.* Here Fanon takes aim at Octave Mannoni's *Prospero and Caliban: The Psychology of the Colonized* (Ann Arbor: University of Michigan Press, 1990), in which Mannoni suggests that the tendency to accept colonial relations of dependency exhibited by some non-Western societies vis-à-vis their colonizers reflects an *inherent or natural* disposition of certain non-Western peoples to accept imposed forms of authority and rule.

48. Fanon, *Black Skin, White Masks* (2008), 188.

49. Ibid., 157. Practices of desubjectification that tactically deploy "reverse" discourses as a means of disrupting a hegemonic field of power is discussed by Michel Foucault in *The History of Sexuality* (New York: Vintage, 1990), 1:101. The transformative potential of reverse discourse in the context of anticolonial "nativist" movements is critically endorsed by Benita Parry in "Resistance Theory/Theorizing Resistance," 221–50.

50. Robert Benasconi, "Eliminating the Cycle of Violence: The Place of a Dying Colonialism within Fanon's Revolutionary Thought," *Philosophia Africana* 4, no. 2 (2001): 19.

51. Gibson, *Fanon*, 81.

52. Fanon, *Black Skin, White Masks* (2008), 89–119.

53. Ibid., 95 (emphasis added).

54. Ibid. (emphasis added).

55. Ibid., 109.

56. Ibid., 110.

57. Ibid., 111.

58. Ibid., 112

59. Ibid., 117.

60. Ibid., xviii, 113.

61. Ibid., 95.

62. Ibid., 19, 28, 132, 197.

63. Frantz Fanon, "Algeria Unveiled," in *The Fanon Reader*, ed. Azzedine Haddour (London: Pluto Press, 2006), 108.

64. McCullock, *Black Soul, White Artifact*.

65. Fanon, *Black Skin, White Masks* (2008), 115.

66. Léopold Senghor, "Negritude and Modernity or Negritude as a Humanism for the Twentieth Century," in *Race*, ed. Robert Benasconi (New York: Blackwell, 2001), 144.

67. Fanon, *Black Skin, White Masks* (2008), 150 (emphasis added).

68. Ibid., 101–11.

69. Ibid., xviii.

70. Ibid., 199.

71. Gibson, *Fanon*, 73–78. Fanon's main charge was that Sartre had ignored or downplayed the importance of the *experiential* worth of negritude for blacks living under the gaze of colonial racism. Sartre had "intellectualized" the lived experience of blackness, and in doing so "destroyed Black zeal" and "impulsiveness." See Fanon, *Black Skin, White Masks* (2008), 113–14. In this sense, Nigel Gibson suggests that Fanon's main criticism of Sartre was that he had largely abandoned the insights of his phenomenological existentialism for a crude Marxist determinism.

72. Fanon, *Black Skin, White Masks* (2008), 80.

73. Ibid., 201.

74. Ibid., 206.

75. Frantz Fanon, "West Indians and Africans," in *Toward the African Revolution* (Boston: Grove Press, 1967), 18.

76. Ibid., 17.

77. Ibid. (emphasis added).

78. Ibid., 21–22.

79. Ibid., 23, 26.

80. Ibid.

81. Fanon, *Black Skin, White Masks* (2008), 63.

82. Frantz Fanon, "Racism and Culture," *Toward the African Revolution* (Boston: Grove Press, 1967), 31–44. This essay was originally presented at the Paris meeting of the First Congress of Negro Writers and Artists in September 1956.

83. Ibid., 32. For "culturalization of racism," see Sharene Razack, *Looking White People in the Eye: Gender, Race and Culture in Courtrooms and Classrooms* (Toronto: University of Toronto Press, 2006), 60; Philomena Essed, *Understanding Everyday Racism: An Interdisciplinary Theory* (London: Sage Publishing, 1991), 14.

84. Fanon, "Racism and Culture," 32.

85. Fanon does not mean to suggest that racism's crude biological variant has "disappeared," however. To be sure, as Fanon continues, he points out that during his day organizations as prominent as the World Health Organization were still conducting studies that advanced "scientific arguments" in "support of a physiological lobotomy of the African Negro." What Fanon is attempting to do, rather, is highlight the capacity of racial discourse to modify itself over time and context. In the early days of "pure"

exploitation, such as slavery, the biological articulation of racism served to justify the domination and exploitation of blacks just fine. But with the gradual advance of scientific and other evidence undermining assumptions about race-based inferiority and superiority, it became increasingly difficult to defend the exploitation of blacks in biological terms. As a result, such "affirmations, crude and massive, [gave] way to a more refined argument" which established a new means to "camouflage" the "techniques by which man is exploited." Racism's turn to culture provided this camouflage. See Fanon, "Racism and Culture," 32.

86. Ibid., 34.

87. Fanon, *The Wretched of the Earth*, 158.

88. Ibid., 154.

89. Fanon, "Racism and Culture," 148.

90. Fanon, *Wretched of the Earth*, 170.

91. Gibson, *Fanon*, ch. 6; Fanon, *The Wretched of the Earth*, 178–79 (emphasis added).

92. Fanon, *The Wretched of the Earth*, 43.

93. Leanne Simpson, *Dancing on Our Turtle's Back: Stories of Nishnaabeg Re-Creation, Resurgence and a New Emergence* (Winnipeg: Arbeiter Ring Press, 2011), 32.

Conclusion

1. See my discussion of the work of Taiaiake Alfred and Leanne Simpson below.

2. Fanon, *The Wretched of the Earth*, 168 (emphasis added).

3. Ibid., 159–60.

4. See in particular, Alfred, *Peace, Power, Righteousness*; Alfred, *Wasáse*; Simpson, *Dancing on Our Turtle's Back*.

5. Alfred, *Peace, Power, Righteousness*, xiii; Alfred, *Wasáse*, 19. Simpson, *Dancing on Our Turtle's Back*, 17.

6. Alfred, *Wasáse*, 19.

7. Simpson, *Dancing on Our Turtle's Back*, 17.

8. Alfred, *Peace, Power, Righteousness*, 5 (emphasis added).

9. Simpson, *Dancing on Our Turtle's Back*, 17–18.

10. Alfred, *Peace, Power, Righteousness*, xviii, 66, 80–88.

11. Ibid., xiii.

12. Simpson, *Dancing on Our Turtle's Back*, 22.

13. Ibid.

14. Alfred, *Peace, Power, Righteousness*, xiii (emphasis added).

15. Ibid., xviii.

16. Simpson, *Dancing on Our Turtle's Back*, 51.

17. Ibid.

18. Alfred, *Peace, Power Righteousness*, xviii.

19. Alfred, *Wasáse*, 22.

20. Ibid., 23.

21. Ibid., 84.

22. Chris Finley, "Decolonizing the Queer Native Body (and Recovering the Native Bull-Dyke): Bringing 'Sexy Back' and out of Native Studies' Closet," in *Queer Indigenous Studies: Critical Interventions in Theory, Politics, and Literature*, ed. Qwo-Li Driskill, Chris Finley, Brian Joseph Gilley, and Scott Lauria Morgensen, 31–42 (Minneapolis: University of Minnesota Press, 2011); and Andrea Smith, "Queer Theory and Native Studies: The Heteronormativity of Settler-Colonialism," in Qwo-Li Driskill, et al., *Queer Indigenous Studies*, 43–65.

23. Leanne Simpson, "Queering Resurgence: Taking on Heteropatriarchy in Indigenous Nation-Building," *Mamawipawin: Indigenous Governence and Community Based Research Space*, June 1, 2012, http://130.179.14.66/blog/.

24. Emma LaRoque, "Métis and Feminist," in *Making Space for Indigenous Feminism*, ed. Joyce Green (Halifax: Fernwood, 2007), 63–64.

25. Simpson, *Dancing on Our Turtle's Back*, 60–61, 105–9.

26. Simpson, "Queering Resurgence."

27. Alfred, *Wasáse*, 40–45.

28. Alfred, *Peace, Power, Righteousness*, 56.

29. Ibid.

30. Monture, *Thunder in My Soul*.

31. Alfred, *Wasáse*, 180.

32. Government of Canada, Bill C-45 Jobs and Growth Act, December 14, 2012, http://www.parl.gc.ca/LegisInfo/BillDetails.aspx?Language=E&Mode=1&Bill=C45 &Parl=41&Ses=1.

33. "9 Questions about Idle No More," CBC News, January 5, 2013, http://www .cbc.ca/news/canada/9-questions-about-idle-no-more-1.1301843.

34. The Canadian Press, "First Nation blockade in Sarnia coming down," *CBC News*, January 2, 2013, http://www.cbc.ca/news/canada/windsor/first-nation-blockade -in-sarnia-coming-down-1.1323922.

35. Kevin Griffin, "Metro Vancouver Idle No More rallies to continue despite Harper's decision to meet native leaders," *Ottawa Citizen*, January 4, 2013, http:// www.cbc.ca/news/canada/windsor/first-nation-blockade-in-sarnia-coming-down-1.13 23922.

36. Christie Blachford, "Inevitable Puffery and Horse Manure Surrounds Hunger Strike While Real Aboriginal Problems Forgotten," *National Post*, December 27, 2012, http://fullcomment.nationalpost.com/2012/12/27/christie-blatchford-inevitable -puffery-and-horse-manure-surrounds-hunger-strike-while-real-aboriginal-problems -forgotten/.

37. Kelly McParland, "Idle No More Has Been Seized by Occupying Forces," *National Post*, January 17, 2013, http://fullcomment.nationalpost.com/2013/01/17/ kelly-mcparland-idle-no-more-has-been-seized-by-occupying-forces/.

38. Pamela Palmater, "Why We Are Idle No More," *Ottawa Citizen*, December 29, 2012, http://www2.canada.com/ottawacitizen/news/archives/story.html?id=63dd9779 -10eb-4807-bd47-223817524aa2.

39. Leanne Simpson, "Fish Broth and Fasting," *DividedNoMore Blog*, January 16, 2013, http://dividednomore.ca/2013/01/16/fish-broth-fasting/.

40. Russell Diabo, "Mr. Harper, One Short Meeting Won't End Native Protests," *Toronto Globe and Mail*, January 11, 2013, http://www.theglobeandmail.com/globe -debate/mr-harper-one-short-meeting-wont-end-native-protests/article7209111/.

41. Arthur Manual, "Idle No More, the Effective Voice of Indigenous Peoples: Current AFN Negotiations with Prime Minister a Go-Nowhere Approach," *The Media Co-op*, January 14, 2013, http://www.mediacoop.ca/fr/story/idle-no-more-effective -voice-indigenous-peoples/15603.

42. Thomson Reuters, "First Nation Chief threatens to Block Resource Develop-ment," *Financial Post*, January 10, 2013, http://business.financialpost.com/2013/01/10/ first-nations-chief-threatens-to-block-resource-development/?__lsa=ff88-c6c5.

43. John Robson, "Don't Brush off Grand Chief Derek Nepinak," *Sun News Straight Talk*, January 13, 2013, http://www.sunnewsnetwork.ca/sunnews/straighttalk/archi ves/2013/01/20130113-101523.html.

44. "Idle No More Protesters Stall Railway Lines, Highways," CBC News, January 16, 2013, http://www.cbc.ca/news/canada/idle-no-more-protesters-stall-railway-lines -highways-1.1303452.

45. Indian Country Today Media Network Staff, "Chief Theresa Spence Ends Fast with 13-Point Declaration of Commitment to First Nations," Indian Country Today, January 24, 2013, http://indiancountrytodaymedianetwork.com/2013/01/24/chief -theresa-spence-ends-fast-13-point-declaration-commitment-first-nations-147195.

46. Natalie Stechyson, "Idle No More Movement Fizzles Out Online, Analysis Finds," *Vancouver Sun*, February 10, 2013, http://www.vancouversun.com/news/natio nal/Idle+More+movement+fizzles+online+analysis+finds/7945480/story.html.

47. Benjamin Aube, "Negotiations, Not Blockades, Lead to Change," *Global News*, January 25, 2013, http://www.timminspress.com/2013/01/25/negotiations-not-block ades-lead-to-change.

48. "Aboriginals Insist Meeting with Stephen Harper Must Fix 'Broken' System," *Calgary Herald*, January 4, 2013, http://o.canada.com/news/national/stephen-harper -to-meet-aboriginal-leaders-next-week/.

49. Armina Ligaya, "Less Than Half of Canadians Support the Idle No More Movement: Poll," *National Post*, January 21, 2013, http://news.nationalpost.com/2013/ 01/21/almost-half-of-canadians-do-not-support-idle-no-more-movement-poll/.

50. Friedrich Nietzsche, *On the Genealogy of Morals and Ecce Homo* (New York: Vintage, 1989), 36–37.

51. Ibid., 37.

52. Fanon, *Black Skin, White Masks* (2008), 197.

53. Miles Howe, "Showdown in Elsipogtog: Seven Months of Shale Gas Resistance in New Brunswick," *The Dominion*, January 14, 2014, http://dominion.mediacoop.ca/ story/showdown-elsipogtog/20423.

54. Shiri Pasternak, "The Economics of Insurgency: Thoughts on Idle No More and Critical Infrastructure," *The Media Co-Op*, January 14, 2013, http://www.media coop.ca/story/economics-insurgency/15610.

55. Naomi Klein, "Dancing the World into Being: A Conversation with Leanne Simpson," *Yes Magazine*, March 5, 2013, http://www.yesmagazine.org/peace-justice/dancing-the-world-into-being-a-conversation-with-idle-no-more-leanne-simpson.

56. Rauna Kuokkanen, "Indigenous Economies, Theories of Subsistence, and Women," *American Indian Quarterly* 35, no. 2 (2011): 219.

57. On the relevance of cooperative and workplace democracy models of economic development to Indigenous societies, see Gurston Dacks, "Worker-Controlled Native Enterprises: A Vehicle for Community Development in Northern Canada," *Canadian Journal of Native Studies*, 3, no. 2 (1983): 289–310; Lou Ketilson and Ian MacPherson, *Aboriginal Co-operatives in Canada: Current Situation and Potential for Growth* (Saskatoon: Centre for the Study of Co-operatives, 2001). Also see Ruttan and T'Seleie, "Renewable Resource Potentials for Alternative Development."

58. Kuokkanen, "Indigenous Economies, Theories of Subsistence, and Women," 223.

59. Environics Institute, *Urban Aboriginal Peoples Study* (Toronto: Published by Environics Institute, 2012), 6. Available online at http://uaps.ca/.

60. Jean Barman, "Erasing Indigenous Indigeneity in Vancouver," *BC Studies* No. 155 (2007), 3–30; Amber Dean, "Space, Temporality, History: Encountering Hauntings in Vancouver's Downtown Eastside," in *The West and Beyond: New Perspectives on an Imagined Region*, ed. Alvin Finkle, Sarah Carter, and Peter Fortna, 113–32 (Athabasca, Alta.: Athabasca University Press, 2010).

61. Jean Barman, "Erasing Indigenous Indigeneity in Vancouver," 6.

62. Ibid., 6–7.

63. John Tobias, "Protection, Civilization, Assimilation: An Outline History of Canada's Indian Policy," in *Sweet Promises: A Reader on Indian–White Relations in Canada*, ed. J. R. Miller (Toronto: University of Toronto Press, 1991), 136.

64. Barman, "Erasing Indigenous Indigeneity in Vancouver," 7.

65. Sherene Razack, "Gendered Racial Violence and Spatialized Justice: The Murder of Pamela George," in *Race, Space and the Law: Unmapping a White Settler Society*, ed. Sherene Razack (Halifax: Between the Lines, 2002), 129.

66. Ibid.

67. Loretta Lees, Tom Slater, and Elvin Wyly, *Gentrification* (New York: Routledge, 2008).

68. Neil Smith, *The New Urban Frontier: Gentrification and the Revanchist City* (New York: Routledge, 1996); Nicholas Blomley, *Unsettling the City: Urban Land and the Politics of Property* (New York: Routledge, 2004); and Dean, "Space, Temporality, History."

69. Lawrence, *"Real" Indians and Others*, 246.

70. Ibid., 232.

71. Ibid., 233–34.

72. Ibid., 233.

73. Ibid., 246.

74. Dory Nason, "We Hold Our Hands Up: On Indigenous Women's Love and Resistance," *Decolonization: Indigeneity, Education, and Society Blog*, February 12, 2013,

http://decolonization.wordpress.com/2013/02/12/we-hold-our-hands-up-on-indig
enous-womens-love-and-resistance/.

75. Native Women's Association of Canada, "Missing and Murdered Aboriginal
Women and Girls in British Columbia, Canada" briefing paper published by the Native
Women's Association of Canada for the Inter-American Commission on Human
Rights, Ottawa, 2012, 3.

76. Pierre Bourdieu, *In Other Words: Essays toward a Reflexive Sociology* (Stanford:
Stanford University Press, 1990), 127.

77. Lawrence, *"Real" Indians and Others*, 69.

78. Nason, "We Hold Our Hands Up."

79. Turner, *This Is Not a Peace Pipe*, 5.

80. Ibid., 31.

INDEX

"Black Orpheus" (Sartre), 131, 136–37, 144
Black Skin, White Masks (Fanon): on the colonized subject, 17–18, 26, 31–32, 44; critique of Hegel's master/slave dialectic, 16–17, 40, 139; on the dual structure of colonialism, 33, 113; on negritude, 131, 139–48; on the value of negation, 169. See also Fanon, Frantz
Blake, Philip, 62–63
Blatchford, Christie, 161
Blomley, Nicholas, 175
Blondin, George, 61
Bound by Recognition (Markell), 29
Bourdieu, Pierre, 177
British Columbia: antipipeline campaigns, 165; Delgamuukw case and, 41; First Nations blockades in, 117, 164; murdered and missing Indigenous women, 167; Nisga'a claim to lands in, 5
Brown, Wendy, 101
Brudholm, Thomas, 107–8, 110–11, 126
Buchanan, Judd, 69

Cairns, Alan, 182n8
Calder, Frank (Chief), 5
Calgary Winter Olympics (1988), 117
Canada: agreement with Dene Nation and Metis Association, 75–76; apology for residential schools (2008), 105, 124–25, 126; assimilationist policy, 3, 4, 5, 12–13, 174; definition of Indigenous status, 84; having "no history of colonialism," 105–6, 108; Idle No More and, 160, 163; legitimacy of sovereignty, 91–92; loss of control over "Indian Problem," 118; as a multinational state, 37; Native claims policy, 5–6, 58–59, 66, 122, 195n12; "recognition" of aboriginal rights, 2, 71–73, 155, 163; role of Indigenous labor in, 12–13; terra nullius argument, 91, 100, 175; turn to reconciliation

politics, 105–7, 118–20, 155–56. See also settler-colonialism; individual provinces
Canadian Labor Congress, 69
Capital (Marx), 7, 10, 186n41
capitalism: colonialism and, 7–8, 10–11, 172; as a condition of cultural accommodation, 66; discourse of sustainability, 77; ecological critique of, 14; incommensurability with Indigenous values, 62, 158–59, 173; primitive accumulation, 7–11, 13, 60, 151–52, 184n35, 186(nn41, 45); racism and, 136, 137–38; as a social relation, 11, 33; state ideology and, 32
Cardinal, Harold, 69
Carrothers Commission, 56
Caute, David, 132
Césaire, Aimé, 138, 145–46, 212n4
Charlottetown Accord (1992), 20, 89–91
Charter of Rights and Freedoms, 87–88, 90, 91, 92, 119, 159
children, 4, 55
Chipewyan Dene, 54
Chrétien, Jean, 6, 173
The Claims of Culture (Benhabib), 80, 81, 99
colonized subjects: dangers of assimilation, 46; internalization of colonial status, 31–33, 39, 42, 112–13, 191n34; "psycho-affective" attachment to colonial structure, 17–18, 26, 152–53; ressentiment and, 109, 113–14, 142; ressentiment-infected nostalgia of, 147; self-essentializing of, 145; self-objectification of, 139; self-recognition of, 43–44, 114–15, 131. See also settler-colonialism
Committee for Original Peoples' Entitlement (COPE), 57
Communist Manifesto (Marx and Engels), 185n39

Constitution Act of 1982, 2, 20, 87–90, 92, 115, 116, 123
Cree, 6, 117
culture: colonialism and the misuse of, 94, 96, 103; defined, 65–66; as a fluid, contested system, 82, 93, 156; hybridity of, 205n54; liberation of territory and, 148; male-dominated interpretations of, 91; preservationist approaches to, 80–81, 92–93; in racism, 146–47, 215n85; separated from politics, 66, 71, 72, 123, 147, 204n46; as transitional category of identification, 153; universal rights and, 70, 92–93. *See also* identity

Dancing on Our Turtle's Back (Simpson), 148, 158
Day, Richard J. F., 3, 35, 102
Dean, Amber, 175
De Angelis, Massimo, 184n35
Dehcho Dene, 54, 76
Deloria, Vine, Jr., 60
democracy: anti-essentialist projects in, 102; deliberative, 79–80, 81, 82, 99; direct or consensus-based, 73
Dene Nation: Agreement in Principle (1976), 67–68, 69–71; Agreement in Principle (1988), 75, 76; on cultural diversity, 51; Declaration (1975), 1, 53, 64, 69–71; "Denendeh" proposal, 73–75, 171–72, 199n76; land claims, 67–75, 202n118; Mackenzie Valley pipeline plan and, 6, 57; Metro Proposal (1977), 70–71; on powerlessness over land administration, 56; withdrawal of funding for secretariat, 76
Denendeh, 53–54
Department of Indian Affairs and Northern Development (DIAND), 85
Dirlik, Arif, 98–99, 102
Dogrib language, 61

Dosman, Edgar, 57
Drury, Charles (Bud), 72

Edmonton Report, 69
Elsipogtog, New Brunswick, 165, 170, 173
Engels, Friedrich, 9, 65, 185n39
Environmental Assessment Act, 127, 160
Erasmus, Georges (Chief), 67, 118, 199n76, 202n118

Fanon, Frantz: advocacy of violence, 31, 47; articulation of colonialism, 16; on cultural racism, 146–47, 215n85; on Hegel's master/slave dialectic, 25; identification of asymmetrical forms of recognition, 25, 190n31; insights into *ressentiment*, 109, 113–15, 128–29; investigation of colonial psychology, 26; lived experience as black person, 32; on negritude, 139–48, 212n4; on Octave Mannoni, 214n47; promotion of self-affirmative cultural practices, 23; on Sartre's characterization of negritude, 141–42, 144, 215n71; on the self-recognition of the colonized, 131; "stretching" of Marxist paradigm, 34; on the value of negation, 169
FBI (Federal Bureau of Investigation), 200n86
Federici, Silvia, 9, 11
Ferro, Marc, 105
Fiddler, Alvin, 164
Finely, Chris, 157
Fisheries Act, 160
Foster, John Bellamy, 13
Foucault, Michel, 25, 214n49
The Fourth World (Manuel and Posluns), 1, 68–69
Fraser, Nancy, 19, 27, 34, 36–37, 52
Front de Libération Nationale (FLN), 47

Gathering Strength (Canada), 121–23, 124–26

T'Seleie, Frank (Chief), 76–77
Tully, James, 189n68
Turner, Dale, 45–46, 107, 178
Turner, Lou, 38
Turner, Terrance, 81

United Nations: Declaration on the
   Rights of Indigenous Peoples, 164;
   International Covenant on Civil and
   Political Rights, 74, 87; study on
   Indigenous populations, 66–67
United States, 37, 56–57, 200n86
United Steelworkers of America, 69
Usher, Peter, 59

A View of the Art of Colonization
   (Wakefield), 10
violence: "cleansing" value, 47; in colonialism, 15, 16, 113, 188n59; Indigenous
   youth and, 118; in neoliberalism, 9; as
   "psychotherapy of the oppressed,"
   44–45; *ressentiment* and, 108, 112; state
   responsibility for, 120; in transition
   to capitalism, 7; against women,
   177–78

Wagamese, Richard, 111–12
Wah-Shee, James, 68
Wakefield, Edward G., 10
Wasáse (Alfred), 51, 151, 154, 157

Weledeh Dene, 19, 54, 61, 76
"West Indians and Africans" (Fanon),
   144–46
White Paper (1969), 4, 5, 58, 95, 161, 163,
   179
Widdowson, Frances, 51
Wilson, Nina, 128, 160
Wolfe, Patrick, 7, 125
women: Charter of Rights and
   Freedoms and, 159; in Idle No More
   movement, 128, 176–77; and the
   Indian Act, 4, 80, 83–96; Indigenous
   feminism, 157–58; Indigenous
   governance principles and, 172; as
   leaders of direct action, 117, 167;
   misrecognition and, 189n68; as
   victims of violence, 164, 167, 177
World Health Organization, 215n85
The Wretched of the Earth (Fanon):
   analysis of misrecognition, 31;
   articulation of colonialism in, 16; on
   cultural self-affirmation, 147, 153;
   influence on Charles Taylor, 33;
   Sartre's preface to, 113; violence in,
   44–45. *See also* Fanon, Frantz

Yellowknife, 55–56
Yellowknives Dene, 19, 54, 61, 76
Young, Robert, 26, 44
Yukon, 78

GLEN SEAN COULTHARD (Yellowknives Dene) is an assistant professor in the First Nations Studies Program and the Department of Political Science at the University of British Columbia.